Keto Cookbook for Beginners

1500+ Easy & Delicious Recipes
That Anyone Can Cook at Home.
With 60-Day Meal Plan and Shopping List

By Natalie Vitale

© **Copyright 2022 – Natalie Vitale - All rights reserved.**

The content in this book may not be reproduced, duplicated or transmitted without direct written permission from the author or the publisher.

Under no circumstances will any blame or legal responsibility be held against the publisher or author for any direct or indirect damages due to the information contained in this book.

Legal Notice:

This book is copyright protected. This book is only for personal use. You cannot amend, distribute, sell, use, quote or paraphrase any part of the content of this book without the written consent of the author or publisher.

Disclaimer:

The information contained in this document is for educational and entertainment purposes only. We have made every effort to present accurate, up-to-date, reliable and complete information. No warranties of any kind are declared or implied. Readers acknowledge that the author is not engaged in the rendering of legal, financial, medical or professional advice. The content within this book has been derived from various sources. Please consult a licensed professional before attempting any techniques outlined in this book. By reading this document, the reader agrees that under no circumstances is the author responsible for any losses, direct or indirect, which are incurred as a result of the use of the information contained within this document, including, but not limited to, errors, omissions, or inaccuracies.

TABLE OF CONTENT

KETO GROCERY LIST 2
Breakfast Recipes And Eggs Recipes 3
    Coconut Crêpes with Vanilla Cream 3
    Morning Chia Pudding 3
    Lemon Crepes 3
    Bread with Pumpkin and Zucchini 3
    Pastrami Gofres and Peanut Butter 4
    Zesty Zucchini Bread with Nuts 4
    Sausage Cakes with Poached Eggs 4
    Winter Squash Pancakes 4
    Chorizo Egg Cups 5
    Bacon and Artichoke Omelet 5
    Deli Ham Eggs 5
    Avocado Chili Omelet 5
    Cheese Cloud Eggs 5
    Avocado and Eggs with Shredded Chicken 6
    Coconut Flaxseed Waffles 6
    Ham and Swiss Waffles 6
    Baked Eggs in Ham Cups 6
    Florentine Breakfast Sandwich 7
    Baked Omelet with Pancetta and Swiss Cheese .. 7
    Eggs with Goat Cheese & Asparagus 7
    Loaded Denver Omelet 7
    Mushroom and Bacon Frittata 8
    Bacon-Wrapped Egg Cups 8
    Spinach, Mushroom, and Cheddar Frittata 8
    Brussels Sprouts & Ground Beef Scrambled Eggs .. 8
    Mexican Egg Casserole 9
    Cheesy Sausage & Egg Muffins 9
    Egg & Cheese Biscuit Casserole 9
    French Toast Egg Muffins 9
    Asparagus Gouda Frittata 10
    Salmon and Egg Scramble 10
    Asparagus, Mushroom & Fennel Frittata 10
    Ham and Cheese Poached Egg Cups 11
    Chorizo Egg Muffins 11
    Bacon Broccoli Crustless Quiche Cups 11
    Scrambled Eggs with Mackerel 11
    Sausage Verde Casserole 12
    Sausage and Cheese Frittata 12
    Turkey Egg Scramble 12
    Bacon Eggs Benedict Cups 12
    Savory Sausage Balls 13
Basic Recipes & Simple Recipes 13
    Green Smoothie 13
    Zucchini Pasta Puttanesca 13
    Green Cheese Bowls 13
    Guacamole 14
    Broccoli Beef 14
    Raspberry Yogurt Parfait 14
    Tuna Pesto Caprese Salad 14
    Creamy Avocado "Pasta" 14
    Golden Saffron Cauli Rice 15
    Coconut Butter Coffee 15
    wrap classic pigs 15
    Avocado Mousse "Croutons" 15
    Scrambled Eggs Smoked Salmon 15
    Bacon Cheddar Egg Muffins 16
    Spinach and Brussels Sprout Salad 16
    Smoked Mackerel Lettuce Cups 16
    Chicken Salad with Parmesan 16
Salads Recipes & Soups Recipes 18
    Artichoke Salad 18
    Turkey Salad 18
    Spinach Salad with Goat Cheese and Nuts 18
    Thai-Style Prawn Salad 18

    Creamy Asparagus Soup 19
    Vegetarian French Onion Soup 19
    Cauliflower-Cheddar Soup 19
    Spiced Pumpkin Soup 19
    Broccoli Cheddar Soup 20
    Tomato Basil Soup 20
    Creamy Broccoli, Bacon, and Cheese Soup 20
    Miso Magic 20
    Loaded Miso Soup with Tofu and Egg 21
    Turnip and Thyme Soup 21
    Creamy Tomato Soup 21
    Easy Herbed Tomato Bisque 21
    Beef Pho 22
    Chilled Avocado-Cilantro Soup 22
    Cream of Cauliflower Gazpacho 22
Poultry Recipes 23
    Stuffed Chicken Breasts 23
    Chicken Breasts 23
    Turnip Greens Artichoke Chicken 24
    Green Bean Broccoli Chicken Stir-Fry 24
    Cheesy chicken Pinwheels 24
    Chicken Nuggets 24
    Thyme Mushroom and turnip Chicken 25
    Paprika Chicken and Pancetta in a Skillet 25
    Baked Zucchini, Chicken and Cheese 25
    Herby Veggies Chicken Casserole 25
    Cabbage and Broccoli Chicken Casserole 26
    Fennel Chicken Wrapped in Bacon 26
    Turkey Patties with Cucumber Salad 26
    Creamed Turkey with Swiss Chard Soup 27
    Sliced Garlic & Cheezy Turkey Breast 27
    Crispy Chicken Thighs with Radishes and Mushrooms .. 28
    Chicken Nuggets 28
    Chicken Thigh Chili with Avocado 28
    Chicken Bacon Burgers 28
    Baked Chicken Tenders 29
    Chicken with Mushrooms, Port, and Cream ... 29
    Creamy Chicken and Spinach Bake 29
    Lemon Chicken and Asparagus Stir-Fry 29
    Loaded Chicken and Cauliflower Nachos 30
    Shredded Chicken 30
    Buffalo Chicken Wings 30
    Curried Chicken Salad 30
    Coconut Chicken 31
    Basil Chicken Zucchini "Pasta" 31
    BBQ Chicken Skewers 31
    Chicken Cordon Bleu Casserole 32
    Roast Turkey 32
    Turkey Meatloaf Muffins 32
Pork Recipes 33
    Baked Pork Sausage 33
    Pork Chops with Tomato Sauce 33
    Cranberry Sauce and Herb Pork Chops 33
    Roasted Pork Stuffed with Ham & Cheese 34
    Barbecued Pork Chops 34
    Citrus Pork with tomatoes Cabbage 34
    Pork Kofta with Spiced Yogurt 34
    Bacon Kale Pizza 35
    Sesame Pork Bites 35
    Pork with Mozzarella 35
    Chinese Style Pork with Noodles 35
    Lettuce Wraps with Pork & Dill Pickles 36
    Cheesy Pork Quiche 36
    Egg and Pork Stuffed Zucchini 36
    Chili Pork Belly with sauce 36
    Meat Lover Sausage Pizza 37

- Pork Steaks and Mushroom Sauce 37
- Pork Shoulder 37
- Gingery Pork Stir-Fry.. 37
- Veggie Bake with Sausage 38
- Prosciutto Pizza 38
- Italian Meatballs... 38
- Green Pork Bake 38

Beef Recipes AND Lamb Recipes 39
- Root Mash Veggie Beef Stew................................ 39
- King Burgers 39
- Beef Cheeseburger 39
- Oven-Roast Veggie Chuck Beef 40
- Bell Peppers Stuffed with Enchilada Beef 40
- Spicy Beef Lettuce Cups 40
- Beef Chili 40
- Asian Broccoli Spiced Beef 41
- Cilantro Beef Balls 41
- Beef Pepper & Green Beans Ragout 41
- Grilled Beef on Skewers and salad 41
- Beef Sausage & Okra Casserole 42
- Grilled Steak and Green Beans 42
- Vegetable Medley with Grilled Beef Steaks 42
- Beef Stew 43
- Beef Cheese & Egg Casserole 43
- Flank Steak Roll... 43
- Beef, Bell Pepper & Mushroom Kebabs 43
- Coconut-Olive Beef with Mushrooms 44
- Eggplant Beef Lasagna 44
- Grandma's Meatballs 44
- Bacon & Mushrooms Beef Steaks 44
- BBQ Rib Sweet Steak 45
- Rosemary Thyme Juicy Beef 45
- Ancho T-Bone Steak 45
- Red Wine Vegetables Beef Roast 45
- Spiralized Zucchini in Bolognese Sauce 46

Fish Recipes And Seafood Recipes 46
- Dijon Sauce Blackened Salmon 46
- Broccoli & Bell Pepper Crispy Salmon 46
- Mediterranean Tilapia Bake 46
- Grilled Salmon with salad 47
- Moroccan Salmon with Cauliflower Rice Pilaf 47
- Grandma Bev's Ahi Poke 47
- Pepper-Crusted Salmon with Wilted Kale 47
- Lemon Salmon and Asparagus 48
- Baked Trout and Asparagus Foil 48
- Green Tuna Traybake 48
- Shirataki Fettucine with Salmon 48
- Tilapia Tortillas with Cauliflower Rice 49
- Cilantro Sauce Coconut Fried Shrimp 49
- Chimichurri Tiger Shrimp 49
- Mustardy Crab Cakes 49
- Shirataki Mussels Pasta 50
- Crispy Fried Cod 50
- Mustard-Crusted Cod with Roasted Broccoli 50
- Cod with Parsley Pistou 50
- Poached Cod over Brothy Veggie Noodles 51
- Parmesan-Crusted Tilapia with Sautéed Spinach 51
- "Spaghetti" with Clams 51
- Brown Butter–Lime Tilapia 51
- Cream-Poached Trout 52
- Tuna Slow-Cooked in Olive Oil 52
- Garlic Parmesan Crusted Salmon 52
- Sesame-Crusted Tuna with Sweet Chili Vinaigrette 53
- Coconut Saffron Mussels 53
- Halibut Curry 53
- Baked Nutty Halibut 53
- Swordfish in Tarragon-Citrus Butter 54
- Spicy Crab Cakes 54

Vegetable Sides & Dairy Recipes 54
- Cheesy Zucchini Muffins 54
- Tomato Gratin with Eggplant 55
- Chilli Dressing Roasted Cauliflower 55
- Stuffed Zucchini with Cheddar 55
- Dinner Vegetarian Pasta Mix 55
- Chia Seeds Coconut-Lime Ice Cream 56
- Vegetable Keto Pasta Gratin 56
- Grilled Asparagus & Carrots 56
- Broccoli & Peppers Balsamic Zoodles 56
- Mushroom & Herb Pizza 57
- Broccoli Nachos Salsa 57
- Tofu Parsnip Spaghetti a la "Bolognese" 57
- Baby Spinach Lasagna with Feta 57
- Roasted Cauliflower Gratin 58
- Cheese Cauliflower Risotto with Mushroom 58
- Coconut Avocado Tart 58
- Green Sauté 59
- Mushrooms Broccoli Noodles 59
- Crispy Avocado with Parmesan Sauce 59
- Broccoli & Mushroom Pizza 59
- Three Cheesy Pizza 60
- Mushroom & Zucchini with Spinach Dip 60
- Tofu Stir-Fry 60
- Butternut Squash Roast 60
- Tofu Roasted Pepper 61
- Feta & Olive Pizza 61
- Avocado Pesto Chargrilled Zucchini 61
- Broccoli Asparagus Flan 61
- Mediterranean Eggplant Squash Pasta 62
- Flavored Stuffed Mushrooms filled with Cajun ... 62
- Cauliflower-Based Waffles 62

Vegan Recipes 63
- Vegan Sandwich with Tofu 63
- Blackberries with Coconut Milk Shake 63
- Grilled Cauliflower Steaks 63
- Stir-Fry Tofu & Vegetable 63
- Grilled Vegetables and Kebab 64
- Vegan Smoothie 64
- Portobello Bun Mushroom Burgers 64
- Roasted Bake tomatoes 64
- Grilled Tofu Kabobs 65
- Thyme & Garlic Steamed Bok Choy 65
- Cucumber & Tomato Salad Sticky with Tofu 65
- Dip with Tofu and Swiss Chard 65
- Ratatouille with Pecans 66
- Fennel & Celeriac with Chili Tomato Sauce 66
- Coleslaw with Poppy Seeds 66
- Roasted Asparagus and Romesco sauce 66
- Vegetable Stew 67
- Zucchini Loaded with Tofu & Hazelnut 67
- Pumpkin & Bell Pepper Noodles 67
- Mushrooms Bake & Curried Cauliflower 67
- Roasted Cauliflower with Bell Peppers 68
- Tofu Vegetable Casserole 68
- Coconut Green Soup 68

Snacks Recipes & Appetizers Recipes 70
- Walnuts & Cheese Mushrooms 70
- Meatball Shakshuka 70
- Avocado & Cauliflower Burritos 70
- Breakfast Bread "Naan" 70
- Rosemary Feta Cheese Bombs 71
- Mushroom Feta Skewers 71
- Mushroom & Kale Pierogis 71
- Parmigiano Cauliflower Cakes 71
- Triple Cheese Chips 72
- Parmesan Zucchini Chips 72
- Crispy Kale Chips 72
- Margarita Pizza Chips 72
- Southern Fried Deviled Eggs 73
- Antipasto Skewers 73

- Rosemary Roasted Almonds 73
- Spicy Barbecue Pecans 73
- Texas Trash 74
- Marinated Artichokes 74
- Fennel and Orange Marinated Olives 74
- Baked Olives and Feta 74
- Loaded Feta 75
- Buffalo Roasted Cauliflower 75
- Prosciutto and Cream Cheese Stuffed Mushrooms 75
- Jalapeño Poppers 76
- Garlic Breadsticks 76
- Cheesy Baked Meatballs 76

Smoothies & Beverages Recipes 78
- Almond Smoothie 78
- Chocolate Protein Cocktail 78
- Hot Chocolate 78
- Cold Matcha Latte 78
- Double Chocolate Shake 79
- Chocolate Protein Shake 79
- Vanilla Bean Smoothie 79
- Vanilla Shake 79
- Strawberries and Cream Shake 79
- Cheesecake Smoothie 79
- Peanut Butter Shake 80
- Peanut Butter Cup Protein Smoothie 80
- Chocolate, Peanut Butter, and Banana Shake 80
- Chocolate-Mint Smoothie 80
- Almond Butter and Cacao Nib Smoothie 80
- Vegan Chocolate Smoothie 81
- Quick Raspberry Vanilla Shake 81
- Blueberry Coconut Smoothie 81
- Creamy Vanilla Cappuccino 81
- Turmeric Latte 81
- Detox Drink 81
- Loaded Denver Omelet 82
- Baked Omelet with Pancetta and Swiss Cheese 82
- Skillet-Baked Eggs with Yogurt and Spinach 82
- Mediterranean Frittata 83
- Asparagus Frittata 83

Keto's Other Favorites 84
- Tofu and Avocado Sandwiches 84
- Broccoli Mushroom Risotto 84
- Quick Strawberry Mousse 84
- Beef Ceeseburgers 84
- Baked Sausage & Peppers 85
- Beef Bolognese Squashed 85
- Ricotta Balls 85
- Broccoli Creamy Cheese Soup 85
- Crunchy Cauliflower with Mash 86
- Mixed Mushroom Pizza with Pepperoni 86
- Cauliflower & Mushroom Arancini 86
- Brussels Sprouts with Spiced Halloumi 86
- Pecan Arugula Pizza 87
- Spinach Pesto 87
- Pepperoni Fat Head Pizza 87
- Berry Pancakes 87

Sweets Recipes And Desserts Recipes 89
- Creamy Avocado Custard 89
- Blackberry Scones 89
- Strawberries Ricotta Parfait 89
- Coconut Panna Cotta Caramel 89
- Almond Cookies 90
- Chocolate Vanilla Cake 90
- Cowboy Cookies 90
- Buttery Dark Chocolate Cookies 90
- Cranberries Cheesecake Bars 91
- Blueberry Soufflé 91
- Ginger Fudge with Chocolate 91
- Chocolate Energy Balls with Lime 91
- American Cheesecake 92
- Chocolate Chips Walnut Biscuits 92
- Almond Cheesecake with Chocolate 92
- Chocolate Fat Bombs 92
- Dark Chocolate Cheesecake Bites 93
- Viennese Coffee Bites 93
- Blueberry Sorbet 93
- Coconut Waffles with Cranberry 93
- Peanut Butter Ice Cream 93
- Chocolate Cupcakes 94
- Strawberry Mini Cakes 94
- Mascarpone Red Velvet Cakes 94
- Chocolate Frosting Cakes 94
- Coconut Macadamia Bars 95
- Almond Butter & Chocolate Bars 95
- Blueberry Ice Balls 95
- Buckeye Fat Bomb Bars 95

Small Keto Appliance Recipes 96
- Beef Meatballs 96
- Chicken Stew with Sorrel 96
- Chipotle Chicken 96
- Green Bean Beef Soup 97
- Pork Ragout 97
- Worcestershire Pork Loin 97
- Pork Neck Casserole 97
- Beef & Broccoli Stew 98
- Chicken Stew with Veggies 98
- Chicken Jardiniere 98
- Chicken with Garlic Sauce 98
- Lamb Shoulder 99
- Pork & Kraut 99
- Goat Cheese Lamb Ribs 99
- Shredded BBQ Roast 99
- Pork with Mushroom Sauce 100
- Touch of Spice Pulled Pork 100
- Buffalo Chicken Wings 100
- Whole Chicken 100
- Chicken Provencal 101
- Chicken in Wine Sauce 101
- Chicken Cacciatore 101
- Turnip Soup with Sour Cream 101
- Smoky Zucchini Chips 102
- Lemon-Garlic Mushrooms 102
- Buttery Green Beans 102
- Sweet and Spicy Pecans 102
- Spiced-Pumpkin Chicken Soup 103
- Cheesy Bacon-Cauliflower Soup 103
- Turkey-Potpie Soup 103
- Faux Lasagna Soup 103
- Pork Kebabs 104
- Pork-and-Sauerkraut Casserole 104
- Cream Cheese Sausage Balls 104
- Bacon-and-Eggs Breakfast Casserole 105
- Carnitas 105
- Lemon Pork 105
- Smoky Pork Tenderloin 105
- Slow Cooker Spanakopita Frittata 106

Appendix 1   Measurement Conversion Chart
.... 107

Appendix 2   Dirty Dozen and Clean Fifteen
.... 108

30-DAY MEAL PLAN 109

Appendix 3   Index 113

KETO GROCERY LIST

Vegetables	MEATS
Avacado	Bacon
Cauliflower	Beef
Broccoli	Turkey
Asparagus	Duck
Spinach	Pork
Cucumbers	Ham
Eggs	**Nuts & Seeds**
Eggs	Pecans
Fats	Almods
Avacado oil	Walnuts
Coconut oil	Macadamias
Olive oil	Chia seeds
Mct oil	Pumpkin seeds
ghee	**Flour**
Cocoa butter	Coconut
Lard	Almond
Bacon fat	Psyllium husk

Breakfast Recipes And Eggs Recipes

Coconut Crêpes with Vanilla Cream

Servings: 4 **Total Time:** approx. 35 minutes

Ingredients:
- 1.4 coconut flour
- 5 large eggs
- 1/4 cup flaxseed milk
- 1/4 cup butter
- 1/4 cup vanilla cream
- 1/2 teaspoon vanilla extract
- 1 tablespoon sugar-free cocoa powder
- 2 tbsp melted coconut oil
- 1/2 cup whipped coconut cream
- 2 tablespoons erythritol

Directions:

In a mixing bowl, whisk the eggs. Mix in the coconut flour, cocoa powder, flax milk, and coconut oil until thoroughly combined. Preheat a skillet over medium heat, spray with cooking spray, and add a ladleful of the batter.

Cook the crepe for 2-3 minutes, swiping the pan quickly to spread the dough around the skillet.

Place the crepe in a flat plate Cook until all of the batter has been used up. In a saucepan over medium heat, melt the butter. Pour in the coconut cream and erythritol, reduce the heat to low, and continue to stir the sauce for 6-8 minutes.

Remove from the heat and stir in the vanilla extract. Drizzle the sauce over the crepes and set aside.

Nutrition: Cal 326; Net Carbs 3g; Fat 23g; Protein 10g

Morning Chia Pudding

Servings: 2 and **Total Time:** approx. 10 min + chilling time

Ingredients:
- 2 tbsp chia seeds
- ½ tsp vanilla extract
- ½ cup blueberries
- ¾ cup coconut milk
- 1 tbsp chopped walnuts

Directions:

In a blender, combine the coconut milk, vanilla, and half of the blueberries. Combine the

ingredients in a food processor and process until the blueberries are completely incorporated into the liquid. Chia seeds should be added last.

Divide the mixture between two jars, cover, and place in the refrigerator for 4 hours to gel. Serve with the remaining blueberries and walnuts as garnish. Serve.

Nutrition: Calories: 299; Net Carbohydrates: 7g; Fat: 28g; Protein: 9g

Lemon Crepes

Servings: 2, **Total Time:** approx. 25 minutes

Ingredients:
- 1 tbsp lemon juice
- 1 tsp butter
- ½ tbsp granulated Swerve
- 1 cup almond flour
- 1 cup almond milk
- 3 large eggs
- A pinch of salt
- ¾ cup powdered Serve

Directions:

In a mixing bowl, combine almond milk, eggs, granulated Swerve, salt, and almond flour. Set a frying pan over medium heat and spray with cooking spray.

Cook the crepes for about 2 minutes, or until the edges begin to brown.

Cook for another 2 minutes on the other side before flipping; repeat with the remaining batter. Arrange the crepes on a plate. In the same pan, combine the powdered Swerve, butter, and 12 cup of water; cook for 6 minutes while stirring.

Mix in the lemon juice and allow to stand until the syrup has thickened. Serve the crepes with the maple syrup.

Nutrition: Cal 421; Net Carbs 10g; Fat 35g; Protein 15g

Bread with Pumpkin and Zucchini

Servings: 4 and **Total Time:** approx. 60 minutes

Ingredients:
- 6 eggs
- 1 cup zucchini, shredded
- 1/3 cup coconut flour
- 1 tbsp cinnamon powder
- 1 tsp apple cider vinegar
- 1 cup pumpkin, shredded
- 1 tbsp olive oil
- ½ cup buttermilk
- ¾ tsp baking soda
- ½ tsp salt

Directions:

Preheat the oven to 360 degrees Fahrenheit. In a mixing bowl, combine all of the ingredients and stir to form a dough.

Pour the batter into a greased loaf pan and bake for 45 minutes, or until a toothpick inserted into the centre comes out clean. Allow for a 5-minute cooling period. Slice and serve.

Nutrition: Cal 185; Net Carbs 5g; Fat 13g; Protein 10g

Pastrami Gofres and Peanut Butter

Servings: 2 and **Total Time:** approx. 20 minutes

Ingredients:

½ tsp baking soda	4 eggs
2 tbsp peanut butter, melted	¼ tsp salt
	3 tbsp tomato puree
4 tbsp coconut flour	
4 oz pastrami, chopped	½ tsp dried rosemary

Directions:

Preheat your waffle maker to high heat. Whisk together the eggs, rosemary, and salt in a mixing bowl. Combine the coconut flour, baking soda, and peanut butter in a mixing bowl.

Continue whisking until everything is thoroughly combined. Cook a third of the batter in the waffle iron for 3 minutes, or until golden. Repeat with the rest of the batter. Top each gofre with the tomato puree and pastrami. Serve.

Nutrition: Cal 411; Net Carbs 8g; Fat 27g; Protein 25g

Zesty Zucchini Bread with Nuts

Servings: 4 and **Total Time:** approx. 50 min + cooling time

Ingredients:

4 eggs	2/3 cup coconut flour
1 cup butter, softened	2 tsp baking powder
1 cup erythritol	1 cup whipped cream
2/3 cup ground almonds	1 tbsp chopped hazelnuts
1 lemon, zested and juiced	1 cup finely grated zucchini

Directions:

Preheat the oven to 380 degrees Fahrenheit. Line a springform pan with parchment paper and grease it. Place aside. In a mixing bowl, cream together the butter and erythritol until creamy and pale.

While whisking, add the eggs one at a time. Stir in the coconut flour, baking powder, and ground cinnamon. Zucchini, almonds, lemon zest, and juice.

Fill the pan halfway with the mixture. Bake for 40 minutes, or until the cake has risen and a toothpick inserted into it comes out clean.

Allow for a 10-minute cooling period inside the pan. Place on a wire rack. On top, spread whipped cream and sprinkle with hazelnuts. Serve and have fun!

Nutrition: Cal 804; Net Carbs 5g, Fat 83g; Protein 12g

Sausage Cakes with Poached Eggs

Servings: 2 and **Total Time:** approx. 20 minutes

Ingredients:

1 tbsp guacamole	½ lb sausage patties
2 eggs	1 tbsp olive oil
1 tbsp cilantro, chopped	½ tsp vinegar
Salt and black pepper to taste	

Directions:

Fry the sausage patties in warm olive oil over medium heat for 6-8 minutes, or until lightly browned. Place the patties on a plate. Top with the guacamole.

In a pot, bring the vinegar and 2 cups of water to a boil over high heat, then reduce to a simmer without boiling.

Each egg should be cracked into a bowl and gently placed in a bowl of simmering water; poach for 2-3 minutes. Remove from the water and pat dry with a paper towel. Serve each cake with a poached egg on top, sprinkled with cilantro, salt, and pepper.

Nutrition: Cal 583; Net Carbs 4.5g; Fat 43g; Protein 28g

Winter Squash Pancakes

Servings 1 | **Prep Time** 5 minutes | **Cook Time** 8 to 10 minutes

Ingredients:

1 large egg	½ cup puréed butternut squash
3 tbsp coconut flour	
2 tablespoons erythritol	¼ tbsp vanilla extract
1 tablespoon coconut oil or butter	

Directions:

Powdered coffee creamer or maple syrup (optional)

In a mixing bowl, combine the egg, butternut squash, flour, erythritol, and vanilla and stir together. In a small sauté pan over medium heat, melt the coconut oil or butter.

Pour your batter in. Cook one side of the pancake until you can easily stick your spatula underneath all sides, 5 to 8 minutes. Carefully flip the pancake over and cook for another 3 to 4 minutes. Plate and top with creamer or syrup, if desired.

Nutrition: Calories: 331; Fat: 22g; Protein: 11g; Total Carbs: 25g

Chorizo Egg Cups

Servings: 2 and **Total Time:** approx. 20 minutes

Ingredients:
- Salt and black pepper to taste
- 1 cup mozzarella, grated
- 1 tsp butter, melted
- 2 chorizo sausages, chopped
- 1 tbsp parsley, chopped
- 4 eggs, beaten

Directions:

In a mixing bowl, combine the eggs, sausages, and cheese; season with salt and pepper to taste. Bake for 8-10 minutes at 400 degrees F in muffin cups greased with butter. To serve, sprinkle with parsley.

Nutrition: Cal 452; Net Carbs 2.4g; Fat 35g; Protein 31g

Bacon and Artichoke Omelet

Servings: 2 and **Total Time:** approx. 20 minutes

Ingredients:
- 1 green onion, chopped
- 4 eggs, beaten
- 1 tbsp olive oil
- 1 tbsp heavy cream
- Salt black pepper to taste
- ¼ cup canned artichoke hearts, drained and chopped
- 4 bacon slices, chopped

Directions:

In a skillet over medium heat, warm the olive oil. 3 minutes of cooking time for the bacon Stir in the green onion, heavy cream, and artichokes for 2 minutes.

Pour the eggs on top. Cook the omelette for 5-6 minutes, flipping once, until the eggs are set. Season with salt and pepper to taste. Serve.

Nutrition: Cal 447; Net Carbs 3.3g; Fat 39g; Protein 19g

Deli Ham Eggs

Servings: 2 and **Total Time:** approx. 20 minutes

Ingredients:
- 2 tbsp butter
- 4 eggs
- ½ cup olives, pitted and sliced
- 1 shallot, chopped
- Salt black pepper to taste
- 2 slices deli ham, chopped
- 1 thyme sprig, chopped

Directions:

In a mixing bowl, lightly beat the eggs with a fork. Combine the feta, flakes, garlic, and coconut milk in a mixing bowl.

Distribute the mixture among greased microwave-safe mugs. For 40 seconds, microwave the mugs. Microwave for another 70 seconds, stirring well. Serve garnished with dill.

Nutrition: Cal 431; Net Carbs 6g; Fat 36g; Protein 21g

Avocado Chili Omelet

Servings: 2 and **Total Time:** approx. 15 minutes

Ingredients:
- 2 tsp olive oil
- 2 spring garlic, chopped
- 4 eggs
- 1 cup buttermilk
- 2 tbsp fresh cilantro, chopped
- 1 ripe avocado, chopped
- 2 spring onions, chopped
- 2 tomatoes, sliced
- 1 green chili pepper, minced
- Salt and black pepper to taste

Directions:

In a mixing bowl, combine the eggs, buttermilk, salt, and black pepper. Warm the olive oil in a pan over high heat. Sauté the garlic and onions until they are soft and translucent.

Pour into the pan and smooth the surface with a spatula; cook until the eggs puff up and become firm. The bottom is brown. To one side of the omelette, combine cilantro, chilli pepper, avocado, and tomatoes. Cut into wedges after folding in half. Serve right away.

Nutrition: Cal 422; Net Carbs 11g; Fat 32g; Protein 19g

Cheese Cloud Eggs

Servings: 2 and **Total Time:** approx. 15 minutes

Ingredients:
- 1 tbsp chives, finely chopped,
- 2 bacon slices
- 3 tbsp grated Pecorino cheese
- 4 eggs, whites and yolks separated
- Salt and black pepper to taste

Directions:

Melt butter in a skillet over medium heat. Cook until the bacon is crispy on both sides, about 5 minutes. Allow it to cool before crumbling it. Beat the egg whites and salt with an electric mixer until stiff peaks form. Combine the Pecorino cheese and bacon in a mixing bowl. Spoon the mixture into four mounds on a baking sheet lined with parchment paper. In each pile, make an indentation. Spoon an egg yolk into each indentation and season with salt and pepper. Bake for 3 minutes, or until the yolks are set, in a 450°F oven. Serve garnished with chives.

Nutrition: Cal 287; Net Carbs 4.7g; Fat 24g; Protein

12g

Avocado and Eggs with Shredded Chicken

SERVINGS 4 | **PREP TIME** 10 minutes | **COOK TIME** 20 minutes

Ingredients:

2 avocados, peeled, halved lengthwise, and pitted
¼ cup shredded Cheddar cheese Sea salt
1 (4-ounce) chicken breast, cooked and shredded
Freshly ground black pepper
4 large eggs

Directions:

Preheat the oven to 425°F. Take a spoon and hollow out each side of the avocado halves until the hole is about twice the original size.

Place the avocado halves in an 8-inch-square baking dish, hollow-side up. Crack an egg into each hollow and divide the shredded chicken between each half. Sprinkle with cheese and season lightly with the salt and pepper.

Bake the avocados until the eggs are cooked through, about 15 to 20 minutes. Serve immediately.

Nutrition: Calories: 324; Fat: 25g; Protein: 19g; Total Carbs: 8g

Coconut Flaxseed Waffles

SERVINGS 4 | **PREP TIME** 15 minutes | **COOK TIME** 5 minutes

Ingredients:

Nonstick cooking spray
⅓ cup coconut oil, melted
2 cups ground flaxseed
2 tablespoons unsweetened coconut flakes
5 to 6 drops liquid stevia
½ cup water
1 tablespoon baking powder
1 teaspoon salt
¼ cup butter
5 large eggs

Directions:

Spray a waffle iron with cooking spray and heat it to a medium-high temperature. Combine the eggs, water, and coconut oil in a blender. Blend on high speed for 30 to 40 seconds.

In a medium bowl, mix the flaxseed, baking powder, and salt until combined. Pour the blender mixture into the flaxseed blend and stir. Allow to sit for 4 to 5 minutes to thicken. Add the coconut flakes and stevia, and mix well. Pour ¼ cup of batter onto the waffle iron and cook.

Repeat until all the batter has been used. Top each waffle with 1 tablespoon of butter.

Nutrition: Calories: 498; Fat: 46g; Protein: 12g; Total Carbs: 9g

Ham and Swiss Waffles

SERVINGS 4 | **PREP TIME** 10 minutes | **COOK TIME** 25 to 35 minutes

Ingredients:

1 cup almond flour, measured and sifted
2 tablespoons granulated erythritol–monk fruit blend
½ teaspoon sea salt
8 ounces (about 1 cup) cream cheese, at room temperature
¼ cup finely chopped ham
½ to ¾ cup water
¼ cup coconut flour
1 tbs psyllium husk powder
2 teaspoons baking powder
1 tbs pure vanilla extract
¼ teaspoon black pepper
5 large eggs, at room temperature
¼ cup finely chopped Swiss cheese
2 tablespoons unsalted butter, melted

Directions:

Preheat the waffle iron. In a large bowl, whisk the almond flour, coconut flour, sweetener, psyllium husk powder, baking powder, salt, and pepper, and set aside. In a medium bowl, using an electric mixer, combine the cream cheese and vanilla.

Add the eggs one at a time, mixing after each. Add the egg mixture to the dry ingredients using a rubber spatula. Fold in the ham and Swiss cheese. Add ½ cup water, and stir to combine. Add up to another ¼ cup water as needed—the batter thickens as it sits. Grease a waffle iron well with the melted butter.

Add spoonfuls of batter evenly. Close the waffle iron, and cook according to the manufacturer's instructions.

Nutrition: Calories: 583; Fat: 49g; Protein: 23g; Total Carbs: 17g

Baked Eggs in Ham Cups

SERVINGS 2 | **PREP TIME** 5 minutes | **COOK TIME** 15 minutes

Ingredients:

Cooking spray for cupcake pan	4 large eggs
1 teaspoon dried parsley	4 slices Black Forest ham

Directions:

Preheat the oven to 400°F. Spray the cupcake pan. Tuck one slice of ham into each cup.

The ham will hang over the sides. Crack one egg into each cup and garnish with the parsley. Place the cupcake pan in the preheated oven. Cook for about 15 minutes, until the egg whites are cooked but the yolk is still runny.

Nutrition: (2 eggs with 2 slices ham): Calories: 221; Fat: 14g;

Florentine Breakfast Sandwich

SERVINGS 1 | **PREP TIME** 10 minutes | **COOK TIME** 5 minutes

Ingredients:

1 teaspoon extra-virgin olive oil	¼ teaspoon salt
¼ teaspoon freshly ground black pepper	1 large egg
	1 tablespoon jarred pesto
	1 Versatile Sandwich Round
¼ ripe avocado, mashed	1 (¼-inch) thick tomato slice
1 (1-ounce) slice fresh mozzarella	

Directions:

In a small skillet, heat the olive oil over high heat. When the oil is very hot, crack the egg into the skillet and reduce the heat to medium.

Sprinkle the top of the egg with salt and pepper and let it cook for 2 minutes, or until set on bottom. Using a spatula, flip the egg to cook on the other side to desired level of doneness (1 to 2 minutes for a runnier yolk, 2 to 3 minutes for a more set yolk). Remove the egg from the pan.

Cut the sandwich round in half horizontally and toast, if desired. Spread the pesto on a toasted bread half. Top with mashed avocado, the tomato slice, mozzarella, and the cooked egg. Top with the other bread half and eat warm.

Nutrition: Calories: 548; Fat: 48g; Protein: 21g; Total Carbs: 8g

Baked Omelet with Pancetta and Swiss Cheese

SERVINGS 4 | **PREP TIME** 10 minutes | **COOK TIME** 40 minutes

1 tablespoon butter, plus more for greasing	10 large eggs
1 cup canned coconut milk	1 cup diced pancetta
Freshly ground black pepper	1 cup shredded Swiss cheese
	2 teaspoons chopped chives Pinch sea salt

Directions:

Preheat the oven to 350°F. Lightly grease a 9-inch-square baking dish with butter, and set aside. In a large skillet over medium-high heat, melt the butter. Cook the pancetta, stirring, until it is crispy, about 4 minutes.

Remove the skillet from the heat, and transfer the pancetta to a medium bowl. Add the eggs, coconut milk, cheese, and chives to the bowl, and whisk to blend. Season the egg mixture with salt and pepper.

Pour the egg mixture into the baking dish, and bake the omelet until it is set, puffy, and golden, about 30 minutes, and serve.

Nutrition: Calories: 496; Fat: 41g; Protein: 27g; Total Carbs: 6g

Eggs with Goat Cheese & Asparagus

SERVINGS 1 | **PREP TIME** 5 minutes | **COOK TIME** 15 minutes

Ingredients:

3 asparagus spears, woody ends removed	1 tablespoon avocado oil
1 tablespoon goat cheese	2 large eggs
A few leaves of cilantro or other fresh herbs	1 tsp extra-virgin olive oil, for drizzling

Directions:

In a small skillet, heat 2 tablespoons of water over medium-high heat. Add the asparagus, cover, and steam until the asparagus is tender.

Place the asparagus on a plate, slice them in half lengthwise, and set aside. In a small bowl, beat the eggs. Pour out any water left in the skillet. Add the avocado oil, and heat over medium heat.

Add the eggs and goat cheese to the skillet, and season with salt and pepper. Cook until the eggs are set and the goat cheese is melted. Serve alongside the asparagus with the olive oil drizzled over top. Garnish with cilantro or fresh herbs of your choice.

Nutrition: Calories: 334; Fat: 29g; Protein: 14g; Total Carbs: 4g

Loaded Denver Omelet

SERVINGS 1 | **PREP TIME** 5 minutes | **COOK TIME** 5 minutes

Ingredients:

1 tablespoon butter	3 large eggs Sea salt
Freshly ground black pepper	1 scallion, white and green parts thinly sliced
¼ bell pepper, seeds and ribs removed, thinly	2 tablespoons shredded Cheddar cheese

sliced
2 tablespoons diced ham

Directions:

Melt the butter in a small nonstick skillet over medium heat. Whisk the eggs in a small bowl and season with salt and pepper. Pour the eggs into the skillet and cook for 1 to 2 minutes, or until barely set around the edges. Lift up the edges with a spatula and tilt the pan so the liquid eggs slide underneath.

Sprinkle the ham, scallion, bell pepper, and shredded cheese over the eggs and continue cooking for another minute.

Fold the omelet in half and cook for 1 minute. Flip carefully and cook for 1 more minute or until the center of the omelet is no longer watery.

Nutrition: Calories: 415; Fat: 33g; Protein: 26g; Total Carbs: 4g

Mushroom and Bacon Frittata

SERVINGS 6 | **PREP TIME** 10 minutes | **COOK TIME** 15 minutes

Ingredients:

2 tablespoons olive oil
ground black pepper
6 bacon slices, cooked and chopped
10 large eggs, beaten
1 cup sliced fresh mushrooms
½ cup crumbled goat cheese Sea salt
1 cup shredded spinach

Directions:

Preheat the oven to 350°F. Place a large ovenproof skillet over medium-high heat and add the olive oil. Sauté the mushrooms until lightly browned, about 3 minutes.

Add the spinach and bacon and sauté until the greens are wilted, about 1 minute. Add the eggs and cook, lifting the edges of the frittata with a spatula so uncooked egg flows underneath, for 3 to 4 minutes.

Sprinkle the top with the crumbled goat cheese and season lightly with salt and pepper. Bake until set and lightly browned, about 15 minutes. Remove the frittata from the oven, and let it stand for 5 minutes. Cut into 6 wedges and serve immediately.

Nutrition: Calories: 316; Fat: 27g; Protein: 16g; Total Carbs: 1g

Bacon-Wrapped Egg Cups

SERVINGS 3 (MAKES 6 EGG CUPS) | **PREP TIME** 10 minutes | **COOK TIME** 20 minutes

Ingredients:

6 bacon slices
6 large eggs
2 tablespoons chopped scallions
1 teaspoon avocado oil
⅛ teaspoon black pepper
¼ teaspoon salt

Directions:

Preheat the oven to 375°F. Line a baking sheet with parchment paper. Add the bacon slides to the baking sheet and cook for 6 minutes in the oven. Remove the bacon slices from the oven and let cool slightly.

Grease a six cup muffin pan with avocado oil. Carefully place each bacon slice inside the muffin cup creating a circle around the edge of each well.

Crack one egg into each muffin cup; top with the scallions, salt, and pepper. Bake for 12 to 14 minutes, until the egg white is cooked but the yolk is still runny. Let cool for 1 to 2 minutes then remove each egg cup carefully with a spoon and serve.

Nutrition: Calories: 244; Fat: 18g; Protein: 19g; Total Carbs: 1g

Spinach, Mushroom, and Cheddar Frittata

SERVINGS 4 | **PREP TIME** 5 minutes | **COOK TIME** 25 minutes, plus 5 minutes to rest

Ingredients:

3 tablespoons olive oil or unsalted butter
6 large eggs
10 ounces fresh baby spinach
Freshly ground black pepper
1 (8-ounce) package white mushrooms, sliced
¾ cup shredded Cheddar cheese, divided
Salt
Chopped fresh parsley, for garnish (optional)

Directions:

Preheat the oven to 400°F. In a 12-inch oven-safe skillet, heat the oil over medium heat. Add the mushrooms and sauté for 5 minutes.

Add the spinach in batches, letting it wilt down before stirring and adding more. Meanwhile, in a large bowl, beat the eggs with ¼ cup of Cheddar and season well with salt and pepper. Drain any excess liquid from the skillet, then add the egg mixture.

Let cook without touching for 5 minutes, or until the edges start to set. Sprinkle the remaining ½ cup of Cheddar over the frittata, then bake for 10 minutes, or until set in the center. Remove from the oven and let rest for 5 minutes before serving. Garnish with the parsley, if using.

Nutrition: Calories: 298; Fat: 23g; Protein: 18g; Total Carbs: 5g

Brussels Sprouts & Ground Beef Scrambled Eggs

1 SERVING | **PREP TIME** 10 minutes | **COOK TIME** 10 to 15 minutes

Ingredients:

- 1 tablespoon butter-flavored coconut oil
- 10 Brussels sprouts, halved
- ¼ pound ground beef (80 percent lean)
- Salt
- 2 large eggs, beaten
- Freshly ground black pepper
- Sugar-free hot sauce (optional)

Directions:

In a sauté pan over medium-high heat, melt the coconut oil and then add the Brussels sprouts. Stir, then cover and cook for 3 to 5 minutes.

Add the ground beef and cook for another 3 to 5 minutes, stirring continuously. Add the eggs, season with salt and pepper, and scramble everything together for 2 to 3 minutes. Pour the mixture onto a plate and top with hot sauce.

Nutrition: Calories: 626; Fat: 46g; Protein: 38g; Total Carbs: 18g

Mexican Egg Casserole

SERVINGS 8 | **PREP TIME** 15 minutes | **COOK TIME** 45 minutes

Ingredients:

- Nonstick cooking spray
- 2 tablespoons olive oil
- ½ cup minced onion
- Freshly ground black pepper
- 3 cups raw spinach
- Salt
- 1½ cups grated Cheddar cheese, divided
- 1 cup chopped green bell pepper
- 2 garlic cloves, minced
- ½ cup unsweetened almond milk
- 12 large eggs
- 1 avocado, sliced
- 1 cup salsa

Directions:

Preheat the oven to 375°F. Spray a nonstick 9-by-13-inch casserole dish with cooking spray and set aside. In a skillet over medium-high heat, warm the olive oil.

Add the bell pepper, onion, and garlic, and sauté for about 3 minutes. Then add the spinach and allow to wilt. Season with a pinch of salt and pepper. Spread the veggies out in the casserole dish. In a medium bowl, whisk the milk, eggs, and 1 cup of Cheddar cheese and pour the egg mixture over the veggies.

Top with the remaining ½ cup of Cheddar cheese. Bake for 40 minutes, or until the edges of the casserole are brown and the eggs are set. Divide the casserole between eight plates. Top with the avocado slices and salsa, and serve warm or cold.

Nutrition: Calories: 271; Fat: 21g; Protein: 15g; Total Carbs: 7g

Cheesy Sausage & Egg Muffins

SERVINGS 12 | **PREP TIME** 10 minutes | **COOK TIME** 30 minutes

Ingredients:

- Nonstick cooking spray (optional)
- 2 tablespoons butter
- ½ teaspoon garlic powder
- ½ cup grated Cheddar cheese
- 6 ounces cream cheese
- 8 large eggs
- ½ tbs ground black pepper
- 4 ounces cooked breakfast sausage

Directions:

Preheat the oven to 350°F. Prepare a 12-cup muffin pan with cooking spray or cupcake liners.

In a blender, mix the eggs, cream cheese, butter, pepper, and garlic powder until fluffy.

Divide the mixture evenly between the prepared muffin cups. Sprinkle each cup evenly with the sausage and cheese. Bake for 30 minutes. Serve warm.

Nutrition: (1 muffin) Calories: 168; Fat: 15g; Protein: 7g; Total Carbs: 1g;

Egg & Cheese Biscuit Casserole

SERVINGS 9 | **PREP TIME** 15 minutes | **COOK TIME** 20 minutes

Ingredients:

- ¼ cup butter, at room temperature, plus more for greasing the pan
- 2 teaspoons baking powder
- 7 large eggs, divided
- 2 tsp heavy cream
- ½ cup coconut flour
- 1 cup grated Cheddar cheese
- ¼ teaspoon salt
- 1 teaspoon salt
- ¼ cup sour cream
- 1 tsp ground black pepper

Directions:

Preheat the oven to 400°F. Grease a 9-inch-square casserole dish and set aside. In a small bowl, whisk the coconut flour, baking powder, and salt. In a medium bowl, whisk 3 eggs, the sour cream, and butter. Pour the dry mixture into the egg mixture, and mix well until just a few lumps remain. Transfer the dough mixture to the casserole dish and spread it evenly across the bottom. In a small bowl, whisk the remaining 4 eggs and the heavy cream, salt, and pepper, and pour over the dough mixture. Bake for 15 minutes.

Pull the casserole out and sprinkle the cheese across the top. Return to the oven for another 3 to 5 minutes or until the cheese is melted. Allow to rest for 5 to 10 minutes before serving.

Nutrition: (⅑ of casserole) Calories 280; Fat: 22g; Protein: 14g; Total Carbs: 9g

French Toast Egg Muffins

SERVINGS 12 | **PREP TIME** 10 minutes | **COOK TIME** 20 to 25 minutes

Ingredients:

- Nonstick cooking spray (optional)
- ½ teaspoon cinnamon
- 8 large eggs
- 1 tablespoon butter
- 1 teaspoon vanilla extract
- 1 (8-ounce) brick cream cheese
- 2 tablespoons sugar-free maple syrup, plus ¾ cup for topping
- 1 teaspoon baking soda

Directions:

Preheat the oven to 350°F. Prepare a 12-cup muffin pan with nonstick cooking spray or cupcake liners. In a blender, combine the eggs, cream cheese, 2 tablespoons of syrup, butter, vanilla, baking soda, and cinnamon and pulse until well blended.

Divide the mixture evenly between the prepared muffin cups. Fill the cups all the way to the top. Bake for 20 to 25 minutes. Cool then drizzle with syrup and serve.

Nutrition: (1 muffin) Calories 122; Fat: 11g; Protein: 5g; Total Carbs: 1g

Asparagus Gouda Frittata

SERVINGS 4 | **PREP TIME** 10 minutes | **COOK TIME** 12 minutes

Ingredients:

- 3 tablespoons butter, divided
- 1 teaspoon minced garlic
- 4 large eggs
- ¼ teaspoon sea salt
- 1 cup shredded mild Gouda cheese
- 2 tablespoons chopped fresh parsley
- ½ onion, chopped
- 2 cups asparagus, cut into 1-inch pieces
- ⅛ teaspoon freshly ground black pepper

Directions:

Preheat the oven to broil. Melt half the butter in a medium ovenproof skillet over medium-high heat. Sauté the onion and garlic until softened, about 3 minutes.

Add the asparagus and sauté until tender, about 4 minutes. Use a spoon to transfer the vegetables to a plate and wipe the skillet. In a medium bowl, whisk the eggs, salt, and pepper. Melt the remaining butter.

Add the egg mixture to the skillet and cook until set, about 4 minutes, lifting the edges of cooked egg to allow the liquid to run underneath. When the eggs are just set, arrange the asparagus mixture evenly on top and top with cheese. Transfer to the broiler and broil until the cheese is melted, about 1 minute. Serve topped with parsley.

Nutrition: Calories: 271; Fat: 22g; Protein: 15g; Total Carbs: 6g

Salmon and Egg Scramble

SERVINGS 6 | **PREP TIME** 5 minutes | **COOK TIME** 10 minutes

Ingredients:

- 8 large eggs
- ¼ teaspoon salt
- ¼ cup butter
- 2 tbs heavy (whipping) cream
- ¼ tbs ground black pepper
- 1 (6-ounce) salmon fillet, skinned and diced into small slivers

Directions:

In a bowl, thoroughly whisk the eggs, cream, salt, and pepper. In a large nonstick skillet over medium heat, melt the butter. Add the eggs and salmon to the pan and cook over medium heat for 6 to 8 minutes or until the eggs are softly scrambled and the salmon pieces are cooked. Stir constantly to create creamy scrambled eggs.

Nutrition: Calories: 226; Fat: 18g; Protein: 15g; Total Carbs: 1g

Asparagus, Mushroom & Fennel Frittata

SERVINGS 4 | **PREP TIME** 5 to 10 minutes | **COOK TIME** 30 minutes

Ingredients:

- 1 teaspoon coconut or regular butter, plus more for greasing
- ½ cup mushrooms, sliced (optional)
- 1 teaspoon salt
- 1 tomato, sliced
- 8 large eggs
- ½ cup diced fennel
- 8 asparagus spears, diced
- ½ cup full-fat regular milk or coconut milk
- ½ teaspoon freshly ground black pepper
- Grated cheese (optional)

Directions:

Preheat the oven to 350°F. Grease a pie dish with butter. Melt 1 teaspoon of butter in a medium skillet over medium-high heat and sauté the asparagus, fennel, and mushrooms (if using) for about 5 minutes, or until fork-tender.

Transfer the vegetables to the prepared pie dish. Whisk the eggs and milk in a medium bowl until combined. Pour the egg mixture over the vegetables in the pie dish, season with salt and pepper, and lightly mix.

Arrange the tomato slices on top and bake for about 30 minutes. Remove from the oven and let cool for 5 to 10 minutes. Slice into wedges and sprinkle with grated cheese, if desired.

Nutrition: Calories: 188; Fat: 12g; Protein: 14g; Total Carbs: 6g

Ham and Cheese Poached Egg Cups

MAKES 12 | **PREP TIME** 5 minutes | **COOK TIME** 20 minutes

Ingredients:

Nonstick cooking spray
1 cup shredded Cheddar cheese
Salt
2 or 3 scallions (green parts only), sliced
12 slices deli ham (about 1 pound)
12 large eggs
ground black pepper
Paprika (optional)

Directions:

Preheat the oven to 400°F. Lightly spray a muffin tin with cooking spray. Place a slice of ham over each muffin cup and press down to form a cup shape. Evenly divide the cheese among the 12 cups.

Carefully crack 1 egg into each cup, keeping the yolk intact. Lightly season with salt, pepper, and a pinch of paprika (if using). Bake for 18 minutes or until the yolks are done to your liking. While still hot, garnish with the scallions, then allow to cool slightly before serving.

Nutrition: Calories: 172; Fat: 11g; Protein: 15g; Total Carbs: 2g

Chorizo Egg Muffins

SERVINGS 12 | **PREP TIME** 10 minutes | **COOK TIME** 32 minutes

Ingredients:

Nonstick cooking spray
¼ tbs ground black pepper
1½ cups shredded Monterey Jack cheese, divided
6 large eggs
1½ tablespoons salsa
12 ounces Mexican chorizo, casing removed
2 ounces cream cheese, at room temperature
2 tablespoons sour cream
½ teaspoon kosher salt

Directions:

Preheat the oven to 325°F. Grease a muffin tin with cooking spray. In a large skillet over medium-high heat, cook the chorizo for 7 to 10 minutes, breaking it up into crumbles, until thoroughly cooked.

Evenly divide the cooked chorizo and Monterey Jack cheese among the prepared muffin cups. In a blender, blend the eggs, cream cheese, sour cream, salsa, salt, and pepper.

Evenly divide the egg mixture among the muffin cups, and bake for 20 to 25 minutes, or until set. Let the muffins cool in the pan for at least 20 minutes before removing them. Serve warm or at room temperature.

Nutrition: Calories: 240; Fat: 20g; Protein: 14g; Total Carbs: 1g

Bacon Broccoli Crustless Quiche Cups

MAKES 12 | **PREP TIME** 10 minutes | **COOK TIME** 20 minutes

Ingredients:

Nonstick cooking spray
½ tbs ground black pepper
1 cup shredded Cheddar or pepper Jack cheese
½ cup heavy (whipping) cream
1 cup chopped fresh broccoli
½ teaspoon salt
½ cup chopped cooked bacon
8 large eggs
½ teaspoon onion powder

Directions:

Preheat the oven to 350°F. Thoroughly coat the cups of a 12-cup muffin tin with cooking spray. Evenly divide the broccoli, cheese, and bacon between the muffin cups.

In a large bowl, whisk the eggs, cream, onion powder, salt, and pepper until well combined. Pour the egg mixture into the muffin cups, distributing it evenly. Bake for 18 minutes or until set.

Nutrition: Calories: 143; Fat: 12g; Protein: 8g; Total Carbs: 1g

Scrambled Eggs with Mackerel

SERVINGS 4 | **PREP TIME** 5 minutes | **COOK TIME** 10 minutes

Ingredients:

6 large eggs
1 teaspoon garlic powder
½ teaspoon freshly ground black pepper
2 Roma tomatoes, chopped
1 (4-ounce) can olive oil–packed mackerel fillets, oil reserved and chopped
2 ounces goat cheese, at room temperature
2 tablespoons minced onion
7 tablespoons extra-virgin olive oil, divided
¼ cup chopped olives
2 tablespoons chopped fresh parsley, oregano, rosemary, or cilantro or 1 teaspoon dried herbs

Directions:

In a small bowl, whisk the eggs, goat cheese, 2 tablespoons of olive oil, garlic powder, and pepper. In a medium nonstick skillet, heat 1 tablespoon of olive oil over medium-low heat. Sauté the tomato and onion for 2 to 3 minutes, until soft and the water from the tomato has evaporated.

Add the egg mixture to the skillet and scramble for 3 to 4 minutes, until set and creamy. Remove the skillet from the heat and stir in the mackerel with the reserved oil, olives, and parsley.

Serve warm with each serving drizzled with an additional 1 tablespoon of olive oil.

Nutrition: Calories: 479; Fat: 45g; Protein: 17g; Total Carbs: 4g

Sausage Verde Casserole

PREP TIME 20 minutes | **COOK TIME** 35 minutes | SERVINGS: 10

Ingredients:

Oil or nonstick cooking spray (optional)
1 (11-ounce) jar green pepper sauce
2 cups shredded Cheddar cheese
¼ teaspoon freshly ground black pepper
2 pounds hot breakfast sausage, cooked drained
½ cup heavy (whipping) cream
¼ teaspoon salt
18 large eggs

Directions:

Preheat the oven to 350°F, and lightly grease a 9-by-13-inch baking dish or line with parchment paper.

In a medium bowl, mix the cooked sausage, eggs, green sauce, heavy cream, cheese, salt, and pepper, and pour into the prepared baking dish. Bake for 35 minutes, or until the center is cooked through. Serve warm.

Nutrition: Calories: 566; Fat: 45g; Protein: 34g; Total Carbs: 5g

Sausage and Cheese Frittata

SERVINGS 8 | **PREP TIME** 10 minutes | **COOK TIME** 35 minutes

Ingredients:

¼ cup butter, melted, plus more for greasing pan
½ teaspoon garlic powder
½ teaspoon paprika
½ teaspoon freshly ground black pepper 1 or 2 dashes favorite hot sauce (optional)
1 cup cooked ground breakfast sausage
¾ cup heavy (whipping) cream
½ teaspoon onion powder
½ teaspoon salt
½ cup shredded Cheddar cheese
10 large eggs
½ cup diced scallion
½ cup diced red bell pepper

Directions:

Preheat the oven to 350°F. Grease a 9-by-13-inch glass casserole dish with butter or cooking spray. In a large bowl, whisk the eggs, cream, butter, garlic powder, onion powder, paprika, salt, pepper, hot sauce (if using), and Cheddar until well combined.

Pour into the prepared casserole dish. Evenly distribute the sausage, scallion, and bell pepper into the egg mixture.

Place on the center rack of the oven and bake for 35 minutes or until the frittata is cooked through and the top is very lightly browned. Allow to rest for 5 minutes and serve.

Nutrition: Calories: 284; Fat: 25g; Protein: 12g; Total Carbs: 2g

Turkey Egg Scramble

SERVINGS 1 | **PREP TIME** 5 minutes | **COOK TIME** 15 minutes

Ingredients:

1 teaspoon avocado oil
¼ red bell pepper, diced
¼ teaspoon chili powder
2 large eggs
¼ medium red onion, diced
4 ounces ground turkey
¼ cup fresh spinach
2 garlic cloves, minced

Directions:

In a skillet, heat the oil over medium heat. Add the onion, bell pepper, and garlic and sauté for 5 to 7 minutes until soft. Add the turkey, then season with the chili powder and salt and freshly ground black pepper to taste.

Continue to cook until the turkey begins to brown. In a small bowl, beat the eggs, and pour them into the skillet over the turkey and vegetables. Layer the spinach on top of the eggs, stir to combine, and continue to cook until the eggs are set.

Nutrition: Calories: 367; Fat: 23g; Protein: 32g; Total Carbs: 8g

Bacon Eggs Benedict Cups

SERVINGS 2 | **PREP TIME** 10 minutes | **COOK TIME** 20 minutes

Ingredients:

Nonstick cooking spray
½ cup butter (1 stick)
Juice of ½ lemon

1 avocado, pitted and sliced, for serving
4 large eggs, plus 3 egg yolks
⅛ teaspoon cayenne pepper Chopped fresh parsley, for
Serving
4 slices vegan bacon

Directions:

Preheat the oven to 350°F. Spray 4 cups of a muffin tin generously with cooking spray. Line each muffin cup with a strip of bacon, covering the sides as much as possible. Break 1 egg into each bacon nest.

Bake the egg cups for 15 to 20 minutes, until the eggs are set in the center. While the eggs are cooking, melt the butter in a cup in the microwave for 30 to 40 seconds. In a blender, combine the egg yolks, lemon juice, and cayenne.

With the blender on the lowest speed, slowly drizzle the melted butter into the blender until it is emulsified. Remove the egg cups from the oven and carefully remove each egg basket from the muffin tin. Drizzle the hollandaise sauce over the eggs. Sprinkle each cup with parsley and top with a few avocado slices.

Nutrition: (2 egg cups) Calories: 822; Fat: 78g; Protein: 19g; Total Carbs: 11g

Savory Sausage Balls

MAKES 30 SAUSAGE BALLS | **PREP TIME** 10 minutes | **COOK TIME** 25 minutes

Ingredients:

1 pound breakfast sausage	1½ cups shredded mozzarella cheese
1 cup coconut flour	
1 (5-ounce) package Boursin cheese, Garlic & Fine Herbs or any other flavor	2 tablespoons butter, at room temperature
	2 teaspoons baking powder
1 teaspoon garlic salt	2 large eggs

Directions:
Preheat the oven to 350°F. Line a baking sheet with parchment paper. In a large bowl, combine all the ingredients and mix well with your hands.
Using a cookie scoop, drop scoopfuls into your hand, roll into balls, and place on the baking sheet. Bake for about 25 minutes or until golden brown.

Nutrition: (2 sausage balls) Calories: 254; Fat: 19g; Protein: 12g; Total Carbs: 9g

Basic Recipes & Simple Recipes

Green Smoothie

Servings: 2 and **Total Time:** approx. 5 minutes

Ingredients:

1 cucumber, peeled and diced Chia seeds to garnish	1 cup collard greens, chopped 3 stalks celery, chopped
1 ripe avocado, pitted, sliced	2 cups spinach, chopped
1 cup ice cubes	

Directions:

In a blender, combine the collard greens, celery, avocado, and ice cubes and blend for 50 seconds. Process for another 40 seconds, or until the spinach and cucumber are smooth.

Pour the smoothie into glasses, top with chia seeds, and serve.

Nutrition: Cal 247; Net Carbs 6.6g; Fat 20g; Protein 5g

Zucchini Pasta Puttanesca

Servings: 4 and **Total Time:** approx. 30 minutes

Ingredients:

2 garlic cloves, sliced	½ teaspoon cayenne pepper
4 anchovies in olive oil, drained	2 teaspoon olive oil
1 teaspoon capers, chopped	2 lb zucchinis, spiralized
	½ tsp dried oregano
¼ cup Parmesan cheese, grated	¼ cup black pitted olives, halved
2 tbsp fresh basil, chopped	2 (14-oz) cans diced tomatoes
Salt and black pepper to taste	

Directions:

In a saucepan, heat the olive oil and toss in the zucchini; stir quickly for about 1 minute. Set aside and season to taste.

Add the garlic, cayenne pepper, oregano, capers, and anchovies to the saucepan and cook for 2-4 minutes, or until the anchovies melt into the oil.

Pour in the tomatoes and cook for 10-12 minutes, stirring frequently, until the sauce thickens slightly; season with salt and pepper. To serve, ladle the sauce over the zucchini pasta and garnish with olives, Parmesan cheese, and basil.

Nutrition: Cal 216; Net Carbs 10g; Fat 15g; Protein 11g

Green Cheese Bowls

Servings: 4 and **Total Time:** approx. 10 minutes

Ingredients:

½ cup baby kale	2 zucchinis, spiralized
½ lemon, juiced	1/3 cup crumbled goat cheese 1/3 cup crumbled feta cheese
1 tbsp olive oil	
2 tbsp toasted pine nuts	¼ tsp Dijon mustard

Salt and black pepper to taste	1 tbsp dill, chopped

Directions:

Season the zucchinis in a bowl with salt and pepper. Combine the lemon juice, olive oil, and mustard in a small bowl. Toss the zucchini with the mixture to coat evenly.

Combine the dill, kale, goat cheese, feta cheese, and pine nuts in a mixing bowl. Toss everything together and serve.

Nutrition: Cal 223; Net Carbs 7g; Fat 15g; Protein 10g

Guacamole

Servings: 4 and **Total Time:** approx. 10 minutes

Ingredients:

2 avocados, peeled, pitted	½ yellow onion, minced
1 tomato, peeled, chopped	½ lime, juiced
2 tbsp fresh cilantro, chopped	Salt and chili powder to taste

Directions:

Fry the bacon for 5 minutes in a skillet over medium heat. Set aside a baking sheet greased with bacon fat. In a mixing bowl, combine the Chèvre cheese, cream cheese, butter, and stir-fried bacon until well combined. Form the mixture into 8 "balls" and arrange them on the baking sheet. 30 minutes in the freezer

Nutrition: Cal 173; Net Carbs 3.4g; Fat 20g; Protein 2g

Broccoli Beef

Servings: 4 and **Total Time:** approx. 25 minutes

Ingredients:

1 lb skirt steak, sliced	1 tsp red pepper flakes
3 tbsp olive oil	Salt and black pepper to taste
1 lb broccoli florets	

Directions:

Steam the broccoli for 5-7 minutes, or until crisp-tender but bright green. Set aside after seasoning with salt and drizzled with olive oil. In a large skillet over medium heat, heat the remaining olive oil. Cook the steak for 6-8 minutes on medium-high heat. Transfer to a plate and season with red pepper flakes, salt, and pepper to taste. Place the broccoli on top of the plate and serve.

Nutrition: Cal 361; Net Carbs 1.9g; Fat 22g; Protein 34g

Raspberry Yogurt Parfait

Servings: 2 and **Total Time:** approx. 10 minutes

Ingredients:

3 mint sprigs, chopped	½ lemon, zested
2 tbsp chia seeds	1 cup fresh raspberries
1 cup Greek yogurt	2 drops liquid stevia

Directions:

In a small mixing bowl, combine the Greek yoghurt and stevia. In medium serving glasses, divide half of the yoghurt, raspberries, lemon zest, mint, and chia seeds. Repeat with the next layer. Serve chilled.

Nutrition: Cal 243; Net Carbs 10g; Fat 10g; Protein 10g

Tuna Pesto Caprese Salad

Servings: 2 and **Total Time:** approx. 10 minutes

Ingredients:

½ cup Parmesan, grated	½ lemon, juiced
4 oz canned tuna chunks in water, drained	1 ball fresh mozzarella, sliced 4 basil leaves
½ cup pine nuts	½ cup extra virgin olive oil
1 tomato, sliced	

Directions:

Blend the basil leaves, pine nuts, Parmesan cheese, and extra virgin olive oil in a food processor until smooth. Add the lemon juice and mix well. Arrange the tomato and cheese slices on a serving plate. Serve with the tuna chunks and pesto scattered on top.

Nutrition: Cal 364; Net Carbs 1g; Fat 31g; Protein 21g

Creamy Avocado "Pasta"

Servings: 4 and **Total Time:** approx. 30 minutes

Ingredients:

1 garlic clove, minced	2 eggs, beaten
1 ½ cups cream cheese	1 avocado, peeled and pitted
5 ½ tbsp psyllium husk	
1 tbsp lime juice	¼ cup olive oil
¼ cup fresh parsley	Salt black pepper to taste
1 oz chopped pecans	2 tbsp grated Parmesan
1 cup heavy cream	

Directions:

Preheat the oven to 300 degrees Fahrenheit. Combine the eggs, cream cheese, psyllium husk, and salt to taste in a mixing bowl. Whisk the batter until it is smooth. LineCover a baking sheet with wax paper, pour in the batter, and cover with another sheet of wax paper. Flatten the dough into a sheet with a rolling pin. After 12 minutes, remove the wax paper and cut the "pasta" into thin strips lengthwise. Cut each piece in half, then place in a bowl and set aside.

Puree avocado, heavy cream, lime juice, parsley, and garlic in a blender until smooth. Apply olive oil to the "pasta." Pour the avocado sauce over the "pasta" and toss to combine. Season with salt, pepper, and freshly grated Parmesan cheese to taste.

Nutrition: Cal 569; Net Carbs 8g; Fat 56g; Protein 20g

Golden Saffron Cauli Rice

Servings: 4 and **Total Time:** approx. 15 minutes

Ingredients:

1 yellow onion, thinly sliced	A pinch of saffron soaked in ¼-cup almond milk
2 cups cauli rice	1 tbsp butter
2 tbsp chopped parsley	¼ cup vegetable broth
2 tbsp olive oil	6 garlic cloves, sliced
Salt and black pepper to taste	

Directions:

In a saucepan over medium heat, warm the olive oil and fry the garlic until golden brown but not burned; set aside. In a saucepan, sauté the butter and onion for 3 minutes. Stir in the cauliflower rice.

Remove the saffron from the milk and combine it with the milk and stock in a saucepan. Cook for 5 minutes with the lid on. Season with salt, pepper, and parsley to taste. Fluff

Place the cauliflower rice on serving plates. Serve with the fried garlic as a garnish.

Nutrition: Cal 102; Net Carbs 6g; Fat 10g; Protein 2g

Coconut Butter Coffee

Servings: 2 and **Total Time:** approx. 3 minutes

Ingredients:

½ tsp ground cinnamon	2 cups freshly brewed coffee
3 tbsp unsalted butter	2 tbsp coconut oil

Directions:

Blend the brewed coffee with the coconut oil and butter in a blender. Blend until the mixture is frothy and smooth. Serve with cinnamon on top.

Nutrition: Cal 229; Net Carbs 0g; Fat 26g; Protein 2g

wrap classic pigs

Servings: 4 and **Total Time:** approx. 30 minutes

Ingredients:

8 Vienna sausages	8 thin bacon slices

Directions:

Preheat the oven to 360 degrees Fahrenheit. Wrap a slice of bacon around each sausage tightly.

Place the bacon-wrapped sausages on a baking sheet that has been greased and bake for 18-20 minutes, or until the bacon is crisp and golden. Serve and have fun!

Nutrition: Cal 320; Net Carbs 1.2g; Fat 26g; Protein 11g

Avocado Mousse "Croutons"

Servings: 4 and **Total Time:** approx. 15 minutes

Ingredients:

½ lime, juiced and zested	2 tbsp cilantro, chopped
Salt black pepper to taste	4 oz bacon, sliced
2 ripe avocados, pitted, halved	1 cup sour cream

Directions:

Stir-fry the bacon in a skillet over medium heat until crispy, about 5 minutes. Transfer to a paper towel to absorb any remaining fat.

Combine the avocado flesh, sour cream, lime juice, lime zest, salt, and pepper in a mixing bowl. Stir until everything is thoroughly combined and smooth.

Fill glass cups halfway with mousse and garnish with bacon and fresh cilantro. Serve hot or cold.

Nutrition: Cal 341; Net Carbs 4.6g; Fat 33g; Protein 10g

Scrambled Eggs Smoked Salmon

Servings: 4 and **Total Time:** approx. 15 minutes

Ingredients:

4 oz smoked salmon, chopped	½ cup sour cream
2 tbsp fresh dill, chopped	8 eggs
	Salt and black pepper to taste

2 tbsp butter

Directions:

In a medium mixing bowl, combine the eggs, sour cream, salt, and pepper. Melt the butter in a skillet over medium heat and quickly whisk in the eggs.

Reduce the heat to low and gently fold in the eggs with a spatula; cook until the eggs are barely set, about 2-3 minutes.

Remove from the heat and add the salmon. Serve garnished with dill.

Nutrition: Cal 395; Net Carbs 5.7g; Fat 31g; Protein 25g

Bacon Cheddar Egg Muffins

Servings: 4 and **Total Time:** approx. 15 minutes

Ingredients:

- 1 green onion, chopped
- 2 tbsp sour cream
- 4 eggs
- 4 bacon slices
- 2 oz cheddar cheese, grated
- 1 teaspoon red chili flakes

Directions:

Cook the bacon for 2 minutes per side in a preheated skillet over medium heat; set aside. 4 ovenproof cups, greased with bacon fat The bacon slices should line the bottom and sides of the cups. Cover with sour cream after spreading half of the cheese on top. Crack an egg into each cup and top with the remaining cheese. Microwave the cups for 1-2 minutes, or until the cheese melts. Serve topped with green onion and red chilli flakes.

Nutrition: Cal 271; Net Carbs 4.3g; Fat 22g; Protein 13g

Spinach and Brussels Sprout Salad

Servings: 2 and **Total Time:** approx. 35 minutes

Ingredients:

- 1 lb Brussels sprouts, halved
- Salt and black pepper to taste
- 1 tbsp balsamic vinegar
- 2 tbsp olive oil
- 2 tbsp extra virgin olive oil
- 1 cup baby spinach
- 1 tbsp Dijon mustard
- ½ cup hazelnuts

Directions:

Preheat the oven to 400 degrees Fahrenheit. Drizzle the Brussels sprouts with olive oil and season with salt and pepper before spreading them out on a baking sheet. Bake for 20 minutes, tossing frequently, until tender.

Toast the hazelnuts in a dry pan over medium heat for 2 minutes, then cool and chop into small pieces. Place the Brussels sprouts in a salad bowl and top with the baby spinach. Mix until everything is well combined. In the case of

In a small mixing bowl, combine the vinegar, mustard, and olive oil. To serve, drizzle the dressing over the salad and sprinkle with hazelnuts.

Nutrition: Cal 511; Net Carbs 10g; Fat 43g; Protein 14g

Smoked Mackerel Lettuce Cups

Servings: 2 and **Total Time:** approx. 20 minutes

Ingredients:

- ½ head Iceberg lettuce, firm leaves removed for cups
- 4 oz smoked mackerel, flaked
- 1 tomato, seeded, chopped
- 2 tbsp mayonnaise
- Salt and black pepper to taste
- 2 eggs
- 1 tbsp chives, chopped
- ¼ red onion, sliced
- 1 tsp lemon juice

Directions:

Boil the eggs for 10 minutes in a small pot of salted water. The eggs should then be run under cold water, peeled, and chopped into small pieces. Place them in a salad bowl.

Mix in the smoked mackerel, red onion, and tomato with a spoon. In a small mixing bowl, combine the mayonnaise, lemon juice, salt, and pepper. Place two lettuce leaves in each cup and divide the salad mixture among them.

Serve garnished with chives.

Nutrition: Cal 334; Net Carbs 8g; Fat 25g; Protein 26g

Chicken Salad with Parmesan

Servings: 2 and **Total Time:** approx. 30 min + chilling time

Ingredients:

- ½ lb chicken breasts,
- 2 tbsp Parmesan, grated

sliced
¼ cup lemon juice
2 garlic cloves, minced
2 tbsp olive oil
2 tbsp extra virgin olive oil
3 Parmesan crisps

1 romaine lettuce, shredded
Dressing
1 tbsp lemon juice
Salt and black pepper to taste

Directions:

Place the chicken, lemon juice, oil, and garlic in a Ziploc bag. Refrigerate for 1 hour after sealing the bag and shaking to combine.

Preheat the grill to medium and cook the chicken for about 2-3 minutes.

1 minute per side In a small mixing bowl, combine all of the dressing

Ingredients and stir well. Arrange the lettuce and Parmesan crisps on a serving platter. Toss the salad with the dressing to coat. To serve, top with the chicken and Parmesan cheese.

Nutrition: Cal 529; Net Carbs 5g; Fat 32g; Protein 34g

Salads Recipes & Soups Recipes

Artichoke Salad

Servings: 4 and **Total Time:** approx. 30 minutes

Ingredients:

- 6 baby artichoke hearts, halved
- ½ lemon, juiced
- 2 tsp balsamic vinegar
- 1 tbsp chopped dill
- ¼ cup olive oil
- 1 tbsp capers
- ½ red onion, sliced
- ¼ cup pitted olives, sliced
- ¼ tsp lemon zest
- Salt and black pepper to taste
- ¼ cup cherry peppers, halved

Directions:

Bring a saucepan of salted water to a boil. Add the artichokes last. Reduce the heat to low and continue to cook for 20 minutes, or until the vegetables are tender. Drain the artichokes and place them in a bowl to cool.

Toss in the remaining Ingredients except the olives, and toss well to combine. Serve with the olives on top.

Nutrition: Cal 204; Net Carbs 9g; Fat 15g; Protein 6g

Turkey Salad

Servings: 4 and **Total Time:** approx. 25 minutes

Ingredients:

- 1 tbsp xylitol
- 4 oz goat cheese, crumbled
- 3 tbsp olive oil
- 1 ¾ cups raspberries
- 1 tbsp Dijon mustard
- ½ lb turkey breasts, boneless
- 1 red onion, chopped
- 2 tbsp lime juice
- 1 cup watercress
- Salt and black pepper to taste 1 cup arugula
- ½ cup walnut halves

Directions:

Begin with the dressing: Combine xylitol, lime juice, 1 cup raspberries, pepper, mustard, 14 cup water, onion, olive oil, and salt in a blender. and blend until smooth. Set aside after straining into a bowl.

Warm a pan over medium heat and lightly coat with cooking spray. Cut the turkey in half and season with salt and black pepper. Put the skin side down in the pan. Cook for 8 minutes before flipping and cooking for another 5 minutes.

Arrange the arugula and watercress on a platter with the remaining raspberries, walnut halves, and goat cheese. To serve, slice the turkey, place it on top of the salad, and drizzle with the raspberry dressing.

Nutrition: Cal 411; Net Carbs 7g; Fat 32g; Protein 24g

Spinach Salad with Goat Cheese and Nuts

Servings: 2 and **Total Time:** approx. 20 min + cooling time

Ingredients:

- 2 cups spinach
- 2 tbsp extra virgin olive oil Salt and black pepper to taste
- ½ cup pine nuts
- 1 cup hard goat cheese, grated 2 tbsp white wine vinegar

Directions:

Preheat the oven to 390 degrees Fahrenheit. Place the grated goat cheese in two circles on two pieces of parchment paper.

Bake for 10 minutes in a preheated oven. Find two identical bowls, flip them over, and carefully place the parchment paper on top to give the cheese a bowl-like shape.

Allow to cool for 15 minutes in this manner. Divide the spinach between the bowls, season with salt and pepper, and drizzle with vinegar and olive oil. To serve, sprinkle with pine nuts.

Nutrition: Calories: 540; Net Carbohydrates: 4.4g; Fat: 52g; Protein: 19g

Thai-Style Prawn Salad

Servings: 2 and **Total Time:** approx. 20 minutes

Ingredients:

- 2 cups watercress
- 1 tbsp cilantro, chopped
- 1 tbsp sesame oil
- 1 Thai chili pepper, sliced
- 1 tomato, sliced
- 2 tsp liquid stevia
- 1 green onion, sliced
- ½ lb prawns, cooked
- 1 avocado, sliced
- ¼ tsp sesame seeds
- 1 tbsp lemon juice
- ½ tsp fish sauce

Directions:

Whisk together the stevia, sesame oil, fish sauce, and lemon juice in a mixing bowl. Toss in the prawns to coat. Refrigerate for 10 minutes, covered.

On a serving platter, combine the watercress, avocado, tomato, Thai chilli pepper, and green onion. Drizzle the marinade over the prawns. Serve with sesame seeds and cilantro on top.

Nutrition: Cal 340; Net Carbs 5.8g; Fat 25g; Protein 25g

Creamy Asparagus Soup

SERVINGS 4 | **PREP TIME** 5 minutes | **COOK TIME** 20 minutes

Ingredients:

- 6 tablespoons extra-virgin olive oil, divided
- ½ cup chopped scallions, green parts only
- ½ teaspoon red pepper flakes
- ¼ cup tahini (ground sesame seed paste)
- Juice and zest of 1 lemon
- 1 pound asparagus, trimmed and cut 2 inch pcs
- 1 teaspoon salt
- 4 garlic cloves, minced
- 2 cups vegetable or chicken stock
- 2 tablespoons toasted pumpkin seeds, for garnish
- 1 cup water

Directions:

In a medium saucepan, heat 2 tablespoons of olive oil over medium heat. Sauté the asparagus for 2 to 3 minutes, until just tender. Add the scallions, garlic, salt, and red pepper flakes and sauté for another 2 to 3 minutes, until fragrant. Add the stock and water, increase the heat to high, and bring to a boil. Reduce the heat to low, cover, and simmer for 8 to 10 minutes, or until the vegetables are tender. Remove from the heat and allow to cool slightly. Add the tahini, remaining ¼ cup of olive oil, and lemon juice and zest. Using an immersion blender, puree the soup until smooth and creamy. Serve warm garnished with toasted seeds.

Nutrition: Calories: 329; Fat: 30g; Protein: 7g; Total Carbs: 12g

Vegetarian French Onion Soup

SERVINGS 6 | **PREP TIME** 10 minutes | **COOK TIME** 30 minutes

Ingredients:

- 1 tablespoon butter
- 1 bay leaf
- 1 tablespoon minced garlic
- 2 cups shredded Gruyère cheese
- 2 large white onions, sliced 6 cups vegetable broth
- ½ teaspoon salt

Directions:

In a large stockpot on medium heat, melt the butter and sauté the onions until translucent, 4 to 5 minutes.

Mix in the broth, garlic, salt, and bay leaf. Bring the soup to a simmer and cook for 20 to 25 minutes, or until the onions are very soft. Sprinkle with the cheese.

Nutrition: (1 cup) Calories: 222; Fat: 14g; Protein: 16g; Total Carbs: 8g

Cauliflower-Cheddar Soup

SERVINGS 8 | **PREP TIME** 10 minutes | **COOK TIME** 30 minutes

Ingredients:

- ¼ cup butter
- 1 head cauliflower, chopped
- 1 cup heavy (whipping) cream Sea salt
- 1 cup shredded Cheddar cheese
- ½ sweet onion, chopped
- ½ teaspoon ground nutmeg
- Freshly ground black pepper
- 4 cups chicken stock

Directions:

Put a large stockpot over medium heat and add the butter. Sauté the onion and cauliflower until tender and lightly browned, about 10 minutes. Add the chicken stock and nutmeg to the pot and bring the liquid to a boil.

Reduce the heat to low and simmer until the vegetables are very tender, about 15 minutes. Remove the pot from the heat, stir in the heavy cream, and purée the soup with an immersion blender or food processor until smooth.

Season the soup with salt and pepper and serve topped with the Cheddar cheese.

Nutrition: Calories: 227; Fat: 21g; Protein: 8g; Total Carbs: 4g;

Spiced Pumpkin Soup

SERVINGS 4 | **PREP TIME** 5 minutes | **COOK TIME** 1 hour on high or 2 hours on low

Ingredients:

- 1 (15-ounce) can pumpkin puree
- 1 cup vegetable broth
- 1 tablespoon onion powder
- 1 teaspoon ground cumin
- Freshly ground black pepper Fresh cilantro leaves, for garnish
- 1 (13.6-ounce) can unsweetened full-fat coconut milk
- ¼ teaspoon ground turmeric Salt

Directions:

In a slow cooker bowl, combine the pumpkin, coconut milk, broth, onion powder, cumin, and turmeric.

Cover and cook for 1 hour on high or 2 hours on low. Season with salt and pepper to taste. Ladle the soup into serving bowls and garnish with cilantro.

Nutrition: Calories: 256; Fat: 22g; Protein: 5g; Total Carbs: 15g

Broccoli Cheddar Soup

SERVINGS 6 | **PREP TIME** 10 minutes | **COOK TIME** 20 minutes

Ingredients:

- ½ cup butter
- 2 celery stalks, diced
- 2 garlic cloves, minced
- 5 cups low-sodium chicken broth
- 1 cup (whipping) cream
- 16 ounces Cheddar cheese, freshly grated, plus more for garnish
- Salt
- ½ medium white onion, diced
- 4 cups diced broccoli florets
- 4 ounces full-fat cream cheese, cubed, at room temperature
- Freshly ground black pepper

Directions:

In a large stockpot over medium heat, melt the butter. Add the onion, celery, and garlic, and sauté until the onion is soft and translucent, 8 to 10 minutes. Add the broccoli and cook for 5 minutes until the broccoli is vibrantly green and soft.

Remove about ½ cup of broccoli and set aside for garnish. Add the broth and cream. Bring to a gentle boil then immediately lower the heat to low. Add the cream cheese and stir. Add the Cheddar, stirring constantly to incorporate.

Continue until all the cheese and stir until incorporated. Add salt and pepper to taste. Divide among bowls and garnish with the reserved broccoli and additional shredded Cheddar.

Nutrition: Calories: 703; Fat: 63g; Protein: 26g; Total Carbs: 11g

Tomato Basil Soup

SERVINGS 4 | **PREP TIME** 5 minutes | **COOK TIME** 20 minutes

Ingredients:

- ¼ cup extra-virgin olive oil
- 1 (28-ounce) can whole plum tomatoes with basil
- 2 cups vegetable broth
- 1 teaspoon minced garlic
- ¼ cup thinly sliced fresh basil
- 1 cup diced onion
- or chicken bone broth

Directions:

Heat the olive oil in a large pot over medium heat. Add the onion and garlic, and cook until soft and fragrant, about 10 minutes. Pour the tomatoes and broth into the pot and simmer uncovered for 10 minutes.

Remove the soup from the heat. Use an immersion blender to purée the soup until very smooth. Stir in the fresh basil, and ladle the portions into soup bowls.

Nutrition: Calories: 167; Fat: 14g; Protein: 2g; Total Carbs: 11g

Creamy Broccoli, Bacon, and Cheese Soup

SERVINGS 6 | **PREP TIME** 15 minutes | **COOK TIME** 30 minutes

Ingredients:

- 2 heads broccoli
- 2 teaspoons minced garlic
- 1 onion, chopped
- ½ teaspoon ground nutmeg
- Freshly ground black pepper
- Sea salt
- 2 tablespoons olive oil
- 4 cups low-sodium vegetable stock
- 1 cup (whipping) cream
- 1 cup shredded Cheddar cheese
- 4 slices uncured bacon, cooked and chopped

Directions:

Chop one head of broccoli, including the stem, and cut the remaining head into small florets and chop the stem. Set the florets aside.

Heat the olive oil in a large saucepan over medium-high heat. Sauté the onion and garlic until tender, about 3 minutes. Add the chopped broccoli, stock, and nutmeg. Bring the soup to a boil, then reduce the heat to low and simmer until the vegetables are tender, about 25 minutes.

While the soup is simmering, place a medium pot of water over high heat and bring to a boil. Blanch the florets until tender-crisp, about 3 minutes, and drain. Transfer the soup to a food processor or use an immersion blender and blend until smooth, then transfer back to the saucepan.

Whisk in the cream and blanched florets. Season with salt and pepper. Serve topped with cheese and bacon.

Nutrition: Calories: 320; Fat: 29g; Protein: 10g; Total Carbs: 7g

Miso Magic

SERVINGS 8 | **PREP TIME** 5 minutes | **COOK TIME** 10 minutes

Ingredients:

- 8 cups water
- shiitake mushrooms
- 1 cup chopped scallions
- 2 cups thinly sliced
- 6 to 7 tsp miso paste
- 1 teaspoon sesame oil
- 3 sheets dried seaweed
- 1 cup drained and cubed sprouted tofu

Directions:

In a large stockpot over medium heat, add the miso paste and seaweed to the water and bring to a low boil. Toss in the mushrooms, tofu, scallions, and sesame oil. Allow to simmer for about 5 minutes and serve.

Nutrition: Calories: 80; Fat: 2g; Protein: 4g; Total Carbs: 12g;

Loaded Miso Soup with Tofu and Egg

SERVINGS 4 | **PREP TIME** 10 minutes | **COOK TIME** 20 minutes

Ingredients:

- 3 cups water
- 3 tablespoons white miso paste
- 2 cups thinly sliced shiitake mushrooms
- 2 garlic cloves, very thinly sliced
- 4 baby bok choy, trimmed and quartered
- 2 hard-boiled eggs, peeled and quartered
- ¼ cup avocado or olive oil
- 3 cups vegetable broth
- 2-inch piece fresh ginger, peeled and minced
- 1 (14-ounce) package firm tofu, drained and cut into bite-sized cubes
- 2 cups spiralized zucchini (or thinly sliced if preferred)
- 2 nori seaweed sheets, cut into 2-inch very thin strips
- 2 tablespoons toasted sesame oil

Directions:

In a large saucepan, bring the water and vegetable broth to a boil over high heat. Reduce the heat to low, whisk in the miso paste and ginger, cover, and simmer for 2 minutes. Add the bok choy, mushrooms, and garlic. Simmer, covered, another 5 minutes or until vegetables are tender. Remove from heat and stir in cubed tofu and zucchini. Divide the mixture between bowls. Add 2 egg quarters and seaweed strips to each bowl. Drizzle 1 tablespoon of avocado oil and ½ teaspoon of sesame oil over each bowl. Serve warm.

Nutrition: Calories: 378; Fat: 29g; Protein: 17g; Total Carbs: 14g

Turnip and Thyme Soup

SERVINGS 4 | **PREP TIME** 10 minutes | **COOK TIME** 20 minutes

- 2 tablespoons olive oil
- 1 teaspoon dried thyme
- ½ teaspoon onion powder
- Freshly ground black pepper
- 3 cups chicken broth
- 1¼ pounds turnips (about 4 medium), peeled and cubed
- Salt
- 2 scallions, green and white parts, finely sliced
- Fresh thyme leaves, for garnish

Directions:

In a large stockpot, heat the oil over medium heat. Add the turnips, thyme, and onion powder. Cover and cook for about 10 minutes, or until the turnips are tender. Add the broth and bring to a boil. Reduce the heat to a simmer, cover, and cook for 10 minutes. Use an immersion blender to blend everything until smooth. Season with salt and pepper to taste. Transfer to serving bowls, sprinkle with the scallions, and garnish with thyme.

Nutrition: Calories: 111; Fat: 7g; Protein: 2g; Total Carbs: 10g;

Creamy Tomato Soup

SERVINGS 3 | **PREP TIME** 5 minutes | **COOK TIME** 15 minutes

Ingredients:

- 1 (14.5-ounce) can diced unsalted tomatoes
- ¼ teaspoon dried thyme
- 1 cup chicken bone broth
- ¼ cup heavy (whipping) cream
- ½ teaspoon salt
- ¼ teaspoon garlic powder Pinch ground nutmeg
- Freshly ground black pepper (optional)

Directions:

In a medium saucepan over medium-high heat, combine the tomatoes, broth, salt, thyme, garlic powder, and nutmeg. Bring to a boil and then reduce the heat to low and simmer for 5 minutes. Either with an immersion blender or in a regular blender, puree the soup. Pour the soup back into the saucepan and turn the heat to medium low. Slowly whisk in the cream and continue whisking until well combined. Simmer for 5 more minutes. Portion into bowls and serve. Season with pepper (if using).

Nutrition: Calories: 119; Fat: 8g; Protein: 5g; Total Carbs: 8g;

Easy Herbed Tomato Bisque

SERVINGS 8 | **PREP TIME** 15 minutes | **COOK TIME** 25 minutes

Ingredients:

- 3 tablespoons olive oil
- 2 garlic cloves, roughly chopped
- ½ cup diced onion
- 1 (28-ounce) can whole tomatoes (San Marzano

1 cup chicken stock or bone broth
1 tablespoon tomato paste
½ teaspoon dried thyme
style are best)
½ cup heavy cream
½ teaspoon dried basil
1 tablespoon freshly squeezed lemon juice

Directions:

In a Dutch oven over medium heat, combine the olive oil and onion. Sauté for 5 minutes until the onion is translucent, but not brown. Add the garlic and cook for 1 minute more. Stir in the tomatoes, chicken stock, tomato paste, basil, and thyme, stirring to break up the chunks of tomato. Reduce the heat to low and simmer for 15 to 20 minutes. Transfer the soup to a blender and blend until smooth. Use caution while blending hot liquids and cover the lid with a towel. Pour the soup back into the pan and stir in the lemon juice and heavy cream.

Nutrition: (½ cup): Calories: 358; Fat: 30g; Protein: 10g; Total Carbs: 12g

Beef Pho

SERVINGS 6 | **PREP TIME** 10 minutes | **COOK TIME** 30 minutes

Ingredients:

10 cups beef broth
1 cinnamon stick
2 scallions, chopped
4 garlic cloves
2 teaspoons raw honey
1 teaspoon salt

1 (7 ounce) package shirataki noodles, prepared according to the package instructions
¼ cup fresh cilantro, chopped

1 (6-inch) piece of ginger, peeled and cut in half lengthwise
¼ cup fish sauce
1 pound flank steak, finely sliced against the grain
¼ cup whole Thai basil leaves, torn into Pieces
1 lime, cut into 6 wedges

Directions:

In a large pot, combine the bone broth, ginger, cinnamon, garlic, fish sauce, honey, and salt. Bring the broth to a boil, cover and reduce the heat to low, and let it simmer for at least 30 minutes.

Strain the broth into a separate pot and discard the solids. Divide the steak, shirataki noodles, basil, cilantro, and scallions into 6 bowls and pour the hot broth into each one. Serve with lime wedges.

Nutrition: Calories: 190; Fat: 7g; Protein: 23g; Total Carbs: 7g;

Chilled Avocado-Cilantro Soup

SERVINGS 4 | **PREP TIME** 10 minutes

Ingredients:

2 very ripe avocados, peeled and pitted
½ cup chopped fresh cilantro leaves
¼ cup freshly squeezed lime juice (about 4 limes)
½ teaspoon freshly ground black pepper
½ teaspoon ground turmeric
½ cup plain Greek yogurt
1 teaspoon salt
¼ cup extra-virgin olive oil
1 teaspoon onion powder
½ teaspoon garlic powder
¼ cup roasted pumpkin seeds, to garnish (optional)

Directions:

Add the avocados, yogurt, cilantro, olive oil, lime juice, salt, onion powder, pepper, garlic powder, and turmeric to a blender or a wide cylindrical container, if using an immersion blender.

Blend until smooth and creamy. Serve chilled topped with pumpkin seeds (if using).

Nutrition: Calories: 268; Fat: 25g; Protein: 4g; Total Carbs: 9g;

Cream of Cauliflower Gazpacho

SERVINGS 4 TO 6 | **PREP TIME** 15 minutes | **COOK TIME** 25 minutes

Ingredients:

1 cup raw almonds
½ cup extra-virgin olive oil, plus 1 tablespoon, divided
1 small onion, minced
2 cups chicken or vegetable stock or broth, plus more if needed
¼ teaspoon freshly ground black pepper
½ teaspoon salt
1 small head cauliflower, stalk removed and broken into florets (about 3 cups)
1 tablespoon red wine vinegar
2 garlic cloves, finely minced

Directions:

Bring a small pot of water to a boil. Add the almonds to the water and boil for 1 minute. Drain in a colander and run under cold water. Pat dry and squeeze the meat of each almond out of its skin.

Discard the skins. In a food processor or blender, blend the almonds and salt. With the processor running, drizzle in ½ cup extra-virgin olive oil, scraping down the sides as needed. Set the almond paste aside. In a large stockpot, heat the remaining 1 tablespoon olive oil over medium-high heat. Add the onion and sauté until golden, 3 to 4 minutes. Add the cauliflower florets and sauté for another 3 to 4 minutes.

Add the garlic and sauté for 1 minute more. Add 2 cups of stock and bring to a boil. Cover, reduce the heat to medium-low, and simmer the vegetables until tender, 8 to 10 minutes. Remove from the heat and allow to cool slightly. Add the vinegar and pepper. Using an immersion blender, blend until smooth.

With the blender running, add the almond paste and blend until smooth, adding extra stock if the soup is too thick. Serve warm, or chill in refrigerator at least 4 to 6 hours to serve a cold gazpacho.

Nutrition: Calories: 505; Fat: 45g; Protein: 10g; Total Carbs: 15g

Poultry Recipes

Stuffed Chicken Breasts

Servings: 2 and **Total Time:** approx. 60 minutes

Ingredients:

- 2 tbsp butter
- 1 tomato, chopped
- ¼ cup goat cheese
- 1 tbsp fresh dill, chopped
- 2 tbsp olive oil
- 2 cucumbers, spiralized
- 2 chicken breasts
- 1 cup baby spinach
- 1 carrot, shredded
- Salt and black pepper to taste
- 1 tsp dried oregano
- 1 tbsp rice vinegar

Directions:

Preheat the oven to 390 degrees Fahrenheit. Coat a baking dish lightly with cooking spray. Heat a skillet over medium heat. Half of the butter should be melted and sautéed.

5 minutes until the spinach, carrot, and tomato are tender. Season with salt and pepper to taste. Allow to cool for 10 minutes in a medium bowl.

Set aside after adding the goat cheese and oregano. Stuff the chicken breasts lengthwise with the cheese mixture. Place in the baking dish. Brush with the remaining butter and season with salt and pepper. Bake for 20-30 minutes, or until thoroughly cooked.

Toss the cucumbers with the dill, salt, black pepper, olive oil, and vinegar on a serving platter to coat. Serve alongside the stuffed chicken.

Nutrition: Cal 861; Net Carbs 9.5g; Fat 58g; Protein 67g

Chicken Breasts

Servings: 2 and **Total Time:** approx. 20 minutes

Ingredients:

- 2 chicken breasts
- 1 cup kale
- Salt black pepper to taste
- 1 cup heavy cream
- 2 tbsp butter
- 1 tsp fresh sage

Directions:

Season both sides of the chicken with salt and pepper. In a skillet over medium heat, melt the butter and cook the chicken breasts for 7-8 minutes, flipping once. Transfer to a flat surface to cool for a few minutes before slicing.

Cook for 2 minutes in the same pan with the heavy cream. Cook for another 2-3 minutes, or until the kale is wilted. Arrange the chicken on a platter and pour the sauce over it. Garnish with sage and serve.

Nutrition: Cal 571; Net Carbs 2.1g; Fat 44g; Protein 33g

Turnip Greens Artichoke Chicken

Servings: 4 and **Total Time:** approx. 40 minutes

Ingredients:

- ½ tbsp onion powder
- 4 oz cream cheese
- 2 chicken breasts, sliced
- 1 cup turnip greens
- Salt and black pepper to taste
- 2 oz Monterrey Jack, shredded
- 4 oz canned artichoke hearts, chopped
- ¼ cup Pecorino cheese, grated
- ½ tbsp garlic powder

Directions:

Line the bottom of a baking dish with parchment paper and layer the chicken slices on top. Season with pepper and salt to taste. Preheat the oven to 350 degrees Fahrenheit and bake for 20-25 minutes.

Combine the remaining

Ingredients in a mixing bowl and thoroughly combine. Remove the chicken from the oven and place it on top of the artichokes. on top of that

Bake for 5 minutes more after adding the Monterrey cheese. Serve hot.

Nutrition: Cal 473; Net Carbs 6.2g; Fat 29g; Protein 41g

Green Bean Broccoli Chicken Stir-Fry

Servings: 2 and **Total Time:** approx. 45 minutes

Ingredients:

- ½ tsp garlic powder
- 2 tbsp olive oil
- 1 tsp red pepper flakes
- 1 tsp onion powder
- ½ cup water
- ½ cup xylitol
- ½ cup green onions, chopped
- 2 chicken breasts, cut into strips
- 1 tbsp fresh ginger, grated
- 10 oz broccoli florets
- ¼ cup tamari sauce
- ½ tsp xanthan gum
- 4 oz green beans, chopped

Directions:

Set aside the green beans and broccoli after steaming for 5-6 minutes, or until crisp-tender but still vibrant green.

In a pan over medium heat, heat the olive oil and cook the chicken and ginger for 4 minutes. Cook for 15 minutes after adding the remaining Ingredients Cook for 6 minutes after adding the green beans and broccoli. Serve.

Nutrition: Cal 411; Net Carbs 6.2g; Fat 25g; Protein 28g

Cheesy chicken Pinwheels

Servings: 4 and **Total Time:** approx. 40 minutes

Ingredients:

- 2 tbsp ghee
- ¼ cup whipping cream
- 4 oz cream cheese
- 1/3 red onion, chopped
- 1 tomato, chopped
- ¼ cup fresh cilantro, chopped
- A pinch of garlic powder
- 1 garlic clove, minced
- 1/3 lb chicken breasts, cubed
- ½ cup chicken stock
- Salt black pepper to taste
- 5 eggs
- 1 tsp creole seasoning
- ½ cup mozzarella, grated

Directions:

Creole seasoning should be used to season the chicken. Warm 1 tbsp ghee in a pan over medium heat. Cook for 2 minutes on each side of the chicken before transferring to a plate.

Melt the remaining ghee and add the garlic and tomato; cook for 4 minutes. Return the chicken to the pan with the stock and cook for 15 minutes. Cook for 2 minutes after adding whipping cream, red onion, salt, mozzarella cheese, and black pepper.

In a blender, combine cream cheese, garlic powder, salt, eggs, and black pepper, and blend until smooth. Place the mixture on a baking sheet lined with parchment paper and bake for 10 minutes at 320 F. Allow the cheese to cool before placing it on a cutting board.

Nutrition: Cal 363; Net Carbs 6.3g; Fat 28g; Protein 20g

Chicken Nuggets

Servings: 2 and **Total Time:** approx. 30 minutes

Ingredients:

- 2 tbsp ranch dressing
- 2 chicken breasts, cubed
- 2 tbsp garlic powder
- ½ cup almond flour
- 1 egg
- Salt and black pepper to taste
- 1 tbsp butter, melted

Directions:

Preheat the oven to 400 degrees Fahrenheit. Butter a baking dish and set aside. Stir together salt, garlic powder, almond flour, and black pepper in a mixing bowl. Beat the egg in a separate bowl.

Dredge the chicken cubes in the flour mixture, then in the egg. Bake for 18-20 minutes, turning halfway through, or until golden and crisp.

Transfer to a plate lined with paper towels, drain the excess grease, and serve with ranch dressing, if desired.

Nutrition: Cal 473; Net Carbs 7.6g; Fat 37g; Protein 31g

Thyme Mushroom and turnip Chicken

Servings: 2 and **Total Time:** approx. 50 minutes

Ingredients:

1 lb chicken breasts, sliced	3 cups mixed mushrooms, teared up
4 tbsp white wine	2 tbsp olive oil
4 tbsp butter, melted	2 cloves garlic, minced
2 tbsp Dijon mustard	4 sprigs thyme, chopped
1 turnip, sliced	Salt and black pepper to taste
1 lemon, juiced	

Directions:

Season the chicken with creole seasoning. 1 tbsp ghee, warmed in a pan over medium heat Cook the chicken for 2 minutes on each side before transferring to a plate.

Melt the remaining ghee and stir in the garlic and tomato; cook for 4 minutes. Return the chicken to the pan and add the stock; cook for 15 minutes.

Preheat the oven to 420°F. Place the turnips on a baking sheet, drizzle with oil, and bake for 15 minutes. In a mixing bowl, combine the chicken, roasted turnips, mushrooms, garlic, thyme, lemon juice, salt, and pepper.

mustard, and pepper Divide the chicken mixture among four large sheets of aluminium foil and top with white wine, olive oil, and butter. To form packets, seal the edges. Put

Nutrition: Cal 394; Net Carbs 4.6g; Fat 29g; Protein 25g

Paprika Chicken and Pancetta in a Skillet

Servings: 2 and **Total Time:** approx. 35 minutes

Ingredients:

1 teaspoon olive oil	5 pancetta strips, chopped
1/3 cup Dijon mustard	Salt and black pepper to taste 1 onion, chopped
2 tbsp oregano, chopped	¼ teaspoon sweet paprika
1 cup chicken stock	
2 chicken breasts	

Directions:

Combine the paprika, black pepper, salt, and mustard in a mixing bowl. The mixture should be rubbed onto the chicken breasts.

In a skillet over medium heat, heat the olive oil. Cook for 3-4 minutes before removing the pancetta to a plate. Cook the chicken breasts in the pancetta fat for 2 minutes per side. Put in the

Stock, black pepper, pancetta, salt, and onion are just a few of the ingredients. Cook for 15-20 minutes. Serve with oregano on top.

Nutrition: Cal 523; Net Carbs 7.6g; Fat 35g; Protein 40g

Baked Zucchini, Chicken and Cheese

Servings: 4 and **Total Time:** approx.. 45 minutes

Ingredients:

1 lb chicken breasts, cubed	1 tbsp olive oil
1 tbsp butter	1 cup mozzarella, shredded
2 zucchinis, cubed	1 red bell pepper, chopped
1 tbsp Worcestershire sauce	1 shallot, sliced
½ cup cream cheese, softened	¼ cup mayonnaise
1 garlic clove, minced	1 tsp thyme
	Salt black pepper to taste

Directions:

Preheat the oven to 370°F. In a pan over medium heat, melt the butter and olive oil and add the chicken. Cook for 5 minutes, or until lightly browned.

Place shallot, zucchini cubes, black pepper, garlic, bell pepper, salt, and thyme in a mixing bowl. Cook for 5 minutes, or until the vegetables are tender; set aside.

Combine the cream cheese, mayonnaise, and Worcestershire sauce in a mixing bowl. Stir in the chicken and vegetables that have been sautéed.

Bake the mixture in a greased baking dish for 20 minutes. Sprinkle with mozzarella cheese and bake for 5 minutes, or until browned.

Nutrition: Cal 448; Net Carbs 5.2g; Fat 31g; Protein 35g

Herby Veggies Chicken Casserole

Servings: 4 and **Total Time:** approx. 35 minutes

Ingredients:

2 chicken breasts, cubed	¾ lb Brussels sprouts, halved
1 tsp chopped rosemary	1 tbsp balsamic vinegar
2 red bell peppers, quartered	2 large zucchinis, chopped
¼ cup olive oil	1 tsp thyme leaves
½ cup toasted walnuts	Salt and black pepper to taste

Directions:

Preheat the oven to 400 degrees Fahrenheit. On a baking sheet, arrange Brussels sprouts, zucchini, bell peppers, and chicken.

Drizzle with olive oil and season with salt and pepper. Toss with balsamic vinegar to taste. Season with thyme and rosemary. Bake for 25 minutes, shaking once halfway through. on top of that

Serve with walnuts.

Nutrition: Cal 491; Net Carbs 6.7g; Fat 34g; Protein 35g

Cabbage and Broccoli Chicken Casserole

Servings: 4 and **Total Time:** 26pprox.. 60 minutes

Ingredients:

- 1 tbsp coconut oil, melted
- 1 head broccoli, cut into florets
- 1 cup mayonnaise
- 1/3 cup chicken stock
- 1 tbsp cilantro, chopped
- 2 cups mozzarella, grated
- ½ head cabbage, shredded
- Salt and black pepper to taste Juice of 1 lemon
- 1 lb chicken breasts, cubed

Directions:

Coat the bottom of a baking dish with coconut oil and place the chicken pieces on top. Sprinkle with half of the mozzarella cheese and top with the green cabbage and broccoli.

In a mixing bowl, combine the mayonnaise, black pepper, stock, and lemon juice.

salt, and lemon juice Spread the mixture over the chicken, then top with the remaining mozzarella cheese and wrap in aluminium foil. Preheat the oven to 350°F for 30 minutes.

Cook for another 20 minutes after removing the aluminium foil. Serve garnished with cilantro.

Nutrition: Cal 533; Net Carbs 6.4g; Fat 32g; Protein 52g

Fennel Chicken Wrapped in Bacon

Servings: 4 and **Total Time:** approx.. 50 minutes

Ingredients:

- 2 tbsp olive oil
- ½ lb fennel bulb, sliced
- 2 tbsp lemon juice
- 2 tbsp cheddar cheese, grated
- 2 chicken breasts
- Salt and black pepper to taste
- 1 tbsp rosemary, chopped
- 4 bacon slices

Directions:

Preheat the grill to high. Season the fennel slices with salt and black pepper after brushing them with olive oil. Grill for 4-6 minutes, turning frequently, until slightly golden. Transfer to a plate and top with lemon juice.

Pour over the cheddar cheese, allowing it to melt slightly when it comes into contact with the hot fennel and form a cheesy dressing.

Preheat the oven to 390 degrees Fahrenheit. Season the chicken breasts with salt and black pepper, then wrap two bacon slices around each one. Place the bacon on a baking sheet lined with parchment paper, drizzle with oil, and bake for 25-30 minutes, or until it is brown and crispy. Serve with rosemary-sprinkled grilled fennel.

Nutrition: Cal 457; Net Carbs 3.2g; Fat 32g; Protein 35g

Turkey Patties with Cucumber Salad

Servings: 4 and **Total Time:** approx. 35 minutes

Ingredients:

- 2 tbsp olive oil
- 1 tbsp chopped dill
- 1 egg
- 1 tsp Cayenne powder
- Cucumber salad
- 2 cucumbers, sliced
- ½ red onion, sliced
- 1 tbsp dried oregano
- 2 spring onions, thinly sliced
- 1 lb ground turkey
- 2 garlic cloves, minced
- Salt and black pepper to taste
- 1 tbsp apple cider vinegar
- 5 radishes, sliced
- 2 tbsp extra virgin olive oil

Directions:

Combine ground turkey, spring onions, egg, garlic, oregano, Cayenne powder, salt, and pepper in a medium mixing bowl. Form the mixture into patties.

In a skillet over medium heat, heat the olive oil and cook the patties for 3 minutes per side. Place aside. Toss cucumber, radishes, red onion, olive oil, apple cider vinegar, salt, and dill in a mixing bowl to coat. Serve with the turkey patties. Serve and have fun!

Nutrition: Cal 352; Net Carbs 3.4g; Fat 28g; Protein 18g

Creamed Turkey with Swiss Chard Soup

Servings: 4 and **Total Time:** approx. 25 minutes

Ingredients:

½ lb turkey breast, cubed	½ tsp chili powder
1 cup Swiss chard, chopped	2 tbsp coconut cream
1 cup canned diced tomatoes	1 garlic clove, minced
2 tbsp coconut oil	1 onion, chopped
½ tsp turmeric	Salt and black pepper to taste

Directions:

Over medium heat, warm the coconut oil and sauté the turkey, onion, and garlic for 3 minutes. Combine the turmeric, tomatoes, chilli powder, salt, and pepper in a mixing bowl. Cook for 10 minutes after adding the tomatoes and coconut cream. Remove from the heat and stir in the Swiss chard.

Using an immersion blender, blend until smooth. Return to the heat and continue to cook for 5 minutes. Serve.

Nutrition: Cal 242; Net Carbs 4g; Fat 15g; Protein 14g

Sliced Garlic & Cheezy Turkey Breast

Servings: 4 and **Total Time:** approx. 25 minutes

Ingredients:

1 tbsp olive oil	1 lb turkey breasts, sliced
½ cup sour cream	1 cup provolone cheese, grated
2 tbsp tomato paste	Salt and black pepper to taste
2 garlic cloves, minced	1 tsp dried oregano

Directions:

Fry the turkey and garlic in a pan with warm olive oil for 5-6 minutes over medium heat; set aside. Cook until thickened, about 4-5 minutes, after adding 1/3 cup water, tomato paste, and sour cream.

Season with salt, pepper, and oregano to taste. Return the turkey to the pan and top with shredded cheese. Allow to sit for 5 minutes, covered, or until the cheese melts. Serve immediately.

Nutrition: Cal 398; Net Carbs 3.3g; Fat 25g; Protein 37g

Crispy Chicken Thighs with Radishes and Mushrooms

SERVINGS 4 | **PREP TIME** 5 minutes | **COOK TIME** 35 minutes

Ingredients:

4 large bone-in, skin-on chicken thighs (6 ounces each)
1 (8-ounce) container white mushrooms, sliced
Chopped fresh parsley
Freshly ground black pepper
Salt
1 pound radishes, halved
3 tablespoons olive oil

Directions:

Preheat the oven to 375°F. Season the chicken with salt and pepper. In a large oven-safe skillet, heat the oil over medium heat. Cooking in batches if needed, place the chicken in the skillet, skin-side down. Cook for 10 minutes, until the skin is golden brown and crispy.

Remove the chicken and set aside. Add the radishes and mushrooms to the skillet. Cook, stirring frequently, for 5 minutes. Return the chicken to the skillet, place it in the oven, and roast for 15 minutes, or until it has reached an internal temperature of at least 165°F or the juices run clear from a cut into the thickest part of the thigh. Garnish with the parsley and serve.

Nutrition: Calories: 433; Fat: 34g; Protein: 26g; Total Carbs: 6g

Chicken Nuggets

MAKES 20 | **PREP TIME** 15 minutes | **COOK TIME** 30 minutes

Ingredients:

Nonstick cooking spray
1 large beaten egg
½ teaspoon sea salt
⅛ teaspoon freshly ground black pepper
¾ teaspoon dried oregano
½ teaspoon paprika
¼ cup almond flour
1 pound ground chicken
¼ teaspoon onion powder
¾ cup finely crushed pork rinds
½ teaspoon garlic powder
3 tbsp Parmesan cheese

Directions:

Preheat the oven to 350°F. Line a baking sheet with parchment paper and spray with cooking spray. In a large bowl, mix the chicken, egg, flour, salt, onion powder, and pepper until well combined. In a medium bowl, combine the pork rinds, Parmesan, oregano, garlic powder, and paprika. Scoop the chicken mixture 1 tablespoon at a time and form into your chosen shape. Completely coat in the pork rind mixture and place on the prepared baking sheet. Bake for 15 minutes, flip, and bake for an additional 15 minutes until golden. Serve immediately.

Nutrition: (5 nuggets): Calories: 275; Fat: 17g; Protein: 28g; Total Carbs: 3g

Chicken Thigh Chili with Avocado

SERVINGS 4 | **PREP TIME** 15 minutes | **COOK TIME** 40 minutes

Ingredients:

3 tablespoons olive oil, divided
2 jalapeño peppers, minced
1 tablespoon minced garlic
1 onion, chopped
1 cup canned coconut milk
Juice of 1 lime
1 pound boneless, skinless chicken thighs, diced
2 cups diced raw or frozen pumpkin
1 cup low-sodium chicken stock
3 tsp chili powder
3 tablespoons no-salt-added tomato paste
1 avocado, diced

Directions:

Heat 2 tablespoons of olive oil in a large skillet over medium-high heat. Sauté the chicken until just cooked through, 10 to 12 minutes. Transfer the chicken to a plate using a slotted spoon.

Add the remaining olive oil and sauté the onion, jalapeños, and garlic until softened, about 5 minutes. Stir in the cooked chicken, pumpkin, chicken stock, coconut milk, tomato paste, chili powder, and lime juice.

Bring the chili to a boil, then reduce the heat to low and simmer until the chicken and vegetables are tender, about 20 minutes. Serve topped with avocado.

Nutrition: Calories: 461; Fat: 36g; Protein: 20g; Total Carbs: 18g

Chicken Bacon Burgers

SERVINGS 6 | **PREP TIME** 10 minutes | **COOK TIME** 25 minutes

Ingredients:

1 pound ground chicken
1 teaspoon chopped fresh basil
Pinch freshly ground black pepper
1 avocado, peeled, pitted, and sliced
¼ cup ground almonds
¼ teaspoon sea salt
8 bacon slices, chopped
4 large lettuce leaves
2 tablespoons coconut oil

Directions:

Preheat the oven to 350°F. Line a baking sheet with parchment paper and set aside. In a medium bowl, combine the chicken, bacon, ground almonds, basil, salt, and pepper until well mixed. Form the mixture into 6 equal patties. Place a large skillet over medium-high heat and add the coconut oil. Pan sear the chicken patties until brown on both sides, about 6 minutes in total. Place the browned patties on the baking sheet and bake until completely cooked through, about 15 minutes. Serve on the lettuce leaves, topped with the avocado slices.

Nutrition: Calories: 374; Fat: 33g; Protein: 18g; Total Carbs: 3g

Baked Chicken Tenders

SERVINGS 4 | **PREP TIME** 15 minutes | **COOK TIME** 20 minutes

Ingredients:

2 large eggs
½ cup shredded Parmesan cheese
¼ teaspoon salt
1 pound boneless chicken thighs, halved
½ cup pork rinds, ground
1 teaspoon onion powder
1 teaspoon garlic powder
⅛ teaspoon freshly ground black pepper

Directions:

Preheat the oven to 400°F. Line a baking sheet with parchment paper. In a medium bowl, beat the eggs. In another medium bowl, combine the pork rinds, Parmesan cheese, garlic powder, onion powder, salt, and pepper. Create a "breading" station: Line up the egg wash, then the pork rind mixture, then the baking sheet. Take one thigh half and dredge thoroughly in the egg wash, then coat in the pork rind mixture, pressing the "breading" into the meat so it adheres. Place the "breaded" thigh on the baking sheet. Repeat with the remaining thigh halves. Place the baking sheet in the preheated oven. Cook for 18 to 20 minutes, or until golden brown.

Nutrition: Calories: 489; Fat: 33g; Protein: 46g; Total Carbs: 2g

Chicken with Mushrooms, Port, and Cream

SERVINGS 4 | **PREP TIME** 10 minutes | **COOK TIME** 20 minutes

Ingredients:

2 tsp canola oil
1 shallot, minced
Freshly ground black pepper
¼ cup port wine
8 boneless, skinless chicken thighs Sea salt
8 ounces mushrooms, sliced
½ cup heavy cream

Directions:

Heat the canola oil in a large skillet over medium-high heat. Pat the chicken thighs dry with paper towels and season generously with salt and pepper. Sear the chicken thighs on each side until well browned and cooked through to an internal temperature of 165°F, about 8 minutes.

Transfer them to a dish. Add the shallot and mushrooms to the pan and cook for 10 minutes, until the mushrooms are browned and most of the moisture has evaporated from the pan. Add the port and cook until reduced to just a couple of tablespoons, about 2 minutes. Stir in the heavy cream and bring to the barest simmer. Return the chicken thighs to the pan, basting with the cream sauce. Season with salt and pepper.

Nutrition: Calories: 389; Fat: 24g; Protein: 30g; Total Carbs: 6g

Creamy Chicken and Spinach Bake

SERVINGS 4 | **PREP TIME** 10 minutes | **COOK TIME** 30 minutes

Ingredients:

Nonstick cooking spray
10 ounces baby spinach
8 ounces cream cheese, at room temperature
¼ cup sour cream
Freshly ground black pepper
1 pound boneless, skinless chicken breasts, cubed
¾ cup shredded mozzarella cheese, divided
2 tsp minced garlic Salt

Directions:

Preheat the oven to 400°F. Coat a 9-by-13-inch baking dish with cooking spray. Spread out the chicken in the dish. Layer the spinach over the top, keeping it as flat as possible. In a medium bowl, combine the cream cheese, ¼ cup of mozzarella, the sour cream, and garlic. Season with salt and pepper to taste.

Spoon the mixture on top of the spinach. Cover with aluminum foil and bake for 20 minutes. Remove from the oven, uncover, and top with the remaining ½ cup of mozzarella. Bake for another 10 to 15 minutes, until the chicken has reached an internal temperature of 165°F.

Nutrition: Calories: 491; Fat: 31g; Protein: 46g; Total Carbs: 6g

Lemon Chicken and Asparagus Stir-Fry

SERVINGS 4 | **PREP TIME** 5 minutes | **COOK TIME** 25 minutes

Ingredients:

2 tablespoons olive oil
1 pound asparagus, ends trimmed, cut 2-inch pieces
¼ cup chicken broth
Salt
1½ pounds boneless, skinless chicken breasts, cut into 1-inch cubes
2 tablespoons soy sauce
Freshly ground black

Juice of 1 lemon

pepper

Directions:

In a large skillet, heat the oil over medium heat. Add the chicken. Cook, stirring frequently, for 10 minutes, or until browned all over. Add the asparagus and cook, stirring frequently, for another 5 minutes. Add the broth and soy sauce and mix well. Cook for 10 minutes, or until the asparagus is tender but still crisp. Stir in the lemon juice and season with salt and pepper.

Nutrition: Calories: 293; Fat: 11g; Protein: 41g; Total Carbs: 6g

Loaded Chicken and Cauliflower Nachos

SERVINGS 4 | **PREP TIME** 10 minutes | **COOK TIME** 25 minutes

Ingredients:

¼ cup olive oil
1 teaspoon ground cumin
1 teaspoon paprika
Freshly ground black pepper
¾ cup shredded Mexican blend cheese
1 tsp onion powder
1 large head cauliflower (about 1 pound)
1 cup cooked chicken, diced or shredded
¼ cup low-carb salsa
Salt

Directions:

Preheat the oven to 375°F. Line a baking sheet with aluminum foil. In a large bowl, combine the oil, onion powder, paprika, and cumin. Set aside.

Cut the cauliflower into quarters and remove any leaves and thick stem. Cut the quarters crosswise into even ½-inch-thick slices. Add the cauliflower to the bowl with the spice mixture and turn to coat. Transfer the cauliflower to the prepared baking sheet and spread in a single layer. Season with salt and pepper. Roast for 20 minutes, then remove from the oven.

Top with the chicken and cheese and return to the oven for 5 to 10 minutes, until the cheese has melted. Remove from the oven, top with the salsa, and serve.

Nutrition: Calories: 297; Fat: 22g; Protein: 16g; Total Carbs: 9g

Shredded Chicken

MAKES 6 CUPS | **PREP TIME** 5 minutes | **COOK TIME** 8 minutes, plus 10 minutes to come to pressure | **RELEASE:** Natural, 10 minutes

Ingredients:

1 cup chicken broth
¼ cup tomato sauce
4 large boneless, skinless chicken breasts (about 6 ounces each)
1 teaspoon salt

Directions:

Pour the broth, tomato sauce, and salt into an electric pressure cooker and stir to mix. Add the chicken breasts and cover in the sauce.

Lock the pressure cooker lid in place with the steam vent set to Sealing. Select high pressure and set the timer for 8 minutes. After cooking, allow a 10-minute natural pressure release.

Open the pressure release valve and let out any remaining steam. Carefully open the pressure cooker and use two forks to shred the chicken into the broth. Let sit for 5 minutes, then use a slotted spoon to remove the chicken.

Nutrition: (1 cup): Calories: 140; Fat: 2g; Protein: 26g; Total Carbs: 2g

Buffalo Chicken Wings

SERVINGS 4 | **PREP TIME** 15 minutes | **COOK TIME** 50 minutes

Ingredients:

1 tablespoon olive oil
½ teaspoon freshly ground black pepper, divided
1 tablespoon butter, melted
1 cup Blue cheese sauce or ranch dressing, or purchased bottled dressing
1 teaspoon salt, divided
¼ cup hot sauce
2 pounds chicken wings
¼ teaspoon cayenne pepper

Directions:

Preheat the oven to 400°F. In a large bowl, mix the olive oil, ½ teaspoon of salt, and ¼ teaspoon of black pepper.

Add the wings and stir to coat. Evenly divide the wings between two baking sheets. Place the sheets in the oven. Bake for 45 to 50 minutes, or until the outer skin is crispy. In another large bowl, mix the hot sauce, butter, cayenne pepper, the remaining ½ teaspoon of salt, and remaining ¼ teaspoon of black pepper.

Add the cooked wings. Toss them in the sauce for 1 minute to coat. Serve with bleu cheese sauce or ranch dressing.

Nutrition: Calories: 507; Fat: 23g; Protein: 67g; Total Carbs: 4g

Curried Chicken Salad

SERVINGS 4 | **PREP TIME** 10 minutes

Ingredients:

½ cup mayonnaise
1 tablespoon lemon

Fresly ground black pepper
1 tbs curry powder
¼ cup roughly chopped toasted cashews
1 celery stalk, minced
juice
16 ounces shredded cooked chicken, light and dark meat
¼ cup diced red onion
Sea salt

Directions:

In a medium bowl, whisk the mayonnaise, lemon juice, and curry powder. Season with salt and pepper. Fold in the chicken, cashews, celery, and red onion. Serve immediately or refrigerate until ready to serve.

Nutrition: Calories: 379; Fat: 28g; Protein: 27g; Total Carbs: 4g

Coconut Chicken

SERVINGS 4 | PREP TIME 15 minutes | COOK TIME 25 minutes

Ingredients:

4 (4-ounce) boneless chicken breasts, cut into 2-inch chunks
1 tablespoon curry powder
¼ cup chopped fresh cilantro
2 tablespoons olive oil
½ cup chopped sweet onion
1 cup coconut milk
1 teaspoon ground coriander
1 teaspoon ground cumin

Directions:

Place a large saucepan over medium-high heat and add the olive oil. Sauté the chicken until almost cooked through, about 10 minutes.

Add the onion and sauté for an additional 3 minutes. In a medium bowl, whisk the coconut milk, curry powder, cumin, and coriander. Pour the sauce into the saucepan with the chicken and bring the liquid to a boil.

Reduce the heat and simmer until the chicken is tender and the sauce has thickened, about 10 minutes. Serve the chicken with the sauce, topped with cilantro.

Nutrition: Calories: 382; Fat: 31g; Protein: 23g; Total Carbs: 5g

Basil Chicken Zucchini "Pasta"

SERVINGS 1 | PREP TIME 10 minutes | COOK TIME 15 minutes

Ingredients:

1 tablespoon butter or ghee
2 boneless chicken thighs, cubed
¼ medium white onion, diced
¼ cup basil pesto
1 teaspoon avocado oil
½ zucchini, peeled into thin ribbons or spiralized
4 cherry tomatoes, halved
2 garlic cloves, minced

Directions:

Melt the butter in a large skillet over medium-high heat. Add the chicken and onion, and cook for several minutes, until the chicken begins to brown.

Add the garlic and cook for another 2 to 3 minutes, until the chicken is cooked through. Turn the heat down to low. In a medium bowl, coat the zucchini in the oil. Add the zucchini to the skillet and cook for 1 minute, stirring occasionally. Transfer the mixture to a medium bowl, and toss with the pesto and tomatoes.

Nutrition: Calories: 875; Fat: 74g; Protein: 37g; Total Carbs: 15g

BBQ Chicken Skewers

SERVINGS 4 | PREP TIME 10 minutes, plus 30 minutes to marinate | COOK TIME 20 minutes

Ingredients:

4 boneless, skinless chicken breasts
2 medium zucchini cut into ½-inch rounds
Freshly ground black pepper
Salt
1 red bell pepper cut into 2-inch chunks
1 (8-ounce) package white mushrooms, stems removed
1 cup low-carb barbecue sauce, divided

Directions:

Cut the chicken into even 2-inch pieces. Set ¼ cup of barbecue sauce aside for basting. Combine the remaining ¾ cup of barbecue sauce and the chicken in a resealable bag. Seal and place in the refrigerator for at least 30 minutes.

Preheat the grill to medium-high. When ready to cook, remove the chicken from the marinade (discard the marinade). Thread each skewer, alternating the ingredients. Each skewer should have 3 pieces of chicken, 1 slice of zucchini, 1 or 2 mushrooms, and 1 or 2 pieces of bell pepper. Season with salt and black pepper. Cook the skewers on the grill, turning occasionally, for about 20 minutes, or until the chicken has reached an internal temperature of 165°F. Brush the cooked skewers with the reserved ¼ cup of barbecue sauce before serving.

Nutrition: (3 skewers): Calories: 360; Fat: 16g; Protein: 41g; Total Carbs: 13g

Chicken Cordon Bleu Casserole

SERVINGS 6 | **PREP TIME** 10 minutes | **COOK TIME** 5 hours on low

Ingredients:

Nonstick cooking spray
8 ounces deli ham, cut into 1-inch cubes
Cheese Sauce using Swiss cheese
Freshly ground black pepper
2¼ pounds boneless, skinless chicken breasts, cubed
½ cup pork rind crumbs
2 tablespoons Dijon mustard

Directions:

Coat the bowl of a slow cooker with cooking spray. Add the chicken, ham, cheese sauce, and mustard. Season with pepper and mix well.

Sprinkle the pork rinds over the top, close the lid, and cook on low for 5 hours, or until the chicken has reached an internal temperature of 165°F.

Nutrition: Calories: 597; Fat: 41g

Roast Turkey

SERVINGS 8 | **PREP TIME** 15 minutes | **COOK TIME** 3 hours

Ingredients:

10- to 12-pound turkey (with no added ingredients)
2 tablespoons chopped sage
1 teaspoon salt
2 tablespoons chopped thyme
1 cup (2 sticks) butter
1 teaspoon freshly ground black pepper

Directions:

The night before cooking, remove the packaging and allow the turkey to sit uncovered in the refrigerator overnight to dry out. In the morning, remove the neck, giblets, and liver from the cavity, and discard. Preheat the oven to 350°F, and place a rack in a roasting pan.

Melt the butter in the microwave, and mix with the thyme and sage. Rub half the mixture all over the skin of the bird, lifting the skin to rub as much on the underside of the skin as possible. Season all over with the salt and pepper. Place on the roasting rack, breast-side up, cover with aluminum foil, and roast for 2 hours (add 15 minutes per pound for a larger turkey).

Remove the foil, increase the oven temperature to 425°F, baste with the remaining butter, and place back in the oven for another hour. Allow to rest for 30 minutes before carving.

Nutrition: Calories: 447; Fat: 21g; Protein: 66g; Total Carbs: 0g

Turkey Meatloaf Muffins

SERVINGS 2 TO 4 | **PREP TIME** 10 minutes | **COOK TIME** 40 minutes

Ingredients:

Nonstick cooking spray
½ cup chopped onions
¼ cup shredded carrots
½ cup chopped green bell pepper
1 teaspoon dried thyme
1 large egg
1 to 2 tablespoons olive oil
1 teaspoon garlic powder
½ cup chopped mushrooms
1 pound ground turkey (the fattier, the better)
1 teaspoon dried rosemary
1 teaspoon mustard

Sugar-free ketchup

Directions:

Preheat the oven to 350°F. Coat a muffin tin with nonstick spray. Heat the olive oil in a large skillet over medium-high heat. Add the onions and season with the garlic powder. Add the carrots, mushrooms, and bell pepper and cook for 3 to 5 minutes, or until the onion is translucent. Put the ground turkey in a medium bowl and add the vegetable mixture.

Add the egg thyme, rosemary, and mustard. Mix until well combined. Divide the turkey mixture evenly among the muffin cups and bake for about 15 minutes. Remove the muffins from the oven and slather each with 1 teaspoon of ketchup. Bake for another 15 minutes, or until the meat is no longer pink.

Nutrition: Calories: 346; Fat: 26g; Protein: 22g; Total Carbs: 6g

Pork Recipes

Baked Pork Sausage

Servings: 2 and **Total Time:** approx. 45 minutes

Ingredients:
- 1 tsp smoked paprika
- 1 tbsp olive oil
- 1 garlic clove, minced
- ½ carrot, sliced
- 1 sprig rosemary, chopped
- 1 small onion, sliced
- 1 red bell pepper, sliced
- ½ lb pork sausages
- 2 tomatoes, chopped
- 1 tbsp balsamic vinegar
- Salt and black pepper to taste

Directions:

Preheat the oven to 360 degrees Fahrenheit. In a saucepan, heat the olive oil and add the tomatoes, bell peppers, garlic, carrot, onion, and balsamic vinegar, cooking for 8-10 minutes, or until softened and lightly golden. Season

seasoned with salt, paprika, and pepper Place in a baking dish. Place the sausages on top of the vegetables. Place the dish in the oven and bake for 20-25 minutes, or until the sausages are browned to your liking. Serve with rosemary on top.

Nutrition: Cal 491; Net Carbs 9.5g; Fat 38g; Protein 18g

Pork Chops with Tomato Sauce

Servings: 2 and **Total Time:** approx. 45 minutes

Ingredients:
- 2 pork chops
- Salt and black pepper to taste
- 1 tbsp olive oil
- 7 oz canned diced tomatoes
- ½ tbsp fresh basil, chopped
- 1 garlic clove, minced
- ½ tbsp tomato paste
- ½ red chili, finely chopped

Directions:

Season the pork with black pepper and salt. Warm the oil in a pan over medium heat. Cook for 3 minutes with the pork chops. Cook for 3 minutes more on the other side before transferring to a bowl.

Cook for 30 seconds after adding the garlic to the pan. Combine the tomato paste, tomatoes, and chilli in a mixing bowl. Bring to a boil, then reduce to a low heat.

Place the pork chops in the pan, cover, and cook for 30 minutes. To serve, transfer the pork chops to plates and top with fresh basil.

Nutrition: Cal 425; Net Carbs 5.5g; Fat 25g; Protein 39g

Cranberry Sauce and Herb Pork Chops

Servings: 2 and **Total Time:** approx. 2 hours 45 minutes

Ingredients:
- 2 pork chops
- ½ onion, chopped
- 1 cup cranberries
- A drizzle of olive oil
- ½ tsp sriracha sauce
- 1 bay leaf
- 1 cup chicken stock
- 1 tbsp parsley, chopped
- ½ tsp garlic powder
- Salt and black pepper to taste
- 1 tsp fresh basil, chopped
- ½ cup xylitol
- ½ cup white wine
- Juice of ½ lemon
- ½ cup water
- 1 tsp fresh rosemary, chopped

Directions:

Preheat the oven to 340 degrees Fahrenheit. Combine the pork, basil, salt, garlic powder, and black pepper in a mixing bowl. Cook the pork in a pan with a drizzle of oil over medium heat until browned, about 4-5 minutes; set aside.

Cook the onion for 2 minutes in the pan. Cook for 4 minutes with the bay leaf and wine. Simmer for 5 minutes after adding the lemon juice and chicken stock. Return the pork to the pan and cook for another 10 minutes. Place the pan in the oven for 2 hours, covered. Bake for 5 minutes, then remove the cover.

Set another pan over medium heat and add the cranberries, rosemary, sriracha sauce, water, and xylitol. Simmer for 15 minutes.

Nutrition: Cal 450; Net Carbs 7.3g; Fat 25g; Protein 42g

Roasted Pork Stuffed with Ham & Cheese

Servings: 2 and **Total Time:** approx. 40 min + cooling time

Ingredients:
- 2 tbsp olive oil
- 1 tbsp mustard
- 1 tbsp fresh cilantro, chopped
- 2 tbsp fresh mint, chopped
- Salt and black pepper to taste
- 2 oz smoked ham, sliced
- Zest and juice from 1 lime
- 1 garlic clove, minced
- 2 pork loin steaks
- 1 pickle, chopped
- 1 tsp cumin
- 2 oz Gruyere cheese sliced

Directions:

In a food processor, combine the lime zest, oil, black pepper, cumin, cilantro, lime juice, garlic, mint, and salt; transfer to a bowl. Organize the Toss the steaks in the marinade to coat. Place in the refrigerator for 2 hours.

Preheat the oven to 360 degrees Fahrenheit. Arrange the steaks on a work surface, top with pickles, mustard, cheese, and ham, roll, and secure with toothpicks. Heat a pan over medium heat, add the pork rolls, and cook for 2 minutes on each side before transferring to a baking sheet. Preheat the oven to 350°F and bake for 25 minutes. Serve and have fun!

Nutrition: Cal 687; Net Carbs 6.2g; Fat 44g; Protein 61g

Barbecued Pork Chops

Servings: 2 and **Total Time:** approx. 20 minutes

Ingredients:
- 2 pork loin chops, boneless
- 2 thyme sprigs, chopped
- ½ tsp ginger powder
- ½ tsp onion powder
- ½ cup BBQ sauce, sugar-free
- Salt and black pepper to taste
- 1 tsp red pepper flakes
- ½ tsp garlic powder

Directions:

In a small bowl, combine black pepper, salt, ginger powder, onion powder, garlic powder, and red pepper flakes. The spices should be rubbed onto the pork chops.

Preheat the grill to medium-high heat. Place the meat in the pan and cook for 2 minutes per side. Reduce the heat to medium and brush the BBQ sauce all over the meat before covering and grilling for another 5 minutes. Turn the key to open the lid

Brush the meat with barbecue sauce once more. Cook for another 5 minutes, covered. Remove from the oven and sprinkle with thyme.

Nutrition: Cal 342; Net Carbs 1g; Fat 18g; Protein 40g

Citrus Pork with tomatoes Cabbage

Servings: 2 and **Total Time:** approx. 25 minutes

Ingredients:
- 3 tbsp olive oil
- ¼ tsp cumin
- 1 tbsp parsley
- 1/3 head cabbage, shredded
- ¼ tsp ground nutmeg
- 1 tomato, chopped
- 2 tbsp lemon juice
- 1 garlic clove, pureed
- 2 pork loin chops
- 1 tbsp white wine
- Salt and black pepper to taste

Directions:

Combine the lemon juice, garlic, salt, pepper, and 1 tablespoon olive oil in a mixing bowl. Brush the mixture over the pork.

Preheat the grill to high. Grill the pork for about 2-3 minutes per side.

until thoroughly cooked Transfer to serving plates. Cook the cabbage for 5 minutes in the remaining olive oil in a pan. Drizzle with white wine and season with cumin, nutmeg, salt, and pepper to taste.

Cook for another 5 minutes, stirring occasionally, after adding the tomato. Serve the sautéed cabbage alongside the chops, sprinkled with parsley.

Nutrition: Cal 565; Net Carbs 8g; Fat 37g; Protein 43g

Pork Kofta with Spiced Yogurt

Servings: 4 and **Total Time:** approx. 30 minutes

Ingredients:
- 1 lb ground pork
- 1 cup plain yogurt
- 1 shallot, chopped
- 1 small egg
- 1/3 tsp paprika
- ½ tsp oregano
- 1 garlic clove, minced
- 2 tbsp olive oil
- 2 tbsp pork rinds, crushed
- 1 tsp Cajun seasoning
- Salt and black pepper to taste
- 2 tbsp parsley, chopped
- 2 tbsp fresh mint, chopped

Directions:

In a mixing bowl, combine the ground pork, shallot, pork rinds, garlic, egg, paprika, oregano, parsley, salt, and black pepper. Form the mixture into balls and place them in an oiled baking pan; drizzle with olive oil. Bake for 18 minutes at 390°F, or until golden brown.

In a mixing bowl, combine the yoghurt, Cajun seasoning, and mint. Seasoning should be adjusted. Serve the kofta with the sauce on the side.

Nutrition: Cal 453; Net Carbs 5g; Fat 32g; Protein 35g

Bacon Kale Pizza

Servings: 3 and **Total Time:** approx. 35 minutes

Ingredients:

1 cup sliced mushrooms
2 oz bacon, chopped
2 cups chopped kale, wilted
6 eggs
1 cup grated mozzarella
9 oz shredded provolone cheese
1 tsp Italian seasoning
4 tbsp tomato sauce

Directions:

Preheat the oven to 380 degrees Fahrenheit. Using parchment paper, line a pizza baking pan.

In a mixing bowl, combine 6 eggs, provolone cheese, and Italian seasoning. Spread the mixture on the pizza baking pan and bake for 15 minutes, or until golden.

Remove from the oven and set aside for 2 minutes to cool. Top the crust with the tomato sauce, kale, mozzarella cheese, bacon, and mushrooms. Bake for 8 minutes at 350°F. Slice and serve. Enjoy!

Nutrition: Cal 590; Net Carbs 4.6g; Fat 42g; Protein 45g

Sesame Pork Bites

Servings: 4 and **Total Time:** approx. 45 min + chilling time

Ingredients:

1 pork tenderloin, cubed
½ cup + 1 tbsp red wine
½ cup sesame seeds
½ cup sugar-free maple syrup
1 tsp pureed garlic
1 tbsp sesame oil
1 tbsp + 1/3 cup tamari sauce
½ tsp freshly grated ginger
1 tbsp scallions, chopped

Directions:

In a zipper bag, combine 1/2 cup red wine and 1 tablespoon tamari sauce. Add the pork cubes, seal the bag, and let the meat marinate in the fridge overnight. Preheat the oven to 350 degrees Fahrenheit. Remove the pork from the refrigerator and drain it. Divide the maple syrup and sesame seeds into two separate bowls; roll the sesame seeds in the maple syrup.

Pork dipped in maple syrup and then sesame seeds Bake for 35 minutes on a greased baking sheet. Combine the remaining red wine, tamari sauce, sesame oil, garlic, and ginger in a mixing bowl. Fill a bowl halfway with the sauce. Serve the pork on a platter garnished with scallions. Pour the sauce over and serve.

Nutrition: Cal 289; Net Carbs 6.4g; Fat 18g; Protein 30g

Pork with Mozzarella

Servings: 4 and **Total Time:** approx. 25 minutes

Ingredients:

1 cup shredded mozzarella
4 boneless pork chops
1 cup tomato sauce
1 cup golden flaxseed meal
1 large egg, beaten
Salt and black pepper to taste

Directions:

Preheat the oven to 380 degrees Fahrenheit. Season the pork with salt and pepper, then coat it in the egg, followed by the flaxseed meal. Place on a baking sheet that has been greased.

Pour on the tomato sauce and top with the mozzarella cheese. Bake for 15 minutes, or until the cheese melts and the pork is thoroughly cooked. Serve and have fun!

Nutrition: Cal 589; Net Carbs 3.7g; Fat 25g; Protein 59g

Chinese Style Pork with Noodles

Servings: 4 and **Total Time:** approx. 60 min + chilling time

Ingredients:

1 lb pork tenderloin, cubed
¼ tsp Chinese five spice
Salt and black pepper to taste
24 oz bok choy, chopped
2 green onions, chopped
2 tbsp sesame seeds
1 tbsp fresh ginger paste
2 tbsp butter
4 large celeriac, spiralized
2 tbsp sesame oil
3 tbsp sugar-free maple syrup
3 tbsp coconut aminos

Directions:

Preheat the oven to 380 degrees Fahrenheit. Combine maple syrup, coconut aminos, ginger paste, five-spice powder, salt, and pepper in a mixing bowl. 3 tablespoons of the

Place the mixture in a bowl and set aside for topping. Refrigerate the pork cubes for 25 minutes in the remaining marinade. In a skillet, melt the butter and sauté the celeriac for 7 minutes; set aside. Remove the pork from the marinade and place it on a baking sheet lined with foil. Bake for 40 minutes.

In a skillet, heat the sesame oil and sauté the bok choy and celeriac pasta for 3 minutes. Serve in serving bowls, topped with the pork. Garnish with green onions and sesame seeds if desired. Serve with the reserved marinade.

Nutrition: Cal 410; Net Carbs 3g; Fat 21g; Protein 44g

Lettuce Wraps with Pork & Dill Pickles

Servings: 4 and **Total Time:** approx. 30 minutes

Ingredients:

2 tbsp avocado oil
½ onion, sliced
1 red bell pepper, chopped
2 dill pickles, finely chopped
1 lb ground pork
1 tbsp ginger paste
Salt and black pepper to taste
1 head Iceberg lettuce

Directions:

In a pan over medium heat, heat the avocado oil and add the pork, ginger paste, salt, and pepper. Cook for 10-15 minutes, breaking up any lumps along the way, until the pork is no longer pink.

Fill each lettuce leaf with 2-3 tablespoons of the pork mixture and top with onion slices, bell pepper slices, and dill pickles. Serve and have fun!

Nutrition: Cal 422; Net Carbs 4.5g; Fat 30g; Protein 31g

Cheesy Pork Quiche

Servings: 4 and **Total Time:** approx. 65 minutes

Ingredients:

2 tbsp melted butter
¼ cup shredded Swiss cheese
1 ¼ cups almond flour
1 yellow onion, chopped
½ lb smoked pork shoulder
6 eggs
1 tbsp butter
1 cup coconut cream
1 tbsp psyllium husk powder 4 tbsp chia seeds
1 tsp dried thyme
Salt black pepper to taste

Directions:

Preheat oven to 360 F. Grease a springform pan with cooking spray, and line with parchment paper; set aside. To a food processor, add

almond flour, psyllium husk, chia seeds, salt, butter, and 1 egg. Mix until a firm dough forms. Oil your hands and spread the dough on the bottom of the springform pan. Place the resulting crust in the fridge while you make the filling.

Melt butter in a skillet and cook the pork and onion until the meat browns, 10-12 minutes. Stir in thyme, salt, and pepper. Remove the crust from the fridge and spoon pork and onion onto the crust. In a bowl, whisk coconut cream, half of the Swiss cheese, and the remaining eggs.

Pour the mixture over the meat filling and top with the remaining cheese. Bake until the cheese melts and a toothpick inserted into the quiche comes out clean, 45 minutes. Slice into wedges and serve.

Nutrition: Cal 693; Net Carbs 8.3g; Fat 54g; Protein 33g

Egg and Pork Stuffed Zucchini

Servings: 4 and **Total Time:** approx. 45 minutes

Ingredients:

2 tbsp olive oil
2 tbsp chopped scallions
1 garlic clove, crushed

1 tsp cumin powder
½ lb ground pork
2 tbsp chopped cilantro
2 zucchinis
1 small plum tomato, diced
1 tsp dried basil
1 tsp smoked paprika
4 oz bacon, chopped
3 large eggs, beaten

Directions:

Scoop out the pulp with a spoon after cutting the zucchini in half lengthwise. In a skillet, heat the olive oil and sauté the garlic, tomato, and

6 minutes with scallions Combine basil, cumin, and paprika in a mixing bowl. Brown the ground pork for 7-8 minutes; set aside.

Cover the zucchini halves with the pork mixture and top with the beaten eggs and bacon. Place in a preheated 380°F oven for 18-20 minutes, or until the eggs are set. Garnish with cilantro and serve.

Nutrition: Cal 372; Net Carbs 4.5g; Fat 25g; Protein 22g

Chili Pork Belly with sauce

Servings: 4 and **Total Time:** approx. 30 min

Ingredients:

2 cups chopped kale
Salt and black pepper to taste
1 white onion, chopped
6 cloves garlic, minced
1 cup coconut cream
1 lb pork belly, chopped
2 tbsp coconut oil
¼ cup ginger thinly sliced
4 long red chilies, halved
1 cup coconut milk

Directions:

Season the pork belly with salt and pepper to taste. In a skillet over medium heat, warm the coconut oil and fry the pork for 10-12 minutes, or until the skin browns and crackles. To avoid burning.

turn the pan a few times. Serve on a plate. Sauté the onion, garlic, ginger, and spices in the same skillet.

5 minutes with the chilies Cook for 1 minute after adding the coconut milk and coconut cream. Cook, stirring occasionally, until the kale is wilted, about 4 minutes. Add the pork and mix well. 2 minutes in the oven Serve hot.

Nutrition: Cal 610; Net Carbs 6.7g; Fat 36g; Protein 51g

Meat Lover Sausage Pizza

Servings: 4 and **Total Time:** approx. 40 minutes

Ingredients:

- ½ cup grated Monterey Jack cheese
- 1 ½ lb Italian pork sausages, crumbled
- 4 cups grated mozzarella
- 1 cup chopped bell peppers
- ¼ cup coconut flour
- 1 cup almond flour
- 1 tbsp olive oil
- 2 eggs
- ¼ cup grated Parmesan
- 1 cup baby spinach
- 2 garlic cloves, minced
- 2 tbsp cream cheese, softened
- 1 onion, thinly sliced
- ½ cup sugar-free pizza sauce

Directions:

Preheat the oven to 380 degrees Fahrenheit. Using parchment paper, line a pizza pan. 1 minute in the microwave with 2 cups mozzarella cheese and cream cheese Remove from the heat and stir in the sausages, coconut flour, almond flour, Parmesan cheese, and eggs.

Spread the mixture on the pizza pan and bake for 15 minutes before removing from the oven. In a skillet, heat the olive oil and sauté the onion, garlic, and bell peppers for 5 minutes. Allow 3 minutes for the baby spinach to wilt.

Top the crust with the bell pepper mixture and pizza sauce. Top with the remaining mozzarella and Monterey Jack cheeses. 5 minutes in the oven Slice and serve.

Nutrition: Cal 1059; Net Carbs 5.3g; Fat 92g; Protein 60g

Pork Steaks and Mushroom Sauce

Servings: 4 and **Total Time:** approx. 25 minutes

Ingredients:

- 8 oz button mushrooms, chopped
- 1 tbsp butter
- 2 tbsp chopped parsley
- 4 bone pork steaks
- 2 tsp lemon pepper seasoning 1 tbsp olive oil
- 1 cup vegetable stock
- 6 garlic cloves, minced

Directions:

In a skillet over medium heat, warm the olive oil and butter and brown the meat for 10 minutes; set aside. Cook until the garlic and mushrooms are softened, about 5 minutes. Pour in the vegetable stock to deglaze the pan; season with lemon pepper seasoning. Return the pork to the pan and cook until the liquid has been reduced by two-thirds. Serve with steamed green beans and garnished with parsley.

Nutrition: Cal 498; Net Carbs 3.2g; Fat 29g; Protein 46g

Pork Shoulder

Servings: 4 and **Total Time:** approx. 25 minutes

Ingredients:

- 2 tbsp ghee ginger
- 2 tbsp pureed garlic
- 6 red onions, sliced
- 1 cup crushed tomatoes
- 2 tbsp Greek yogurt
- 2 tbsp garam
- 1 ½ lb pork shoulder, cubed
- 1 tbsp freshly grated
- 1 bunch cilantro, chopped
- ½ tsp chili powder masala
- 2 green chilies, sliced

Directions:

Bring a pot of water to a boil. Add the pork and blanch for 3 minutes; drain and set aside. Melt ghee in a skillet and sauté ginger, garlic, and onions for 5 minutes, or until caramelised. Toss in the tomatoes.

Return the pork and the yoghurt. Season with chilli powder and garam masala to taste. Cook for 10 minutes, stirring occasionally. Combine the cilantro and green chilies in a mixing bowl. Serve the pork masala with cauliflower rice.

Nutrition: Cal 359; Net Carbs 4.2g; Fat 30g; Protein 38g

Gingery Pork Stir-Fry

Servings: 4 and **Total Time:** approx. 25 minutes

Ingredients:

- 2 tbsp coconut oil
- 1 green bell pepper, diced
- 1 small red onion, diced
- 1/3 cup walnuts
- 1 tsp olive oil
- 1 habanero pepper, minced
- 1 ½ lb pork tenderloin
- 1 tbsp freshly grated ginger
- 3 garlic cloves, minced
- 2 tbsp tamari sauce
- Salt and black pepper to taste

Directions:

Pork should be cut into strips. In a wok, heat the coconut oil, season the pork with salt and pepper, and cook until no longer pink, about 10 minutes.

Add the bell pepper, onion, walnuts, ginger, and garlic to one side of the wok.

Garlic, olive oil, and habanero pepper are just a few of the Ingredients 5 minutes later, the onion should be softened and fragrant. Season with tamari sauce and mix well. Stir-fry for 1 minute, or until everything is well combined. With cauliflower rice, serve.

Nutrition: Cal 318; Net Carbs 4.8g; Fat 16g; Protein 41g

Veggie Bake with Sausage

Servings: 4 and **Total Time:** approx. 40 minutes

Ingredients:

- 1 lb pork sausage, sliced
- 1 cup mayonnaise
- ½ cup celery stalks, chopped
- 1 green bell pepper, chopped
- Salt and black pepper to taste
- 10 oz cauliflower florets
- 2 oz butter
- 1 onion, chopped
- 4 oz Parmesan cheese, grated
- 1 tsp red chili flakes

Directions:

Preheat the oven to 400 degrees Fahrenheit. In a pan over medium heat, melt the butter and stir-fry the onion, celery, and bell pepper for 5 minutes. Cook for another 4-5 minutes after adding the sausage. Season with salt and pepper to taste.

Combine cauliflower, mayonnaise, Parmesan cheese, and red chilli flakes in a mixing bowl. Pour the mixture into a baking dish and top with the sausage mixture. Bake for 20 minutes, or until golden brown. Serve hot.

Nutrition: Cal 611; Net Carbs 7.4g; Fat 47g; Protein 32g

Prosciutto Pizza

Servings: 4 and **Total Time:** approx. 40 minutes

Ingredients:

- ⅓ cup tomato sauce
- 1 egg, beaten
- 2 tbsp cream cheese, softened
- ½ cup almond flour
- 2 cups grated mozzarella
- 4 prosciutto slices, cut into thirds
- 6 fresh basil leaves, to serve
- ⅓ cup sliced mozzarella

Directions:

Preheat the oven to 380 degrees Fahrenheit. Using parchment paper, line a pizza pan. 1 minute in the microwave with mozzarella cheese and 2 tbsp cream cheese Mix in the almond flour and the egg. Bake for 15 minutes after spreading the mixture on the pizza pan.

Cover the crust with the tomato sauce. Arrange the mozzarella slices on top of the sauce, followed by the prosciutto. Bake for another 15 minutes, or until done.

until the cheese has melted Remove from the oven and top with the basil. Cut into slices and serve.

Nutrition: Cal 209; Net Carbs 4.5g; Fat 11g; Protein 19g

Italian Meatballs

Servings: 4 and **Total Time:** approx. 50 minutes

Ingredients:

- ¾ cup pork rinds
- ½ lb ground Italian sausage
- ½ cup grated Parmesan
- 1 tsp onion powder
- ½ lb ground pork
- 2 eggs
- 1 tsp garlic powder
- 1 tbsp chopped fresh basil
- 2 tsp dried Italian seasoning
- 3 tbsp olive oil
- 2 ½ cups marinara sauce
- Salt and black pepper to taste

Directions:

Combine ground pork, Italian sausage, pork rinds, Parmesan cheese, eggs, onion powder, garlic powder, basil, salt, pepper, and parsley in a mixing bowl.

Seasoning from Italy. Form the mixture into meatballs. In a skillet, heat the olive oil and brown the meatballs for 10 minutes. Cook for 30 minutes after adding the marinara sauce and submerging the meatballs in it. Serve and have fun!

Nutrition: Cal 509; Net Carbs 8.2g; Fat 24g; Protein 35g

Green Pork Bake

Servings: 4 and **Total Time:** approx. 50 minutes

Ingredients:

- 1 lb ground pork
- ½ cup Monterey Jack cheese, grated
- ¼ cup heavy cream
- 5 eggs
- 1 onion, chopped
- 1 garlic clove, minced
- 1 zucchini, sliced
- ½ lb green beans, chopped
- Salt and black pepper to taste

Directions:

Combine the onion, green beans, ground pork, garlic, black pepper, and salt in a mixing bowl. In a small greased baking dish, layer the meat mixture.

Top with zucchini slices. Combine Monterey Jack cheese, eggs, and heavy cream in a separate bowl. Pour the solution over the

Bake for 40 minutes at 360 degrees F, or until the edges and top are brown.

Nutrition: Cal 445; Net Carbs 5.9g; Fat 31g; Protein 29g

Beef Recipes AND Lamb Recipes

Root Mash Veggie Beef Stew

Servings: 2 and **Total Time:** approx. 2 hours 10 minutes

Ingredients:
- Salt and black pepper to taste 1 ¼ cups beef stock
- ¼ celeriac, chopped
- 2 tbsp butter
- ½ parsnip, chopped
- 1 garlic clove, minced
- ½ carrot, chopped
- 2 bay leaves
- ½ lb stewing beef, cut into chunks
- ¼ cauliflower head, cut into florets 1 tbsp olive oil
- ½ onion, chopped
- 2 tbsp red wine
- 1 celery stalk, chopped
- ½ tbsp rosemary, chopped
- 1 tomato, chopped

Directions:

Cook the celery, onion, and garlic in warm oil for 5 minutes over medium heat in a pot. Cook for 3 minutes after adding the beef chunks. Season with salt and black pepper to taste.

Using the red wine, deglaze the bottom of the pot. Combine the carrot, parsnip, beef stock, tomato, and bay leaves in a mixing bowl.

Bring the mixture to a boil, then reduce to a low heat and cook for 1 hour and 30 minutes.

In the meantime, heat a pot of water over medium heat. Cover and simmer for 10 minutes with the celeriac. Cook for 15 minutes with the cauliflower florets, then drain and combine with the butter, pepper, and salt.

Mash the potatoes with a potato masher and divide the mash between two plates. Serve with vegetable mixture on top.

Nutrition: Cal 465; Net Carbs 9.8g; Fat 24g; Protein 32g

King Burgers

Servings: 4 and **Total Time:** approx. 25 minutes

Ingredients:
- 2 tbsp olive oil
- ½ tbsp Worcestershire sauce
- ½ tbsp chopped parsley
- 1 tbsp thyme
- 1 lb ground beef
- 2 green onions, chopped
- 1 garlic clove, minced
- 2 tbsp almond flour
- 2 tbsp beef broth

Directions:

Preheat your grill to 370 degrees Fahrenheit. In a mixing bowl, combine all ingredients except the parsley. Mix well with your hands and shape the mixture into two patties. Arrange on a baking sheet that has been lined with parchment paper. Bake for 18-20 minutes, or until the bacon is nice and crispy. Garnish with parsley before serving.

Nutrition: Cal 363; Net Carbs 3g; Fat 26g; Protein 25g

Beef Cheeseburger

Servings: 2 and **Total Time:** approx. 25 minutes

Ingredients:
- 2 tbsp olive oil
- 2 portobello mushroom caps
- ½ tsp Worcestershire sauce Salt and black pepper to taste
- ½ lb ground beef
- ½ tsp fresh parsley, chopped
- 2 slices mozzarella cheese

Directions:

Mix the beef, parsley, Worcestershire sauce, salt, and black pepper in a mixing bowl with your hands until evenly combined. Form the mixture into medium-sized patties.

Preheat the grill to 400 degrees Fahrenheit and

season the mushroom caps with olive oil, salt, and black pepper. Place the portobello caps and burger patties, rounded side up, on a hot grill pan and cook for 5 minutes. Cook for 1 minute after turning the mushroom caps.

Place a slice of mozzarella on top of each patty. Cook for 4 to 5 minutes more, or until the mushroom caps are softened and the beef patties are no longer pink in the centre. Turn the patties over and top with cheese. Cook for another 2-3 minutes until the cheese is melted.

Nutrition: Cal 505; Net Carbs 2.2g; Fat 39g; Protein 38g

Oven-Roast Veggie Chuck Beef

Servings: 4 and **Total Time:** approx. 1 hour 45 minutes

Ingredients:

2 tbsp olive oil	1 lb beef chuck roast, cubed
1 cup canned diced tomatoes	1 carrot, chopped
Salt and black pepper to taste	½ cup beef stock
½ lb mushrooms, sliced	1 onion, chopped
1 celery stalk, chopped	1 tbsp almond flour
1 bell pepper, sliced	1 tbsp rosemary, chopped
½ tsp dry mustard	1 bay leaf

Directions:

Preheat the oven to 350 degrees Fahrenheit. Warm the olive oil in a pot over medium heat and brown the beef on each side for 4-5 minutes.

Combine the tomatoes, onion, mustard, carrot, mushrooms, bell pepper, celery, bay leaf, and stock in a mixing bowl.

Season with salt and pepper to taste. 12 cup water and flour in a mixing bowl, stir in the pot Place in a baking dish and bake for 90 minutes, stirring every 30 minutes. Scatter the rosemary over the top and serve hot.

Nutrition: Cal 325; Net Carbs 8.6g; Fat 18g; Protein 31g

Bell Peppers Stuffed with Enchilada Beef

Servings: 6 and **Total Time:** approx. 60 minutes

Ingredients:

3 tbsp butter, softened	6 bell peppers, deseeded
½ white onion, chopped	3 tsp enchilada seasoning
3 cloves garlic, minced	1 cup cauliflower rice
2 ½ lb ground beef	Sour cream for serving
¼ cup grated cheddar cheese	Salt and black pepper to taste

Directions:

Preheat the oven to 380 degrees Fahrenheit. In a skillet over medium heat, melt the butter and sauté the onion and garlic for 3 minutes.

Combine the beef, enchilada seasoning, salt, and pepper in a mixing bowl. Cooking time is 10 minutes. Mix in the cauliflower rice until well combined. Fill the peppers with the mixture, then top with the cheese.

Place the stuffed peppers in a greased baking dish and top with cheddar cheese. 40 minutes in the oven Serve with generous dollops of sour cream on top of the peppers.

Nutrition: Cal 479; Net Carbs 5.4g; Fat 32g; Protein 38g

Spicy Beef Lettuce Cups

Servings: 4 and **Total Time:** approx. 30 minutes

Ingredients:

3 tbsp ghee, divided	1 lb chuck steak
¼ cup sour cream for topping	1 large white onion, chopped
1 jalapeño pepper, chopped	1 cup cauliflower rice
2 tsp red curry powder	8 small lettuce leaves
Salt and black pepper to taste	2 garlic cloves, minced

Directions:

2 tbsp ghee, warmed in a large deep skillet Cook the beef thinly against the grain for 10 minutes, or until brown and cooked through; set aside. In a skillet, sauté the onion for 3 minutes. Cook for 1 minute after adding the garlic, salt, pepper, and jalapeo.

Combine the remaining ghee, curry powder, and beef in a mixing bowl. Cook for 5 minutes before adding the cauliflower rice. Sauté for 2 to 3 minutes, or until thoroughly combined and the cauliflower is slightly softened. Season with salt and pepper to taste.

Place the lettuce leaves on a clean, flat surface and spoon the beef mixture into the centre of each one, 3 tbsp per leaf. Serve topped with sour cream and wrapped in lettuce leaves.

Nutrition: Cal 302; Net Carbs 5.3g; Fat 21g; Protein 32g

Beef Chili

Servings: 4 and **Total Time:** approx. 40 minutes

Ingredients:

2 tbsp olive oil	1 onion, chopped
15 oz canned tomatoes, diced	1 tsp chopped cilantro
½ cup pickled jalapeños, diced	1 garlic clove, minced
	2 lb ground beef

1 tsp onion powder
1 tsp garlic powder
Salt and black pepper to taste
1 tsp chipotle chili paste

3 celery stalks, chopped
2 tbsp coconut aminos
2 tbsp cumin

Directions:

In a pan over medium heat, heat the olive oil and sauté the onion, celery, garlic, beef, pepper, and salt until the meat browns. Cook for 30 minutes after adding the remaining Ingredients. Serve and have fun!

Nutrition: Cal 5451; Net Carbs 5.8g; Fat 36g; Protein 46g

Asian Broccoli Spiced Beef

Servings: 2 and **Total Time:** approx. 30 minutes

Ingredients:

½ cup coconut milk
2 tbsp coconut oil
½ tbsp sesame seeds
½ tbsp coconut aminos
1 head broccoli, cut into florets
½ tbsp Thai green curry paste

¼ tsp garlic powder
1 tsp ginger paste
¼ tsp onion powder
1 lb beef steak, cut into strips
Salt and black pepper to taste
1 tbsp cilantro, chopped

Directions:

In a pan over medium heat, warm the coconut oil, then add the beef and season with garlic powder, pepper, salt, ginger paste, and onion powder.

4 minutes in the oven Stir in the broccoli and cook for 5 minutes. Cook for 15 minutes after adding the coconut milk, coconut aminos, and Thai curry paste. Garnish with cilantro and sesame seeds before serving.

Nutrition: Cal 623; Net Carbs 2.3g; Fat 43g; Protein 53g

Cilantro Beef Balls

Servings: 4 and **Total Time:** approx. 45 minutes

Ingredients:

1 garlic clove, minced
1 small onion, chopped
1 cup flax meal
½ tsp allspice
1 tsp cumin
½ cup mascarpone cheese
¼ cup coconut flour
¼ tsp baking powder

1 lb ground beef
1 jalapeño pepper, chopped
Salt and black pepper to taste
1 tbsp butter + 1 ½ tbsp melted
¼ tsp turmeric
2 tsp cilantro

Directions:

In a blender, combine the onion, garlic, jalapeo, and 14 cup of water. 1 tbsp butter melted in a pan over medium heat Cook the beef for 3 minutes on high heat. Cook for 2 minutes after adding the onion mixture. Cook for 3 minutes after adding the cilantro, salt, cumin, turmeric, allspice, and pepper.

Combine the coconut flour, flax meal, and baking powder in a mixing bowl. Melted butter and mascarpone cheese should be combined in a separate bowl. To make a dough, combine the two mixtures. Form the mixture into balls, place them on parchment paper, and roll each one into a circle.

Spread the beef mixture on half of the dough circles, then cover with the other half, seal the edges, and place on a lined baking sheet. 25 minutes in the oven

Nutrition: Cal 374; Net Carbs 9g; Fat 26g; Protein 33g

Beef Pepper & Green Beans Ragout

Servings: 4 and **Total Time:** approx. 2 hours

Ingredients:

1 lb chuck steak, trimmed and cubed
2 tbsp olive oil
4 green onions, diced
2 tsp Worcestershire sauce
½ cup dry white wine
1 cup beef broth
3 tsp smoked paprika

Salt and black pepper to taste
2 tbsp almond flour
4 oz tomato puree
1 yellow bell pepper, diced
1 cup green beans, chopped
Parsley leaves to garnish

Directions:

Set aside the meat after dredging it in the almond flour. Heat 1 tablespoon of oil in a large skillet over medium heat, then sauté the green onion, green beans, and bell pepper for 3 minutes.

Combine the paprika and the remaining olive oil in a mixing bowl. Cook the beef for 10 minutes, turning halfway through. Stir in the white wine, reduce it by half (about 3 minutes), and then add the Worcestershire sauce, tomato puree, and beef broth.

Allow the mixture to boil for 2 minutes, then reduce to the lowest heat and allow to simmer for 12 hours, stirring occasionally. Adjust the seasoning and serve the ragout.

Nutrition: Cal 334; Net Carbs 5.9g; Fat 22g; Protein 33g

Grilled Beef on Skewers and salad

Servings: 2 and **Total Time:** approx. 20 minutes

Ingredients:

1 lb sirloin steak, boneless, cubed
¼ cup ranch dressing

Salt to taste
1 cucumber, sliced
½ tbsp white wine

1 red onion, sliced

2 tbsp fresh parsley, chopped

vinegar

1 tbsp virgin olive oil

2 ripe tomatoes, sliced

Directions:

Thread the beef cubes onto the skewers, 4–5 cubes per skewer. Half of the ranch dressing should be applied to the skewers (all around).

Preheat the grill to high heat. Cook the skewers for 6 minutes on the grill. Cook for another 6 minutes after turning the skewers. Brush the remaining ranch dressing over the meat and cook for 1 more minute one minute on each side

Toss red onion, tomatoes, and cucumber in a salad bowl with salt, vinegar, and extra virgin olive oil to combine. Skewers should be placed on top of the salad, and parsley should be scattered evenly.

Nutrition: Calories 423; Net Carbs 2.4g; Fat 24g; Protein 45g

Beef Sausage & Okra Casserole

Servings: 4 and **Total Time:** approx. 35 minutes

Ingredients:

½ cup marinara sauce, sugar-free
1 celery stalk, chopped
1 lb beef sausage, chopped Salt and black pepper to taste
¼ tsp red pepper flakes
2 green onions, chopped
½ tsp garlic powder
½ cup ricotta cheese

½ cup okra, trimmed
1 tbsp olive oil
¼ cup almond flour
½ tbsp dried parsley
1 egg
¼ cup Parmesan cheese, grated
¼ tsp dried oregano
1 cup cheddar cheese, grated

Directions:

Mix the sausage, pepper, pepper flakes, oregano, egg, Parmesan cheese, green onions, almond flour, salt, parsley, celery, and garlic powder in a mixing bowl.

Form the balls, place them on a baking sheet lined with parchment paper, and bake for 15 minutes at 390°F. Take the balls out of the oven and top with half of the marinara sauce and okra.

Pour the rest of the marinara sauce over the ricotta cheese. Scatter the cheddar cheese over the top and bake for 10 minutes. Allow to cool completely before serving.

Nutrition: Cal 702; Net Carbs 7.3g; Fat 33g; Protein 33g

Grilled Steak and Green Beans

Servings: 2 and **Total Time:** approx. 20 minutes

Ingredients:

2 rib-eye steaks
1 tbsp fresh thyme, chopped

½ cup green beans, sliced
Salt black pepper to taste

2 teaspoon unsalted butter
1 tsp olive oil
1 tbsp rosemary
1 teaspoon fresh parsley, chopped,

Directions:

Preheat a grill pan over medium-high heat. Season the steaks with salt and black pepper after brushing them with olive oil. Cook the steaks for 4 minutes per side; set aside. Green beans should be steamed for 3-4 minutes, or until tender.

Season with salt and pepper. Melt the butter in the pan and cook the herbs for 1 minute before adding the green beans. Serve with the steaks on top. Enjoy!

Nutrition: Cal 626; Net Carbs 2.3g; Fat 39g; Protein 65g

Vegetable Medley with Grilled Beef Steaks

Servings: 2 and **Total Time:** approx. 30 minutes

Ingredients:

½ cup mushrooms, sliced
2 sirloin beef steaks
Salt and black pepper to taste 2 tbsp olive oil

¼ lb asparagus, trimmed
1 small onion, quartered

1 red bell pepper, seeded, cut into strips

1 ½ tbsp balsamic vinegar
1 garlic clove, sliced
½ cup snow peas

Directions:

Asparagus, mushrooms, snow peas, bell pepper, onion, and garlic should all be combined in a bowl.

In a small bowl, combine the salt, pepper, olive oil, and balsamic vinegar; pour half of the mixture over the vegetables and stir to combine. Toss the beef in the remaining oil mixture to coat well.

Preheat a grill pan over medium-high heat. Sear the steaks for 6-8 minutes on each side in a grill pan.

Remove the beef from the pan and set it aside. Cook for 5 minutes, turning once, with the vegetables and marinade in the pan. Divide the vegetables among the plates. Serve with the beef on top and a drizzle of the pan sauce.

Nutrition: Cal 488; Net Carbs 7g; Fat 31g; Protein 37g

Beef Stew

Servings: 4 and **Total Time:** approx. 40 minutes

Ingredients:

1 garlic clove, minced	14 oz canned tomatoes with juice
1 cup beef stock	1 celery stick, chopped
1 lb ground beef	Salt and black pepper to taste 3 tbsp fresh parsley, chopped
1 lb butternut squash, diced	
1 tbsp Worcestershire sauce	1 onion, chopped
1 tsp dried sage	1 carrot, chopped
3 tsp olive oil	2 bay leaves

Directions:

Cook the onion, garlic, celery, carrot, and beef in warm oil for 10 minutes over medium heat. Bring to a boil with the butternut squash, Worcestershire sauce, bay leaves, stock, canned tomatoes, and sage.

Simmer for 20 minutes on low heat. Seasonings should be adjusted. Take out the bay leaves and set them aside. Serve garnished with parsley.

Nutrition: Cal 353; Net Carbs 15g; Fat 16g; Protein 26g

Beef Cheese & Egg Casserole

Servings: 4 and **Total Time:** approx. 25 minutes

Ingredients:

2 tbsp olive oil	½ tsp nutmeg
¼ cup heavy cream	1 lb ground beef
2 zucchinis, sliced	5 eggs, beaten
1 cup Gouda cheese, grated	2 cups tomatoes, chopped
Salt and black pepper to taste	1 Banana pepper, chopped
1 yellow onion, chopped	2 garlic cloves, chopped

Directions:

Preheat the oven to 360 degrees Fahrenheit. In a skillet over medium heat, warm the olive oil. Stir-fry the garlic, banana pepper, and onion for 2 minutes, or until the garlic is fragrant.

tender. Sauté the ground beef for 4-6 minutes, stirring frequently.

Season with nutmeg, salt, and pepper to taste. Place the mixture in a baking dish. Arrange the zucchini slices on top of the tomatoes. 30 minutes in the oven

Combine the eggs, cheese, and heavy cream in a mixing bowl. Season with salt and pepper to taste. Remove the baking dish from the oven and top it with the cheese mixture. Bake for another 10-15 minutes, or until the eggs are set. Enjoy!

Nutrition: Cal 658; Net Carbs 6.4g; Fat 46g; Protein 56g

Flank Steak Roll

Servings: 2 and **Total Time:** approx. 40 minutes

Ingredients:

1 lb flank steak	Salt black pepper to taste
1 tbsp basil leaves, chopped	½ cup ricotta, crumbled
½ cup baby kale, chopped	1 serrano pepper, chopped

Directions:

Wrap the steak in plastic wrap, place it on a flat surface, and gently flatten with a rolling pin.

Remove the wraps. Season with salt and pepper, then top with kale, serrano pepper, and the remaining cheese.

Secure the steak with toothpicks after rolling it over on the stuffing. Cook for 30 minutes at 390 F, flipping once, until nicely browned on the outside and the cheese is melted on the inside.

Allow to cool for 3 minutes before slicing and serving with basil.

Nutrition: Cal 445; Net Carbs 2.8g; Fat 21g; Protein 53g

Beef, Bell Pepper & Mushroom Kebabs

Servings: 4 and **Total Time:** approx. 15 min + cooling time

Ingredients:

1 lb cremini mushrooms, halved	2 tbsp coconut oil
2 yellow bell peppers	1 lime, juiced
1 tbsp tamari sauce	1 tbsp ginger powder
½ tsp ground cumin	2 lb beef tri-tip steak, cubed

Directions:

Remove the seeds from the bell peppers and cut them into squares.

Combine the coconut oil, tamari sauce, lime juice, ginger, and cumin powder in a mixing bowl. Toss in the beef, mushrooms, and bell peppers until evenly coated. Cover the bowl with plastic wrap and set aside for 1 hour to marinate. Preheat the grill to medium-high.

Remove the plastic wrap and thread the mushrooms, beef, and bell peppers on skewers in this order until all of the Ingredients are used. Cook the skewers for 5 minutes per side on a hot grill. Take away to

Serve warm with steamed cauliflower rice or braised asparagus on serving plates.

Nutrition: Cal 379; Net Carbs 4.2g; Fat 23g; Protein 49g

Coconut-Olive Beef with Mushrooms

Servings: 4 and **Total Time:** approx. 30 minutes

Ingredients:

3 tbsp black olives, sliced
1/3 cup coconut milk
3 tbsp butter
2 tbsp coconut cream
1/2 tsp dried thyme
¼ cup button mushrooms, sliced
1 yellow onion, chopped
2 tbsp chopped parsley
4 rib-eye steaks

Directions:

In a large skillet over medium heat, melt 2 tablespoons butter. Sauté the mushrooms for 4 minutes, or until tender.

Cook for 3 minutes more after adding the onion; set aside. Cook the beef for 10 minutes on both sides in the skillet with the remaining butter. Return the mushrooms and onion to the skillet and stir in the milk, coconut cream, thyme, and 1 teaspoon salt.

1 tbsp parsley Simmer for 2 minutes, stirring occasionally. Remove from the heat and stir in the black olives. Garnish with the remaining parsley and serve.

Nutrition: Cal 743; Net Carbs 2.9g; Fat 48g; Protein 71g

Eggplant Beef Lasagna

Servings: 4 and **Total Time:** approx. 65 minutes

Ingredients:

2 large eggplants, sliced lengthwise
2 tbsp olive oil
2 garlic cloves, minced
Salt and black pepper to taste 2 tsp sweet paprika
1 cup mozzarella cheese, grated
½ red chili, chopped
1 lb ground beef
1 shallot, chopped
1 cup tomato sauce
1 tsp dried thyme
1 tsp dried basil
1 cup chicken broth

Directions:

In a skillet, heat the oil and cook the beef for 4 minutes, breaking up any lumps as you stir. Add shallot, garlic, chilli, tomato sauce, salt, paprika, and black pepper to taste. Cook for 5 minutes more, stirring occasionally.

1/3 of the eggplant slices should be placed in a greased baking dish. Top with a third of the beef mixture and repeat the layering process twice more with the same amounts.

Season with basil and thyme to taste. Add the chicken broth. Place the baking dish in the oven and top with the mozzarella cheese. Preheat the oven to 380°F and bake for 35 minutes. Remove the lasagna from the oven and set aside for 10 minutes before serving.

Nutrition: Cal 438; Net Carbs 9.8g; Fat 20g; Protein 41g

Grandma's Meatballs

Servings: 4 and **Total Time:** approx. 30 minutes

Ingredients:

1 tbsp olive oil
1 lb ground beef
1 red onion, finely chopped
2 tbsp tamari sauce
Salt and black pepper to taste
1 tbsp melted butter
2 garlic cloves, minced
1 tsp dried basil
1 tbsp dried rosemary
2 red bell peppers, chopped

Directions:

Preheat the oven to 380 degrees Fahrenheit. Combine the beef, onion, bell peppers, garlic, butter, basil, tamari sauce, salt, pepper, and rosemary in a mixing bowl. Form the mixture into 1-inch meatballs and place them on a greased baking sheet.

Drizzle olive oil over the beef and bake for 20 minutes, or until the meatballs are golden brown on the outside. Serve with ranch dressing on the side.

Nutrition: Cal 352; Net Carbs 4.5g; Fat 23g; Protein 29g

Bacon & Mushrooms Beef Steaks

Servings: 2 and **Total Time:** approx. 50 minutes

Ingredients:

2 oz bacon, chopped
1 garlic clove, chopped
1 cup heavy cream
¼ cup coconut oil
Salt and black pepper to taste
1 cup mushrooms, sliced
1 shallot, chopped
½ lb beef steaks
1 tsp ground nutmeg
1 tbsp parsley, chopped

Directions:

Cook the bacon for 2-3 minutes in a pan over medium heat; set aside. Warm the oil in the same pan, then add the shallot, garlic, and mushrooms. 4 minutes in the oven

Season the beef with salt, pepper, and nutmeg and sear until done. 2 minutes per side until browned

Preheat the oven to 360 degrees Fahrenheit and bake the pan for 25 minutes. Transfer the beef steaks to a bowl and wrap in foil.

Heat the heavy cream in the pan over medium heat, then add the reserved bacon and cook for 5 minutes before removing from the heat. Serve the bacon/mushroom sauce over the beef steaks, sprinkled with parsley.

Nutrition: Cal 705; Net Carbs 3.8g; Fat 68g; Protein 32g

BBQ Rib Sweet Steak

Servings: 4 and **Total Time:** approx. 2 hours 40 minutes

Ingredients:

- 2 tbsp avocado oil
- 3 tbsp maple syrup, sugar-free
- 1 ½ lb rib steaks
- 3 tbsp barbecue dry rub

Directions:

Preheat the oven to 300 degrees Fahrenheit. Remove the steaks' membranes. Aluminum foil should be used to line a baking sheet.

Combine the avocado oil and maple syrup in a bowl and brush the mixture over the meat. Rub the BBQ sauce all over the ribs. Place them on a baking sheet and bake for 2 12 hours, or until the meat is tender and crispy on top. Serve with buttered broccoli and green beans on the side.

Nutrition: Cal 487; Net Carbs 1.8g; Fat 26g; Protein 51g

Rosemary Thyme Juicy Beef

Servings: 4 and **Total Time:** approx. 30 minutes

Ingredients:

- 2 garlic cloves, minced
- 1 tsp xylitol
- 1 tbsp rosemary, chopped
- 1 lb beef rump steak, sliced
- ½ cup heavy cream
- ½ cup beef stock
- 1 tbsp mustard
- A sprig of thyme
- 2 tbsp butter
- 2 tbsp olive oil
- Salt and black pepper to taste
- 1 shallot, chopped
- A sprig of rosemary
- 2 tsp soy sauce, sugar-free
- 2 tsp lemon juice

Directions:

Heat a tbsp olive oil in a pan over medium heat, then add the shallot and cook for 3 minutes. Cook for 8 minutes after adding the stock, soy sauce, xylitol, thyme sprig, cream, mustard, and rosemary sprig.

Combine the butter, lemon juice, pepper, and salt in a mixing bowl. Remove the rosemary and thyme. Place aside. Combine the remaining oil, black pepper, garlic, rosemary, and salt in a mixing bowl. Toss in the beef and set aside for a few minutes to coat.

Heat a pan over medium-high heat, add the beef steak, and cook for 6 minutes, flipping halfway; set aside and keep warm. Plate the beef slices, top with the sauce, and serve.

Nutrition: Cal 341; Net Carbs 2.6g; Fat 27g; Protein 28g

Ancho T-Bone Steak

Servings: 4 and **Total Time:** approx. 30 minutes

Ingredients:

- 2 (8-oz) T-bone steaks
- Salt and black pepper to taste 4 oz butter, softened
- 2 tbsp fresh parsley, chopped
- 1 tsp ancho chile powder
- ¼ tsp garlic powder
- 2 tbsp avocado oil
- 1 tsp lemon juice

Directions:

In a mixing bowl, combine the butter, garlic powder, parsley, salt, pepper, and lemon juice. Place aside.

Preheat the grill to medium-high heat. Season the steaks with ancho chilli powder, salt, and pepper before brushing with avocado oil.

Cook for 12-14 minutes on both sides, or until the meat reaches an internal temperature of 150 F for medium-rare. Serve the beef with parsley butter on top. Serve and have fun!

Nutrition: Cal 486; Net Carbs 1.2g; Fat 44g; Protein 34g

Red Wine Vegetables Beef Roast

Servings: 4 and **Total Time:** approx. 2 hours 20 minutes

Ingredients:

- 1 tbsp olive oil
- 1 tbsp fresh thyme, chopped 1 cup red wine
- 2 stalks celery, cut into chunks 1 garlic clove, minced
- 1 lb brisket
- ½ cup carrots, peeled
- 1 red onion, quartered
- Salt and black pepper to taste 1 bay leaf

Directions:

Season the brisket generously with salt and pepper. Brown the meat for 6-8 minutes on both sides in warm olive oil over medium heat.

Place in a large casserole dish. Arrange the carrots, onion, garlic, thyme, celery, and bay leaf around the brisket and add the red wine and 12 cup of water.

water. Cover the pot and place it in a preheated oven set to 370 degrees Fahrenheit.

2 hours in the oven Remove the casserole when it is done. Transfer the beef to a cutting board and thinly slice it. To serve, top the beef with vegetables.

Nutrition: Cal 446; Net Carbs 8.6g; Fat 22g; Protein 52g

Spiralized Zucchini in Bolognese Sauce

Servings: 4 and **Total Time:** approx. 35 minutes

Ingredients:
- 4 zucchinis, spiralized
- 1 tsp rosemary
- 1 tsp sage
- 1 onion, chopped
- 7 oz canned diced tomatoes
- 1 lb ground beef
- 2 bacon slices, chopped
- 2 garlic cloves
- 1 tsp dried oregano
- 2 tbsp olive oil

Directions:

Cook the zoodles in warm olive oil for 3-4 minutes over medium heat before transferring to a serving plate.

Cook for 3 minutes in the same pan with the bacon, onion, and garlic. Cook until the beef is browned, about 4-5 minutes.

Combine the herbs and tomatoes in a mixing bowl. Cook for 15 minutes, then serve over zoodles.

Nutrition: Cal 378; Net Carbs 3.9g; Fat 24g; Protein 31g

Fish Recipes And Seafood Recipes

Dijon Sauce Blackened Salmon

Servings: 2 and **Total Time:** approx. 15 minutes

Ingredients:
- 2 salmon fillets
- Salt black pepper to taste
- ¼ cup Dijon mustard
- 2 tbsp white wine
- ¾ tsp fresh thyme
- ¼ cup heavy cream
- ½ tsp tarragon
- 1 tbsp butter

Directions:

Thyme, salt, and pepper should be used to season the salmon. Melt the butter in a small saucepan over medium heat.

Cook for about 4-5 minutes on both sides, or until golden and charred.Transfer to a plate and wrap in foil to keep warm. Add the mustard, white wine, heavy cream, and tarragon to the same pan. Reduce the heat to low and continue to stir until the sauce thickens slightly.

Cook for 60 seconds to infuse the flavours; season with salt and pepper to taste. Pour the sauce over the chicken. salmon to be served

Nutrition: Cal 637; Net Carbs 2.5g; Fat 36g; Protein 67g

Broccoli & Bell Pepper Crispy Salmon

Servings: 2 and **Total Time:** approx. 35 minutes

Ingredients:
- 2 salmon fillets
- 2 tbsp fennel seeds
- ½ head broccoli, cut in florets
- 1 red bell pepper, sliced
- Salt black pepper to taste
- 2 lemon wedges
- 1 tbsp olive oil
- 2 tbsp mayonnaise

Directions:

Season the salmon with salt and black pepper after brushing it with mayonnaise.

Coat with fennel seeds and bake for 15 minutes at 370 F in a lined baking dish.

In a pot over medium heat, steam the broccoli for 5-6 minutes, or until tender. In a saucepan, heat the olive oil and sauté the red bell pepper for 5 minutes.

Remove from the heat and stir in the broccoli. Allow the pan to sit on a warm burner for 2 to 3 minutes. Serve the vegetables alongside the salmon. Garnish with lemon slices wedges.

Nutrition: Cal 663; Net Carbs 6.5g; Fat 37g; Protein 64g

Mediterranean Tilapia Bake

Servings: 2 and **Total Time:** approx. 30 minutes

Ingredients:
- 2 tilapia fillets
- ¼ tbsp chili powder
- 2 tbsp white wine
- 10 black olives, halved
- 1 tbsp parsley, chopped
- 2 garlic cloves, minced
- 1 tbsp olive oil
- 1 cup canned tomatoes
- ½ red onion, chopped
- 1 tsp basil, chopped

Directions:

Preheat the oven to 350 degrees Fahrenheit. In a skillet over medium heat, heat the olive oil and stir-fry the onion and garlic for about 3 minutes.

Bring the tomatoes, olives, chilli powder, and wine to a boil in a saucepan. Reduce the heat to low and continue to cook for 5 minutes.

Place the tilapia in a baking dish and season with

salt and pepper.

Pour the sauce over the top and bake for 12-15 minutes. Garnish with basil and parsley before serving.

Nutrition: Cal 282; Net Carbs 5.6g; Fat 15g; Protein 23g

Grilled Salmon with salad

Servings: 2 and **Total Time:** approx. 20 minutes

Ingredients:

¼ cup parsley, chopped	1 lb skinned salmon, cut into 4 steaks each
8 green olives, chopped	
Salt and black pepper to taste	1 cup arugula
2 green onions, sliced	2 large tomatoes, diced
3 tbsp olive oil	3 tbsp red wine vinegar
1 cup radishes, sliced	

Directions:

Combine the radishes, olives, arugula, tomatoes, vinegar, green onion, 2 tablespoons olive oil, and parsley in a mixing bowl. Place in the refrigerator while preparing the salmon.

Preheat the grill to high heat. Season the salmon steaks with salt and pepper to taste.

season with pepper and drizzle with the remaining olive oil Grill the salmon for 8 minutes total, on both sides. Serve immediately with the radish salad.

Nutrition: Cal 338; Net Carbs 7g; Fat 22g; Protein 28g

Moroccan Salmon with Cauliflower Rice Pilaf

SERVINGS 4 | **PREP TIME** 5 minutes | **COOK TIME** 10 minutes

Ingredients:

1 medium head of cauliflower, riced	3 tablespoons coconut oil, melted, divided
1 teaspoon white wine vinegar	1 tablespoon minced preserved lemons
¼ cup roughly chopped mint	¼ cup roughly chopped pistachios
ground black pepper	1 tsp extra-virgin olive oil
½ teaspoon coarse sea salt, plus more for seasoning pilaf, divided	4 (5-ounce) salmon fillets
	1 teaspoon ground cumin
1 tsp ground coriander	1 teaspoon paprika
1 teaspoon ground ginger	

Directions:

Heat 1 tablespoon of the coconut oil in a large skillet over medium-high heat. Stir-fry the cauliflower for 5 minutes, until just heated through.

Sprinkle in the olive oil, white wine vinegar, preserved lemons (if using), mint, and pistachios, and toss gently to mix. Season with salt and pepper. Set aside. Heat a separate large skillet over medium-high heat until hot.

In a small bowl, combine the salt, cumin, coriander, ginger, and paprika. Coat the salmon fillets with the remaining 2 tablespoons of coconut oil and season with the spice mixture, ½ teaspoon salt, and pepper.

Sear the salmon for about 2 minutes on each side, until it flakes easily with a fork but is still a deeper shade of pink on the inside. Serve each salmon fillet alongside a serving of the cauliflower rice.

Nutrition: Calories: 409; Fat: 24g; Protein: 41g; Total Carbs: 10g

Grandma Bev's Ahi Poke

SERVINGS 6 | **PREP TIME** 10 minutes

Ingredients:

3 scallions, both white and green parts diced	½ cup soy sauce
	1 teaspoon salt
2 teaspoons sesame oil	1 tsp sesame seeds
¼ teaspoon ground ginger	2 pounds fresh ahi tuna, cut into ½-inch cubes
1 teaspoon garlic powder	

Directions:

In a medium bowl, mix the scallions, soy sauce, sesame oil, sesame seeds, ginger, garlic powder, and salt. Combine the soy sauce mixture with the tuna, and toss well. Serve immediately.

Nutrition: Calories: 241; Fat: 9g; Protein: 38g; Total Carbs: 2g;

Pepper-Crusted Salmon with Wilted Kale

SERVINGS 4 | **PREP TIME** 5 minutes | **COOK TIME** 5 minutes

Ingredients:

4 (6-ounce) salmon fillets	2 tsp coconut oil, melted
1 tablespoon freshly ground black pepper	½ teaspoon coarse sea salt, divided
1 bunch kale, tough ribs removed and roughly chopped	1 teaspoon red wine vinegar
	2 tsp extra-virgin olive oil
¼ cup roughly chopped hazelnuts	½ cup fresh blueberries (optional)

Directions:

Preheat a large skillet over medium-high heat. Coat the salmon fillets with the oil and then season liberally with the pepper and salt. In the hot skillet, sear the salmon for about 2 minutes on each side, until it flakes easily with a fork but is still a deeper shade of pink on the inside.

While the salmon is cooking, place the kale in a large bowl, season with a generous pinch of sea salt, and drizzle with the olive oil.

Using your hands, massage the oil and salt into the kale until it releases some of its liquid and becomes soft. Season with the red wine vinegar.

Divide the kale among the serving plates and top with equal amounts of the hazelnuts and blueberries (if using). Serve the salmon fillets alongside the kale.

Nutrition: Calories: 442; Fat: 29g; Protein: 37g; Total Carbs: 8g

Lemon Salmon and Asparagus

SERVINGS 1 | **PREP TIME** 5 minutes | **COOK TIME** 15 minutes

Ingredients:

2 tablespoons avocado oil, divided	1 (6-ounce) salmon fillet
Juice of ½ lemon	2 garlic cloves, minced
Half a lemon, sliced thinly	6 asparagus spears, woody ends removed

Directions:

Preheat the oven to 425°F; line a baking sheet with parchment paper. Combine 1 tablespoon of avocado oil and the garlic in a bowl. Place the salmon on the baking sheet.

Rub the salmon with the garlic and oil mixture until it is evenly coated. Squeeze the lemon juice over the salmon, and season with salt and pepper. Arrange the asparagus around the salmon in a single layer, drizzle the spears with the remaining 1 tablespoon of avocado oil, and place the lemon slices over them. Roast for 12 to 15 minutes, until the salmon is cooked through.

Nutrition: Calories: 527; Fat: 39g; Protein: 36g; Total Carbs: 8g

Baked Trout and Asparagus Foil

Servings: 2 and **Total Time:** approx. 25 minutes

Ingredients:

½ lb asparagus spears	½ lb deboned trout, butterflied
1 tbsp garlic puree	
Salt black pepper to taste	2 sprigs rosemary
2 sprigs thyme	½ red onion, sliced
2 tbsp butter	2 lemon slices

Directions:

Preheat the oven to 400 degrees Fahrenheit. Garlic puree, salt, and pepper should be applied to the trout. Prepare two squares of aluminium foil.

Put a fish on each square. Divide the asparagus and onion among the squares, then top with a pinch of salt and pepper, a sprig of rosemary and thyme, and 1 tablespoon of butter. Place the lemon slices on top of the fish. Wrap and tuck

Place the fish packets on a baking sheet and secure them. Bake for 15 minutes at 350°F. Serve.

Nutrition: Cal 305; Net Carbs 4g; Fat 19g; Protein 27g

Green Tuna Traybake

Servings: 4 and **Total Time:** approx. 40 minutes

Ingredients:

1 (15 oz) can tuna in water, drained and flaked	1 cup grated Parmesan cheese
1 bunch asparagus, trimmed and cut into 1-inch pieces	1 tbsp butter
	2 tbsp arrowroot starch
2 cups coconut milk	1 cup green beans, chopped
	3 zucchinis, spiralized

Directions:

Preheat the oven to 370 degrees Fahrenheit. In a skillet, melt the butter and sauté the green beans and asparagus until softened, about 5 minutes; set aside.

Combine arrowroot starch and coconut milk in a saucepan over medium heat. Bring to a boil and cook, stirring frequently, for 3 minutes, or until thickened. Add half of the Parmesan cheese and stir until melted.

Combine the green beans, asparagus, zucchini, and tuna in a large mixing bowl.

Spread the mixture in a baking dish and top with the remaining Parmesan cheese.

Bake 18-20 minutes, or until the cheese is melted and golden. Serve.

Nutrition: Cal 522; Net Carbs 10.8g; Fat 38g; Protein 29g

Shirataki Fettucine with Salmon

Servings: 4 and **Total Time:** approx. 35 minutes

Ingredients:

4 salmon fillets, cubed	8 oz shirataki fettuccine
3 garlic cloves, minced	½ cup dry white wine
1 ¼ cups heavy cream	1 tsp lemon zest
1 cup baby spinach	Salt and black pepper to taste
5 tbsp butter	

Directions:

Pour 2 cups of water into a pot and bring it to a boil. Strain the shirataki pasta and rinse well under hot running water.

Allow proper draining and pour the shirataki pasta into the boiling water.

Cook for 3 minutes and strain again. Place in a dry skillet over medium heat and stir-fry the shirataki pasta until visibly dry, 1-2 minutes; set aside.

Melt half of the butter in the skillet. Season the salmon with salt and pepper and cook for 8 minutes, stirring occasionally; set aside.

Melt the remaining butter in the skillet and stir-fry the garlic for 30 seconds. Mix in heavy cream, wine, lemon zest, salt, and pepper.

Cook over low heat for 5 minutes. Stir in spinach, let wilt for 2 minutes. Stir in shirataki fettuccine and salmon. Serve.

Nutrition: Cal 803; Net Carbs 9g; Fats 46g; Protein 69g

Tilapia Tortillas with Cauliflower Rice

Servings: 2 and **Total Time:** approx. 15 minutes

Ingredients:

1 tsp avocado oil	1 cup cauli rice
¼ tsp taco seasoning	2 tilapia fillets, cut into cubes
1 tbsp cilantro, chopped	2 whole cabbage leaves
2 tbsp guacamole	Salt and hot paprika to taste

Directions:

In a microwave-safe bowl, heat the cauli rice for 4 minutes. Set aside after fluffing with a fork.

Warm the avocado oil in a skillet over medium heat, then season the tilapia with taco seasoning, salt, and hot paprika and cook until brown on all sides, about 8 minutes total

Distribute the fish among the cabbage leaves and top with the cauli rice.

Guacamole and cilantro are optional. Serve.

Nutrition: Cal 170; Net Carbs 2.4g; Fat 7g; Protein 24g

Cilantro Sauce Coconut Fried Shrimp

Servings: 2 and **Total Time:** approx. 20 minutes

Ingredients:

2 tsp coconut flour	2 tbsp grated Pecorino cheese
½ cup coconut cream	½ oz Paneer cheese, grated
¼ tsp curry powder	Sauce
2 tbsp ghee	1 egg, beaten in a bowl
½ lb shrimp, shelled	½ onion, diced
2 tbsp coconut oil	Salt to taste
2 tbsp cilantro leaves, chopped	

Directions:

In a mixing bowl, combine the flour, Pecorino, curry, and salt. Melt the coconut oil in a saucepan.

medium-high heat in a skillet Coat the shrimp in the cheese mixture after dipping them in the beaten egg. Fry for 5 minutes, or until golden and crispy.

Melt the ghee in a separate skillet. Cook for 3 minutes with the onion.

Cook until the coconut cream and Paneer cheese are thickened, about 3-4 minutes. Coat the shrimp thoroughly. Serve warm, garnished with cilantro.

Nutrition: Cal 641; Net Carbs 7.3g; Fat 54g; Protein 31g

Chimichurri Tiger Shrimp

Servings: 4 and **Total Time:** approx. 10 min + chilling time

Ingredients:

¼ cup extra-virgin olive oil	1 lime, juiced
1 lb tiger shrimp, peeled and deveined	2 cups parsley, minced
Juice of 1 lime	1 garlic clove, minced
Salt and black pepper to taste	2 tbsp olive oil
¼ tsp red pepper flakes	Chimichurri
	¼ cup red wine vinegar
	2 garlic cloves, minced

Directions:

In a mixing bowl, combine the shrimp, olive oil, garlic, and lime juice. Refrigerate for 30 minutes to allow the flavours to meld.

To make the chimichurri dressing, combine all of the chimichurri ingredients in a blender and blend until smooth; set aside.

Preheat your grill to medium-high heat. Cook the shrimp for 2 minutes on each side. Serve the shrimp with a drizzle of chimichurri.

Nutrition: Cal 323; Net Carbs 3.5g; Fat 22g; Protein 24g

Mustardy Crab Cakes

Servings: 4 and **Total Time:** approx. 15 minutes

Ingredients:

1 tbsp coconut oil	1 lb lump crab meat
1 egg	1 tsp Dijon mustard
¼ cup mayonnaise	1 tbsp cilantro, chopped
Salt black pepper to taste	2 tbsp coconut flour

Directions:

Combine the crab meat, mustard, mayonnaise, coconut flour, egg, cilantro, salt, and pepper in a mixing bowl. Make patties out of the mixture after thoroughly mixing it.

In a skillet over medium heat, melt the coconut oil. Brown the patties for about 2-3 minutes per side. Drain on kitchen paper after removing with a perforated spoon. If desired, serve with tartare sauce.

Nutrition: Cal 218; Net Carbs 0.6g; Fat 13g; Protein 23g

Shirataki Mussels Pasta

Servings: 4 and **Total Time:** approx. 25 minutes

Ingredients:

- 8 oz angel hair shirataki
- 1 ½ lb mussels
- 1 ½ cups heavy cream
- 2 tbsp chopped fresh parsley
- Salt black pepper to taste
- 1 cup white wine
- 4 tbsp olive oil
- 6 garlic cloves, minced
- 3 shallots, finely chopped
- 2 tsp red chili flakes

Directions:

Pour 2 cups of water into a pot and bring to a boil. Strain the pasta and rinse well under hot running water. Drain and transfer to the boiling water. Cook for 3 minutes and strain again. Place a large dry skillet and stir-fry the pasta until visibly dry, 1-2 minutes; set aside.

Add the mussels, wine, and 1 cup of water in a pot over medium heat and bring to a boil. Cook covered for 3-4 minutes. Strain the mussels and reserve the cooking liquid. Let them cool, and discard any closed mussels.

Remove the meat out of ¾ of the mussel shells. Set aside the remaining mussels with shells.

Heat olive oil in a skillet and sauté shallots, garlic, and chili flakes for 3 minutes. Mix in the reserved cooking liquid and cook until reduced by half, about 2-5 minutes. Whisk in the heavy cream.

Season with salt and pepper. Pour in shirataki pasta and shell-less mussels and toss to combine. Top with parsley and decorate with the remaining mussels with shells. Serve.

Nutrition: Cal 469; Net Carbs 6g; Fat 34g; Protein 21g

Crispy Fried Cod

SERVINGS 4 | **PREP TIME** 15 minutes | **COOK TIME** 15 minutes

Ingredients:

- 1 cup crushed pork rinds
- ½ cup heavy (whipping) cream
- 1 large egg
- 1 (10-ounce) can original Ro-Tel (drained)
- ¼ cup grated Parmesan cheese
- 4 (4-ounce) cod fillets, patted dry Extra-virgin olive oil, for frying
- 2 tablespoons lemon juice (optional)

Directions:

In a small bowl, combine the pork rinds and grated Parmesan. In another bowl, whisk the heavy cream and egg. Dip each cod fillet completely in the egg mixture, then dip on both sides into the pork rind mixture, making sure the entire fillet is covered. Place the fillets on a plate and refrigerate while the oil heats. In a large skillet over medium heat, heat 2 to 3 inches of oil. Heat the oil to 365°F. Working in batches if necessary, fry each fillet for about 2 minutes on each side or until the outside is golden brown. Drain on a paper towel if needed, then plate and serve, topping each fillet with one-quarter of the can of Ro-Tel.

Nutrition: (1 fillet): Calories: 375; Fat: 28g; Protein: 36g; Total Carbs: 6g

Mustard-Crusted Cod with Roasted Broccoli

SERVINGS 4 | **PREP TIME** 5 minutes | **COOK TIME** 10 minutes

Ingredients:

- 1 pound broccoli, cut into florets
- ½ cup Dijon mustard
- ¾ cup pork rind crumbs
- Parsley leaves, for garnish
- Salt
- 2 tablespoons olive oil
- 4 skinless cod fillets (4 ounces each)

Directions:

Preheat the oven to 400°F. Line a large baking sheet with parchment paper. In a medium bowl, combine the broccoli, oil, and ½ teaspoon salt and toss to combine. Spread the broccoli in a single layer on one side of the baking sheet. Roast for 15 minutes. Meanwhile, spread the mustard onto one side of each fillet. Press the pork rind crumbs onto the mustard. Place the cod on the empty side of the baking sheet. Roast for 8 to 10 minutes, until the fish is opaque and flakes easily with a fork. Season the broccoli with salt to taste. Serve the broccoli with the cod, garnished with the parsley.

Nutrition: Calories: 337; Fat: 17g; Protein: 37g; Total Carbs: 9g

Cod with Parsley Pistou

SERVINGS 4 | **PREP TIME** 15 minutes | **COOK TIME** 10 minutes

Ingredients:

- 1 cup packed roughly chopped fresh flat-leaf
- Zest and juice of 1 lemon

Italian parsley
1 teaspoon salt
1 cup extra-virgin olive oil, divided
1 to 2 small garlic cloves, minced
½ teaspoon freshly ground black pepper
1 pound cod fillets, cut into 4 equal-sized pieces

Directions:

In a food processor, pulse the parsley, garlic, lemon zest and juice, salt, and pepper. While the food processor is running, slowly stream in ¾ cup olive oil until well combined. In a large skillet, heat the remaining ¼ cup olive oil over medium-high heat. Add the cod fillets, cover, and cook for 4 to 5 minutes on each side, or until cooked through. Remove from the heat and keep warm. Add the pistou to the skillet and heat over medium-low heat. Return the cooked fish to the skillet, flipping to coat in the sauce. Serve warm, covered with pistou.

Nutrition: Calories: 581; Fat: 55g; Protein: 21g; Total Carbs: 3g

Poached Cod over Brothy Veggie Noodles

SERVINGS 2 | **PREP TIME** 15 minutes | **COOK TIME** 15 minutes

Ingredients:

1 teaspoon olive oil
1 small shallot sliced
ground black pepper
1 large zucchini, spiralized
3 or 4 radishes, spiralized
Lemon wedges, for serving
1 garlic clove, smashed
2 (6-ounce) fillets cod
Salt
1 large turnip, spiralized
1 to 2 tablespoons chopped fresh parsley
1½ cups chicken broth

Directions:

In a small saucepan (big enough to hold the fish) over medium heat, heat the olive oil. Add the garlic and shallot. Sauté for 2 to 3 minutes, or until fragrant. Pour in the chicken broth and bring to a simmer. Season the fish with salt and pepper and gently add to the broth. Cover the pan and cook for about 10 minutes, or until the flesh is opaque and flakes easily with a fork. Assemble the bowls by dividing the turnip, zucchini, and radish noodles evenly between them. Top each with cooked fish and ladle the broth over each bowl. Serve topped with parsley and with a lemon wedge on the side for squeezing.

Nutrition: Calories: 203; Fat: 4g; Protein: 29g; Total Carbs: 14g

Parmesan-Crusted Tilapia with Sautéed Spinach

SERVINGS 2 | **PREP TIME** 15 minutes | **COOK TIME** 15 minutes

Ingredients:

½ cup grated Parmesan cheese
¼ teaspoon salt
2 tilapia fillets
2 tsp olive oil, divided
½ teaspoon garlic powder
1 teaspoon paprika
2 tsp almond flour
⅛ teaspoon freshly ground black pepper
1½ cups spinach
1 tsp chopped parsley

Directions:

Preheat the oven to 400°F. In a medium bowl, mix the Parmesan cheese, almond flour, paprika, salt, and pepper. Place the tilapia fillets on a plate and drizzle with 1 tablespoon of olive oil. Massage the oil into the fish, and then dredge them in the Parmesan mix, coating thoroughly.

Line a baking dish with aluminum foil. Place the fillets inside. Put the dish in the preheated oven and bake for 10 to 15 minutes, depending on the thickness of the fillets. While the fillets cook, add the remaining tablespoon of olive oil to a large skillet and heat over medium-high heat. Add the spinach and sauté until tender, about 6 minutes. Add the garlic powder. Cover, and reduce the heat to medium-low.

Cook for 3 to 5 minutes. Remove the baking dish from the oven. Check the fillets for doneness. Plate the spinach with the fillets on top and serve immediately, garnished with the parsley.

Nutrition: Calories: 376; Fat: 27g; Protein: 32g; Total Carbs: 4g

"Spaghetti" with Clams

SERVINGS 2 | **PREP TIME** 10 minutes | **COOK TIME** 10 minutes

Ingredients:

1 tablespoon olive oil
2 large zucchini, spiralized Salt
1 (6-ounce) can clams, drained and minced
Juice of ½ lemon
½ cup chicken broth
Freshly ground black pepper
2 tablespoons chopped fresh parsley, for garnish
1 garlic clove, minced

Directions:

In a large skillet over medium heat, heat the olive oil. Add garlic and sauté for just under 1 minute. Add the chicken stock and bring to a simmer. Add the zucchini noodles and gently toss to combine. Taste and season with salt and pepper. Stir in the clams and lemon juice. Toss again to combine and cook for 2 to 3 minutes to warm through. Serve immediately topped with fresh parsley.

Nutrition: Calories: 214; Fat: 9g; Protein: 20g; Total Carbs: 16g

Brown Butter–Lime Tilapia

SERVINGS 4 | **PREP TIME** 10 minutes | **COOK TIME** 15 minutes

Ingredients:

½ cup unsalted butter
4 (4-ounce) tilapia fillets
Sea salt
Juice of 1 lime
¼ cup chopped fresh dill
Freshly ground black pepper
4 teaspoons coconut oil

Directions:

In a small saucepan over medium-high heat, heat the butter until it starts to foam up and fizz. Swirl the saucepan until tiny brown specks form and the butter smells nutty, about 1 minute. Remove from the heat, and set aside. In a blender, purée the dill and lime juice until a paste forms.

Slowly pour the brown butter into the blender while it is running until an emulsified sauce forms and all the butter is used. Rinse the tilapia fillets, and pat them dry with paper towels. Season the fish lightly with salt and pepper on both sides. In a large skillet over medium-high heat, heat the coconut oil. Brown the fish on both sides, turning once, for about 10 minutes total. Serve with the brown butter sauce.

Nutrition: Calories: 347; Fat: 28g; Protein: 22g; Total Carbs: 3g

Cream-Poached Trout

SERVINGS 4 | **PREP TIME** 10 minutes | **COOK TIME** 20 minutes

Ingredients:

4 (4-ounce) skinless trout fillets Sea salt
3 tablespoons butter
1 teaspoon minced garlic
1 leek, white and green parts, halved lengthwise, thinly sliced, and thoroughly washed
Freshly ground black pepper
1 teaspoon chopped fresh parsley, for garnish
1 cup heavy (whipping) cream Juice of 1 lemon

Directions:

Preheat the oven to 400°F. Pat the trout fillets dry with paper towels and lightly season with salt and pepper. Place them in a 9-inch-square baking dish in one layer. Set aside.

Place a medium saucepan over medium-high heat and melt the butter. Sauté the leek and garlic until softened, about 6 minutes. Add the heavy cream and lemon juice to the saucepan and bring to a boil, whisking. Pour the sauce over the fish and bake until the fish is just cooked through, 10 to 12 minutes. Serve topped with the parsley.

Nutrition: Calories: 449; Fat: 37g; Protein: 24g; Total Carbs: 5g

Tuna Slow-Cooked in Olive Oil

SERVINGS 4 | **PREP TIME** 5 minutes | **COOK TIME** 45 minutes

Ingredients:

1 cup extra-virgin olive oil, plus more if needed
2 large garlic cloves, thinly sliced
2-inch strips lemon zest
½ teaspoon freshly ground black pepper
8 (3- to 4-inch) sprigs fresh thyme
1 teaspoon salt
4 (3- to 4-inch) sprigs fresh rosemary
1 pound fresh tuna steaks (about 1 inch thick)

Directions:

Combine the olive oil, rosemary, thyme, garlic, lemon zest, salt, and pepper over medium-low heat and cook until warm and fragrant, 20 to 25 minutes. Remove from the heat and allow to cool for 25 to 30 minutes, until warm but not hot.

Add the tuna to the bottom of the pan, adding additional oil if needed so that tuna is fully submerged, and return to medium-low heat. Cook for 5 to 10 minutes, or until the oil heats back up and is warm and fragrant but not smoking. Lower the heat if it gets too hot. Remove the pot from the heat and let the tuna cook in warm oil for 4 to 5 minutes, to your desired level of doneness. For a tuna that is rare in the center, cook for 2 to 3 minutes.

Remove from the oil and serve warm, drizzling 2 to 3 tablespoons seasoned oil over the tuna. When both have cooled, remove the herb stems with a slotted spoon and pour the cooking oil over the tuna.

Nutrition: Calories: 363; Fat: 28g; Protein: 27g; Total Carbs: 1g

Garlic Parmesan Crusted Salmon

SERVINGS 8 | **PREP TIME** 15 minutes | **COOK TIME** 15 minutes

Ingredients:

4 pounds salmon fillets, skin on
1 teaspoon salt
3 garlic cloves, minced
½ cup finely crushed pork skins
½ cup (1 stick) butter, melted
½ teaspoon freshly ground black pepper
½ cup grated Parmesan cheese
1 lemon, for squeezing

Directions:

Preheat the oven to 350°F, and line a baking sheet with parchment paper. Place the salmon fillets, skin-side down, on the lined baking sheet. In a small bowl, mix the butter and minced garlic. Spread or brush over the salmon. Season the fillets with the salt and pepper, and then sprinkle with the crushed pork skins and Parmesan. Bake for 15 minutes, remove from the oven, and squeeze lemon over the top (if using).

Nutrition: Calories: 532; Fat: 32g; Protein: 56g; Total Carbs: 1g

Sesame-Crusted Tuna with Sweet Chili Vinaigrette

SERVINGS 4 | **PREP TIME** 10 minutes | **COOK TIME** 5 minutes

Ingredients:

1 tablespoon Thai chili sauce, such as sambal	¼ cup light olive oil or canola oil
4 to 6 drops liquid stevia	6-ounce ahi tuna steaks
2 tablespoons toasted sesame oil Sea salt	Freshly ground black pepper
½ cup sesame seeds	4 packed cups mixed spring greens
1 tsp rice wine vinegar	

Directions:

In a small bowl, combine the chili sauce, vinegar, oil, and stevia. Preheat a large skillet over medium-high heat. Pat the tuna steaks dry with paper towels. Coat each side of the steaks with the sesame oil, and season with the salt and pepper. Spread the sesame seeds in a shallow dish. Press the tuna steaks into the seeds to coat them on both sides. Immediately place the tuna steaks into the hot skillet. Sear on each side for 1½ minutes for rare. Divide the greens among the serving plates and drizzle each salad with the chili vinaigrette. Transfer the tuna to a cutting board and slice each steak on an angle into ½-inch pieces. It will still be dark and barely warm in the center. Place equal portions of the tuna on each serving plate.

Nutrition: Calories: 475; Fat: 32g; Protein: 41g; Total Carbs: 11g

Coconut Saffron Mussels

SERVINGS 4 | **PREP TIME** 15 minutes | **COOK TIME** 12 minutes

Ingredients:

¼ cup low-sodium vegetable or chicken stock Pinch saffron	3 tablespoons coconut oil
	2 tablespoons chopped fresh cilantro
1 scallion, white and green parts, thinly sliced	1 teaspoon peeled, grated fresh ginger
2 teaspoons minced garlic	1 cup canned coconut milk
Juice and zest of 1 lime	1½ pounds fresh mussels, scrubbed and debearded

Directions:

Put the stock in a small bowl and sprinkle in the saffron. Set aside for 15 minutes. Heat the oil in a large skillet and sauté the scallions, garlic, and ginger until softened, about 3 minutes. Stir in the coconut milk, saffron and liquid, lime juice, and lime zest and bring to a boil. Add the mussels, cover, and steam until the shells are open, about 8 minutes. Discard any unopened shells and take the skillet off the heat. Stir in the cilantro. Serve immediately with the sauce.

Nutrition: Calories: 245; Fat: 22g; Protein: 7g; Total Carbs: 7g

Halibut Curry

SERVINGS 4 | **PREP TIME** 5 minutes | **COOK TIME** 35 minutes

Ingredients:

1 tablespoon avocado oil	½ cup finely chopped celery
½ cup frozen butternut squash cubes	½ cup seafood stock
1 tsp dried cilantro	1 cup full-fat canned coconut milk
1½ tablespoons curry powder	½ tablespoon garlic powder
½ tablespoon ground turmeric	1 pound skinless halibut fillet, cut into chunks
1 teaspoon ground ginger	Cooked cauliflower rice

Directions:

In a large saucepan with a lid, heat the avocado oil over medium-high heat. Add the celery and cook for about 3 minutes. Add the squash and cook for 5 minutes. Add the coconut milk and seafood stock and cook, stirring, for 3 minutes. Stir in the curry powder, cilantro, garlic, turmeric, and ginger. Add the halibut to the pot, reduce the heat to medium, cover, and cook for 15 to 20 minutes, or until the fish is completely white and flakes easily with a fork. Serve the halibut curry over cauliflower rice if you'd like, or just eat it by itself!

Nutrition: Calories: 362; Fat: 22g; Protein: 33g; Total Carbs: 8g

Baked Nutty Halibut

SERVINGS 4 | **PREP TIME** 20 minutes | **COOK TIME** 15 minutes

Ingredients:

½ cup heavy (whipping) cream	½ cup finely chopped pecans
ground black pepper	2 tsp extra-virgin olive oil
¼ cup finely chopped almonds	4 (4-ounce) boneless halibut fillets
	Sea salt

Directions:

Preheat the oven to 400°F. Line a baking sheet with parchment. Pour the heavy cream into a bowl and set it on your work surface. In another bowl, stir the pecans and almonds and set beside the cream. Pat the halibut fillets dry with paper towels and lightly season with salt and pepper.

Dip the fillets in the cream, shaking off the excess; then dredge the fish in the nut mixture so that both sides of each piece are thickly coated. Place the fish on the prepared baking sheet and brush both sides of the pieces generously with olive oil. Bake the fish until the topping is golden and the fish flakes easily with a fork, 12 to 15 minutes. Serve.

Nutrition: Calories: 392; Fat: 31g; Protein: 26g; Total Carbs: 3g

Swordfish in Tarragon-Citrus Butter

SERVINGS 4 | **PREP TIME** 5 minutes | **COOK TIME** 20 minutes

Ingredients:

- 1 pound swordfish steaks, cut into 2-inch pieces
- ¼ cup extra-virgin olive oil, plus 2 tablespoons, divided 2 tablespoons unsalted butter
- 2 tsp fresh tarragon
- ¼ teaspoon freshly ground black pepper
- Zest and juice of 2 clementines
- Zest and juice of 1 lemon
- 1 teaspoon salt

Directions:

In a bowl, toss the swordfish with salt and pepper. In a large skillet, heat ¼ cup olive oil over medium-high heat. Add the swordfish chunks to the hot oil and sear on all sides, 2 to 3 minutes per side, until they are golden brown. Using a slotted spoon, remove the fish from the skillet and keep warm. Add the remaining 2 tablespoons olive oil and butter to the oil already in the skillet and return the heat to medium-low. Once the butter has melted, whisk in the clementine and lemon zests and juices, along with the tarragon. Season with salt. Return the fish pieces to the pan and toss to coat in the butter sauce.

Nutrition: Calories: 379; Fat: 31g; Protein: 23g; Total Carbs: 3g

Spicy Crab Cakes

SERVINGS 4 | **PREP TIME** 20 minutes, plus 1 hour to chill | **COOK TIME** 20 minutes

Ingredients:

- 1 pound crab
- 1 teaspoon Dijon mustard
- ½ red bell pepper, minced
- 3 tsp minced red onion
- 1 teaspoon chopped fresh dill Splash Tabasco sauce
- ½ cup almond flour, plus additional for dusting
- ¼ cup mayonnaise
- 1 tsp Worcestershire sauce
- 3 tsp extra-virgin olive oil

Directions:

In a large bowl, stir the crab, almond flour, red pepper, Mayonnaise, red onion, Dijon mustard, Worcestershire sauce, dill, and Tabasco sauce until the mixture holds together when pressed. Form the crab mixture into 12 patties, and refrigerate them on a plate, covered, for 1 hour. Dust with additional almond flour. In a large skillet over medium-high heat, heat the olive oil. Cook the crab cakes in batches, until golden brown and heated through, about 10 minutes per side. Serve.

Nutrition: Calories: 349; Fat: 29g; Protein: 16g; Total Carbs: 6g

Vegetable Sides & Dairy Recipes

Cheesy Zucchini Muffins

Servings: 6 and **Total Time:** approx. 40 minutes

Ingredients:

- 1 large egg
- 1 spring onion, chopped
- ½ tsp baking soda
- 1 tsp baking powder
- ½ cup grated cheddar cheese
- 5 tbsp olive oil
- ½ cup almond flour
- 1 red bell pepper, chopped
- 1/3 cup almond milk
- 2 zucchinis, grated
- 1 ½ tsp mustard powder
- 6 green olives, sliced
- 1 tbsp chopped thyme
- Salt black pepper to taste

Directions:

Preheat the oven to 340 degrees Fahrenheit. Combine almond flour, baking powder, baking soda, mustard powder, salt, and pepper in a mixing bowl. In a separate bowl, whisk together the almond milk, egg, and oil.

Combine the wet and dry ingredients: then stir in

the cheddar cheese, zucchini, olives, spring onion, bell pepper, and thyme.

Bake for 30 minutes, or until the muffins are golden brown, in greased muffin cups. Allow to cool for 5 minutes before serving.

Nutrition: Cal 169; Net Carbs 1.6g; Fat 16g; Protein 4g

Tomato Gratin with Eggplant

Servings: 4 and **Total Time:** approx. 45 minutes

Ingredients:
- 1/3 cup melted butter
- 2 tbsp Parmesan, grated
- 7 oz tomato sauce
- Salt and black pepper to taste
- 2 eggplants, sliced
- 1 red onion, sliced
- 1/4 cup chopped fresh parsley
- 2 garlic cloves, minced

Directions:

Preheat the oven to 400 degrees Fahrenheit. Preheat the oven to 350°F. Line a baking sheet with parchment paper.

Brush the eggplants with butter. Bake for 20 minutes, or until lightly browned.

In a skillet, melt the remaining butter and sauté the garlic and onion until fragrant and soft, about 3 minutes. Season with salt and pepper and stir in tomato sauce. Cook for 10 minutes.

Remove the eggplants from the oven and top with the tomato sauce. Garnish with Parmesan

Serve with cheese and parsley.

Nutrition: Cal 213; Net Carbs 9g; Fat 15g; Protein 6g

Chilli Dressing Roasted Cauliflower

Servings: 4 and **Total Time:** approx. 35 minutes

Ingredients:
- 1 head cauliflower, chopped
- 1 lemon, zested and juiced
- 1 tbsp red chili flake
- Salt and black pepper to taste
- 3 tbsp olive oil
- 2 tbsp capers, drained
- 2 tbsp cilantro, chopped
- 1 tbsp chili oil

Directions:

Preheat the oven to 360 degrees Fahrenheit. Put the cauliflower in a baking dish and drizzle with half of the olive oil.

Season with salt and pepper to taste. Cook for 20-25 minutes, or until golden. Whisk together the remaining olive oil, chilli oil, lemon zest, lemon juice, and salt in a mixing bowl.

Combine capers and red chilli flakes in a mixing bowl.

Place the cauliflower on a plate and drizzle with the dressing. Serve warm, garnished with cilantro.

Nutrition: Cal 138; Net Carbs 2.6g; Fat 14g; Protein 1.4g

Stuffed Zucchini with Cheddar

Servings: 4 and **Total Time:** approx. 40 minutes

Ingredients:
- 4 tbsp butter
- 2 garlic cloves, minced
- 2 tbsp tomato sauce
- Salt and black pepper to taste
- 1 zucchini, halved
- 1 cup cheddar cheese
- 1 1/2 oz baby kale

Directions:

Preheat the oven to 375 degrees Fahrenheit. Using a spoon, scoop out the zucchini pulp. Save the flesh. Coat a baking sheet with cooking spray and arrange the zucchini boats on it.

Melt butter in a skillet over medium heat and sauté garlic for 4 minutes, or until fragrant and slightly browned.

Mix in the kale and zucchini pulp. Season with salt and pepper after the kale has wilted.

Distribute the tomato sauce evenly among the boats. Sprinkle with cheddar cheese and top with kale mixture. 25 minutes in the oven

Nutrition: Cal 517; Net Carbs 5g; Fat 51g; Protein 19g

Dinner Vegetarian Pasta Mix

Servings: 4 and **Total Time:** approx. 30 min + chilling time

Ingredients:
- 1 cup shredded mozzarella cheese
- 3 tbsp olive oil
- 1 head broccoli, cut into florets
- 1 egg yolk
- 1 lb green beans, halved
- 3 tbsp balsamic vinegar
- 2 garlic cloves, minced
- 1 cup grated Parmigiano-Reggiano cheese
- 2 tbsp chopped walnuts
- 1 red bell pepper, sliced
- 1 red onion, thinly sliced
- 1 tsp dried oregano
- Salt and black pepper to taste

Directions:

Microwave the mozzarella cheese for 2 minutes on high. Allow to cool for 1 minute. Incorporate the egg yolk until well combined.

Place a piece of parchment paper on a flat surface, top with the cheese mixture, and cover with another piece of parchment paper. Flatten the dough to a thickness of 1/8-inch.

Remove the parchment paper and cut the dough into penne-sized pieces. Refrigerate overnight in a bowl.

Bring 2 cups of water to a boil before adding the keto penne. Cook for 1 minute, then drain and set aside. In a skillet, heat the olive oil and sauté the onion, garlic, green beans, broccoli, and bell pepper for 5 minutes.

Season with salt, pepper, and oregano, to taste. Cook for 1 minute, then toss in the balsamic vinegar.

Nutrition: Cal 332; Net Carbs 9g; Fat 21g; Protein 19g

Chia Seeds Coconut-Lime Ice Cream

Servings: 4 and **Total Time:** approx. 20 min + chilling time

Ingredients:

- 2 avocados, mashed
- Juice and zest of 3 limes
- 1/3 cup erythritol
- 1 ¾ cups coconut cream
- ¼ tsp vanilla extract
- 2 tbsp chia seeds

Directions:

Combine the mashed avocado, chia seeds, lime juice and zest, erythritol, coconut cream, and vanilla extract in a mixing bowl and beat with an electric mixer until creamy and uniform.

Pour the mixture into an ice cream maker and process according to the manufacturer's instructions. Transfer to a freezer-safe container and freeze for 2 hours, or until firm. Fill dessert cups halfway with ice cream and serve.

Nutrition: Cal 559; Net Carbs 9g; Fat 52g; Protein 7g

Vegetable Keto Pasta Gratin

Servings: 4 and **Total Time:** approx. 35 min + chilling time

Ingredients:

- 1 cup shredded mozzarella cheese
- 1 cup sliced white button mushrooms
- 1 cup chopped bell peppers
- 1 yellow squash, chopped
- ¼ tsp red chili flakes
- 1 cup grated Parmesan cheese
- 2 tbsp olive oil
- 1 egg yolk
- Salt and black pepper to taste
- 1 red onion, sliced
- 1 cup grated mozzarella
- 1 cup marinara sauce

Directions:

Microwave the mozzarella cheese for 2 minutes on high. Remove the bowl and set aside for 1 minute to cool. Mix in the egg yolk until well-combined.

Place a piece of parchment paper on a flat surface, top with the cheese mixture, and cover with another piece of parchment paper.

Flatten the dough to a thickness of 1/8-inch. Remove the parchment paper from the dough and cut it into penne-size pieces. Place in a bowl and place in the refrigerator overnight. Bring 2 cups water to a boil, then add the "penne." Cook for 1 minute, then drain and set aside.

In a skillet, heat the oil and sauté the bell peppers, squash, onion, and mushrooms. 5 minutes in the oven Season with salt, pepper, and chilli flakes if desired. Cook for 5 minutes after adding the marinara sauce.

Nutrition: Cal 290; Net Carbs 9.5g; Fat 15g; Protein 31g

Grilled Asparagus & Carrots

Servings: 2 and **Total Time:** approx. 20 minutes

Ingredients:

- 4 tbsp butter, melted
- 2 carrots, quartered lengthwise
- Salt and black pepper to taste
- 1 lb asparagus, trimmed
- 2 tbsp Parmesan, grated
- 1 tsp dried thyme

Directions:

Preheat a grill pan to medium-high heat. Season the asparagus and carrots in a bowl with salt, pepper, and thyme.

Drizzle with melted butter. Sear the vegetables in the pan for 10 minutes, turning frequently. Garnish with Parmesan. Serve.

Nutrition: Cal 289; Net Carbs 8.8g, Fat 23g, Protein 10g

Broccoli & Peppers Balsamic Zoodles

Servings: 4 and **Total Time:** approx. 20 minutes

Ingredients:

- 1 cup sliced mixed bell peppers
- 2 tbsp olive oil
- 4 shallots, finely chopped
- 2 garlic cloves, minced
- 2 tbsp balsamic vinegar
- Salt, black pepper to taste
- ½ lemon, juiced
- 4 zucchinis, spiralized
- 1 head broccoli, cut into florets
- ¼ tsp red pepper flakes
- 1 cup chopped kale
- 1 cup grated Parmesan cheese

Directions:

Warm the oil in a skillet and sauté the broccoli, bell peppers, and shallots for 7 minutes, or until softened. Cook until the garlic and red pepper flakes are fragrant.

30 seconds, fragrant Cook until the kale and zucchini spaghetti are tender, about 3 minutes. Mix in the vinegar and lemon juice, and season with salt and pepper to taste. Garnish with

Parmesan cheese if desired. Serve.

Nutrition: Cal 201; Net Carbs 8g; Fat 13g; Protein 10g

Mushroom & Herb Pizza

Servings: 4 and **Total Time:** approx. 40 minutes

Ingredients:

2 ½ cups grated mozzarella cheese
1 egg, beaten
1 garlic clove, minced
Salt black pepper to taste
6 black olives, sliced
1 tsp olive oil
1 tsp dried basil
1 tsp dried oregano
½ cup grated Parmesan
2 medium cremini mushrooms, sliced
2 tbsp cream cheese, softened
½ cup almond flour
½ cup tomato sauce
1 tbsp erythritol
½ tsp paprika

Directions:

Preheat the oven to 380 degrees Fahrenheit. Using parchment paper, line a pizza pan. 1 minute in the microwave with 2 cups mozzarella cheese and 2 tablespoons cream cheese Mix in the almond flour and the egg. Bake for 5 minutes after spreading the mixture on the pizza pan.

In a skillet, heat the olive oil and sauté the mushrooms and garlic for 5 minutes, or until softened. Combine tomato sauce, erythritol, oregano, basil, paprika, salt, and pepper in a mixing bowl. 2 minutes in the oven Spread the sauce over the crust, then top with the remaining mozzarella, Parmesan, and olives. 15 minutes in the oven Cut into slices and serve.

Nutrition: Cal 317; Net Carbs 3.6g; Fat 25g; Protein 22g

Broccoli Nachos Salsa

Servings: 4 and **Total Time:** approx. 30 minutes

Ingredients:

2 eggs, beaten
½ lime, juiced
3 tbsp coconut flour
1 tsp smoked paprika
½ tsp garlic powder
4 plum tomatoes, chopped
¼ cup grated Monterey Jack
½ tsp coriander powder
1 tsp cumin powder
1 avocado, chopped
4 sprigs cilantro, chopped
2 heads broccoli, chopped

Directions:

Preheat the oven to 360 degrees Fahrenheit. Place broccoli in a food processor and pulse until it resembles rice. Warm a skillet over low heat, then pour in

Fry the broccoli rice for 4-5 minutes. Transfer to a mixing bowl. 2 baking sheets should be lined with parchment paper. Add the coconut flour, paprika, coriander powder, cumin, garlic, and eggs to the broccoli. Form a ball out of the mixture. Divide the dough in half and make two equal-sized crusts. Place them on the baking sheets and bake for 10 minutes in batches. Remove from the oven, cut into triangles, and top with Monterey Jack cheese; set aside to cool. Combine the tomatoes, lime, cilantro, and avocado in a mixing bowl. Toss the nachos with the salsa.

Nutrition: Cal 250; Net Carbs 4.5g, Fat 15g, Protein 10g

Tofu Parsnip Spaghetti a la "Bolognese"

Servings: 4 and **Total Time:** approx. 35 minutes

Ingredients:

2 tbsp olive oil
2 parsnips, spiralized
1 garlic clove, minced
2 celery stalks, chopped
¼ cup vegetable broth
1 cup grated Parmesan cheese
2 tbsp butter
1 cup crumbled firm tofu
1 onion, chopped
2 cups sugar-free passata
2 tbsp fresh basil, chopped
Salt black pepper to taste

Directions:

In a skillet, melt butter and sauté parsnips for 5 minutes. Set aside after seasoning with salt and pepper. In a pot, heat the olive oil and cook the tofu for 5 minutes.

Cook for 5 minutes after adding the onion, garlic, and celery. Season with salt and pepper and stir in the passata and broth.

Cook, covered, for 8-10 minutes, or until the sauce thickens. Stir in the basil. Distribute the pasta among the plates and top with the sauce. Serve with the Parmesan cheese on top.

Nutrition: Cal 385; Net Carbs 12.5g; Fat 24g; Protein 20g

Baby Spinach Lasagna with Feta

Servings: 4 and **Total Time:** approx. 60 minutes

Ingredients:

2 tbsp butter
1 cup baby spinach
2 ½ cups feta, crumbled
Salt black pepper to taste
4 eggs
3 tbsp tomato paste
5 tbsp psyllium husk powder
2 cups heavy cream
5 oz mozzarella, shredded
1 onion, chopped
1 garlic clove, minced
½ tbsp dried oregano
Keto pasta
1 ½ cups cream cheese
1 tsp salt
Cheese topping
Salt and black pepper
½ cup fresh parsley, chopped

2 oz Parmesan cheese,

Directions:

Melt the butter in a pot over medium heat. Add in the onion and garlic and sauté until fragrant and soft, about 3 minutes. Mix in the tomato paste, oregano, salt, and black pepper. Pour in ½ cup of water, stir, and simmer until most of the liquid has evaporated.

While cooking the sauce, make the lasagna sheets. Preheat oven to 300 F Combine the eggs with cream cheese and salt. Add the psyllium husk a bit while whisking, and allow the mixture to sit for a few more minutes. Line a baking sheet with parchment paper and spread in the mixture. Cover with another parchment paper and use a rolling pin to flatten the dough into the sheet.

Bake the batter in the oven for 10-12 minutes, remove after, take off the parchment papers, and slice the pasta into sheets that fit your baking dish.

In a bowl, combine the heavy cream and two-thirds of the mozzarella cheese. Fetch out 2 tablespoons of the mixture and reserve. Mix in the Parmesan cheese, salt, black pepper, and parsley. Set aside. Grease a baking dish with cooking spray and lay in one-third of the pasta sheet; spread half of the tomato paste on top, add another one-third set of the pasta sheets, the remaining tomato paste, and the rest of the pasta sheets.

Grease a baking dish with cooking spray, layer a single line of pasta, spread with some tomato sauce, 1/3 of the spinach, 1/3 of the feta cheese, and ¼ of the heavy cream mixture. Season with salt and pepper. Repeat layering the Ingredients twice in the same manner, making sure to top the final layer with the heavy cream mixture and the reserved cream cheese.

Bake in the oven for 30 minutes at 400 F or until the lasagna has a beautiful brown surface. Remove the dish, allow cooling for a few minutes, and slice. Serve the lasagna with a green salad.

Nutrition: Cal 1062; Net Carbs 13g; Fat 95g Protein 40g

Roasted Cauliflower Gratin

Servings: 4 and **Total Time:** approx. 35 minutes

Ingredients:

1/3 cup butter	2 tbsp melted butter
10 oz cauliflower florets	1 tbsp parsley, chopped
Salt black pepper to taste	¼ cup almond milk
½ cup almond flour	1 ½ cups cheddar, grated
1 onion, chopped	1 tbsp ground almonds

Directions:

Steam the cauliflower for 4-5 minutes in salted water. Set aside after draining. In a saucepan over medium heat, melt the 1/3 cup butter.

For 3 minutes, sauté the onion. Season the cauliflower with salt and pepper, then stir in the almond milk. Cook for 3 minutes. Combine the

Combine the almond flour and the remaining melted butter. Combine the cauliflower and half of the cheese in a mixing bowl.

Garnish with the remaining cheese and ground almonds. Bake for 10 minutes, or until the top is golden brown, in a preheated 380 F oven.

Garnish with parsley before serving.

Nutrition: Cal 455; Net Carbs 6.5g; Fat 38g; Protein 16g

Cheese Cauliflower Risotto with Mushroom

Servings: 4 and **Total Time:** approx. 25 minutes

Ingredients:

3 tbsp olive oil	1 onion, chopped
1 large head cauliflower, break into florets	¼ cup vegetable broth
	2 tbsp parsley, chopped
1/3 cup Parmesan cheese	3 tbsp chives, chopped
	2 lb mushrooms, sliced
4 tbsp heavy cream	

Directions:

In a food processor, pulse the cauliflower florets until they resemble rice. In a saucepan, heat 2 tbsp oil.

Cook the mushrooms for about 3 minutes over medium heat, then set aside. Cook the onion for 2 minutes in the remaining oil.

Cook until the liquid is absorbed, about 7-8 minutes, after adding the cauliflower and broth.

Combine the heavy cream and Parmesan cheese in a mixing bowl. To serve, sprinkle with chives and parsley.

Nutrition: Cal 255; Net Carbs 5.3g; Fat 21g; Protein 10g

Coconut Avocado Tart

Servings: 4 and **Total Time:** approx. 70 minutes

Ingredients:

1¼ ups grated Parmesan	½ cup cream cheese
4 tbsp coconut flour	¾ cup almond flour
4 tbsp chia seeds	1 egg
2 tbsp fresh parsley, chopped	1 tbsp psyllium husk powder
3 tbsp coconut oil	2 ripe avocados, mashed
1 tsp baking powder	1 cup mayonnaise
1 jalapeño pepper,	½ tsp onion powder

minced

Directions:

Preheat the oven to 350 degrees Fahrenheit. Combine coconut flour, chia seeds, almond flour, psyllium husk, baking powder, coconut oil, and 4 tbsp water in a mixing bowl.

Blend until the dough comes together in a ball.

Spread the dough in a springform pan lined with parchment paper. 15 minutes in the oven Mix avocados, mayonnaise, egg, parsley, jalapeo pepper, onion powder, cream cheese, and Parmesan cheese in a mixing bowl.

When the piecrust is ready, remove it from the oven and fill it with the creamy mixture. Bake for 35 minutes, or until the top is lightly golden brown.

Nutrition: Cal 891; Net Carbs 6g; Fat 76g; Protein 24g

Green Sauté

Servings: 4 and **Total Time:** approx. 20 minutes

Ingredients:

- 1 tbsp olive oil
- 1 garlic clove, minced
- 4 tbsp chopped parsley
- 2 shallots, finely sliced
- 2 tbsp pine nuts
- 1 tsp cumin powder
- 2 tbsp butter
- 2 heads large broccoli, riced
- 2 zucchinis, sliced
- 1 tsp Swerve sugar
- 2 tbsp red wine vinegar

Directions:

Set aside shallots, Swerve sugar, and vinegar in a bowl. In a skillet, melt the butter and stir in the cumin and garlic for 1 minute. Sauté the broccoli for 5 minutes, or until softened. Stir in the zucchini.

Reduce the heat to low and continue to cook for another 4-5 minutes. Mix in the parsley. To serve, drizzle with olive oil and garnish with pine nuts.

Nutrition: Cal 111; Net Carbs 7.5g; Fat 9g; Protein 2g

Mushrooms Broccoli Noodles

Servings: 4 and **Total Time:** approx. 20 minutes

Ingredients:

- 1 cup cremini mushrooms, sliced
- 4 scallions, chopped
- 4 large heads broccoli
- 1 ½ cups almond milk
- Salt black pepper to taste
- 2 tbsp olive oil
- 1 cup grated Gruyere cheese
- 2 garlic cloves, minced
- 2 tbsp almond flour
- ¼ cup chopped fresh parsley

Directions:

Remove the florets from the broccoli heads, leaving only the stems. Cut the stem ends flat and evenly. To make the noodles, spiralize the stems.

In a skillet, heat the olive oil and sauté the broccoli noodles, mushrooms, garlic, and scallions until softened, about 5 minutes. Combine the almond flour and almond milk in a mixing bowl and pour over the vegetables. Allow for a 2-3 minute thickening period after stirring.

Whisk in half of the Gruyere cheese to melt and season with salt and black pepper to taste. Garnish with the remaining Gruyere cheese and parsley and serve.

Nutrition: Cal 269; Net Carbs 3.4g; Fat 19g; Protein 12g

Crispy Avocado with Parmesan Sauce

Servings: 4 and **Total Time:** approx. 20 minutes

Ingredients:

- 2 tbsp olive oil
- ¼ tsp garlic powder
- 1 cup grated cheddar cheese
- ¼ tsp mustard powder
- 5 tbsp melted butter
- 3 tbsp almond flour
- 1 ½ cups almond milk
- ¼ cup grated Parmesan
- 2 avocados, sliced
- 2 tbsp sriracha sauce
- Black pepper to taste
- 4 oz cream cheese, softened

Directions:

In a saucepan, combine 3 tbsp butter and almond flour and cook until golden.

Whisk in the almond milk, mustard powder, garlic powder, and salt and pepper to taste.

pepper, black Cook, whisking constantly, for 2 minutes, or until the sauce thickens. Set aside the cheeses after they have melted.

Toss the avocado with the remaining butter and sriracha sauce in a mixing bowl. In a pan, heat the olive oil and cook the avocado until golden, turning halfway through, about 4 minutes total. To serve, spoon the cheese sauce over the plate.

Nutrition: Cal 551; Net Carbs 5.2g; Fat 51g; Protein 10g

Broccoli & Mushroom Pizza

Servings: 4 and **Total Time:** approx. 30 minutes

Ingredients:

- 2 tablespoon olive oil
- ½ cup sugar-free pizza sauce
- ½ cup almond flour
- 2 tbsp ground psyllium
- 1 ½ cups grated mozzarella
- ⅓ cup grated Parmesan
- ¼ tsp salt
- 1 cup sliced fresh

husk
4 tomatoes, sliced
2 garlic cloves, minced

mushrooms 1 white onion, thinly sliced
3 cups broccoli florets

Directions:

Preheat the oven to 380 degrees Fahrenheit. Preheat the oven to 350°F. Line a baking sheet with parchment paper.

In a mixing bowl, combine almond flour, salt, psyllium powder, 1 tablespoon olive oil, and

1 cup lukewarm water and combine until a dough forms. Bake for 10 minutes after spreading the mixture on the pizza pan. In a skillet, heat the remaining olive oil and sauté the mushrooms, onion, garlic, and broccoli for 5 minutes.

Top the crust with the pizza sauce, broccoli mixture, tomato, mozzarella, and Parmesan. 5 minutes in the oven Slice and serve.

Nutrition: Cal 160; Net Carbs 4.6g; Fat 10g; Protein 17g

Three Cheesy Pizza

Servings: 2 and **Total Time:** approx. 35 minutes

Ingredients:

3 tbsp grated Parmesan
½ cup almond flour
2 tbsp ground psyllium husk
¼ tsp salt
1 cup grated Gruyère

1 cup sliced mozzarella
1 cup lukewarm water
1 tbsp olive oil

½ cup sugar-free pizza sauce 2 tsp Italian seasoning

Directions:

Preheat the oven to 380 degrees Fahrenheit. Using parchment paper, line a pizza pan. Place almond flour, salt, psyllium husk, olive oil, and water in a mixing bowl and gently combine until a dough forms. Bake for 10 minutes after spreading the mixture on the pizza pan. Remove the crust and top it with the pizza sauce.

top. Combine the sliced mozzarella, grated Gruyère, Parmesan cheese, and Italian seasoning in a mixing bowl. 18-20 minutes in the oven Cut into slices and serve.

Nutrition: Cal 323; Net Carbs 2g; Fat 24g; Protein 22g

Mushroom & Zucchini with Spinach Dip

Servings: 4 and **Total Time:** approx. 20 minutes

Ingredients:

Spinach Dip
1 avocado, halved and pitted 2 tbsp fresh lemon juice
Salt and black pepper to taste
Zucchini:
Salt and black pepper to taste

1 oz spinach, chopped
1 garlic clove, minced
2 oz pecans
¾ cup olive oil

2 zucchinis, sliced
½ lb mushrooms, sliced
2 tbsp olive oil

Directions:

In a food processor, combine the spinach and avocado pulp.

Lemon juice, garlic, and pecans are some of the ingredients in this dish. Season with salt and pepper after blending the ingredients until smooth. Process a little more after adding the olive oil.

Place the pesto in a bowl and set aside. In a mixing bowl, combine the zucchinis and mushrooms. Season with salt, pepper, and oil to taste.

Preheat a grill pan over medium heat and cook the mushroom and zucchini slices until both sides are browned. Serve the vegetables with the spinach dip.

Nutrition: Cal 683; Net Carbs 5.5g; Fat 72g; Protein 5g

Tofu Stir-Fry

Servings: 4 and **Total Time:** approx. 45 minutes

Ingredients:

2 ½ cups baby bok choy, quartered lengthwise
1 tsp garlic powder
1 tsp onion powder
1 tbsp fresh ginger, grated
3 green onions, sliced

5 oz butter
1 tbsp plain vinegar
2 garlic cloves, minced
1 tsp chili flakes
Salt black pepper to taste
2 cups extra firm tofu, cubed

Directions:

In a wok, melt half of the butter over medium heat, then add the bok choy and stir-fry until softened. Season with salt, pepper, garlic, onion, and vinegar powders, as well as plain vinegar. Set aside after 2 minutes of sautéing. Melt the chocolate

Sauté garlic, chilli flakes, and ginger in the remaining butter in the wok until fragrant. Cook until the tofu is browned. Cook for 2 minutes after adding the green onions and bok choy.

Nutrition: Cal 591; Net Carbs 5g; Fat 44g; Protein 32g

Butternut Squash Roast

Servings: 4 and **Total Time:** approx. 25 minutes

Ingredients:

1 lb butternut squash
3 tbsp toasted pine nuts

1 tbsp butter, melted
Salt and black pepper to taste

Chimichurri:

½ red bell pepper, chopped
2 garlic cloves, minced
1 cup olive oil
Zest and juice of 1 lemon
1 jalapeño pepper, chopped
½ cup chopped fresh parsley

Directions:

In a food processor, combine all of the chimichurri Ingredients and pulse until the desired consistency is reached; season to taste. Refrigerate until ready to use.

Remove the seeds from the squash and slice it into rounds. Season with salt and pepper and drizzle with butter.

Cook the squash for 5-6 minutes on each side in a grill pan heated over medium heat. Serve with chimichurri and pine nuts on top.

Nutrition: Cal 547; Net Carbs 11.6g; Fat 54g; Protein 2g

Tofu Roasted Pepper

Servings: 4 and **Total Time:** approx. 25 minutes

Ingredients:

2 ½ cups cubed tofu
1 tsp dried parsley
1 large tomato, chopped
3 oz cream cheese
Salt and black pepper to taste
4 orange bell peppers
1 cucumber, diced
¾ cup mayonnaise
1 tbsp melted butter
1 tsp dried basil

Directions:

Preheat the broiler to 450 degrees Fahrenheit. Preheat the oven to 350°F.

Line a baking sheet with parchment paper. Refrigerate cream cheese, mayonnaise, cucumber, tomato, salt, pepper, and parsley in a salad bowl.

Arrange the bell peppers and tofu on a baking sheet, drizzle with melted butter, and season with salt and pepper.

seasoned with basil, salt, and pepper. Bake for 15 minutes, or until the peppers are lightly charred and the tofu is browned. Enjoy with a chilled salad on the side!

Nutrition: Cal 508; Net Carbs 9.5g; Fat 41g; Protein 31g

Feta & Olive Pizza

Servings: 4 and **Total Time:** approx. 30 minutes

Ingredients:

1 tbsp olive oil
½ cup almond flour
2 tbsp ground psyllium husk
¼ tsp red chili flakes
¼ tsp dried Greek seasoning 1 cup crumbled feta cheese
3 plum tomatoes, sliced
¼ tsp salt
6 Kalamata olives, chopped
5 basil leaves, chopped

Directions:

Preheat the oven to 390 degrees Fahrenheit. Preheat the oven to 350°F. Line a baking sheet with parchment paper.

Mix almond flour, salt, psyllium powder, olive oil, and 1 cup lukewarm water in a mixing bowl until a dough forms.

Bake for 10 minutes after spreading the mixture on a baking sheet.

Sprinkle the crust with the red chilli flakes and Greek seasoning, then top with the feta cheese. Arrange the tomatoes and olives on top of the salad. 10 minutes in the oven Slice the pizza and serve it warm, garnished with basil.

Nutrition: Cal 181; Net Carbs 9.5g; Fat 12g; Protein 8g

Avocado Pesto Chargrilled Zucchini

Servings: 4 and **Total Time:** approx. 20 minutes

Ingredients:

1 avocado, chopped
¾ cup olive oil
2 zucchinis, sliced
1 garlic clove, minced
Juice of 1 lemon
3 oz spinach, chopped
2 tbsp melted butter
2 oz pecans
Salt and black pepper to taste

Directions:

In a food processor, combine the spinach, avocado, lemon juice, garlic, olive oil, and pecans and blend until smooth; season with salt and pepper.

Place the pesto in a bowl and set aside. Zucchini should be seasoned with salt, pepper, and butter.

Preheat a grill pan over medium heat and brown the zucchini slices for 8-10 minutes.

Transfer to a plate and serve with the pesto on the side.

Nutrition: Cal 394; Net Carbs 4g; Fat 42g; Protein 15g

Broccoli Asparagus Flan

Servings: 4 and **Total Time:** approx. 65 minutes

Ingredients:

2 tbsp butter, melted
1 tbsp butter, softened
½ cup whipping cream
2 tbsp Parmesan, grated
Salt and black pepper to taste
1 lb asparagus, stems trimmed
3 eggs
2 tbsp tarragon, chopped
1 cup almond milk
1 cup broccoli florets

Directions:

For 6 minutes, steam asparagus and broccoli in salted water over medium heat. Drain and cut the asparagus tips, reserving them for garnish.

Cut the rest of the asparagus into small pieces. Blend the asparagus and broccoli in a blender until smooth. Blend in the cream, almond milk, tarragon, salt, pepper, and Parmesan until smooth. Pour the mixture through a sieve into a mixing bowl and whisk in the eggs.

Preheat the oven to 350 degrees Fahrenheit. Divide the asparagus mixture among the ramekins and grease them with softened butter.

Place 2-3 asparagus tips on top of each one and drizzle with melted butter. Fill a baking dish halfway with boiling water, add the ramekins, and place in the oven. 45 minutes in the oven

Nutrition: Cal 268; Net Carbs 7.5g; Fat 24g; Protein 11g

Mediterranean Eggplant Squash Pasta

Servings: 4 and **Total Time:** approx. 20 minutes

Ingredients:

2 tbsp butter
2 tbsp parsley, chopped
¼ cup Parmesan cheese
3 tbsp scallions, chopped
10 oz butternut squash, spirals
1 cup cherry tomatoes
1 eggplant, cubed
1 tsp lemon zest
1 cup green beans

Directions:

Melt the butter in a saucepan over medium heat. Cook the spaghetti squash for 4-5 minutes before transferring to a plate.

Cook the eggplant in the same saucepan for 5 minutes, or until tender.

Cook for 5 minutes more after adding the tomatoes and green beans.

Remove the pan from the heat and stir in the parsley, zest, and scallions. Mix in the spaghetti squash. To serve, sprinkle with Parmesan cheese.

Nutrition: Cal 258; Net Carbs 7.6g; Fat 14g; Protein 12g

Flavored Stuffed Mushrooms filled with Cajun

Servings: 2 and **Total Time:** approx. 40 minutes

Ingredients:

1 cup Parmesan, shredded
1 onion, chopped
½ head broccoli, cut into florets
1 bell pepper, chopped
Salt and black pepper to taste
1 lb cremini mushrooms, stems removed
¼ cup almonds, chopped
1 garlic clove, minced
1 tsp cajun seasoning mix
2 tbsp coconut oil

Directions:

Preheat the oven to 380 degrees Fahrenheit. In a mixing bowl, combine the almond flour, cinnamon, xylitol, and baking powder.

In a separate bowl, cream the eggs with a low-speed electric mixer. Mascarpone cheese, heavy cream, butter, and lemon zest are all mixed in. While mixing, gradually add in the flour mixture.

blending until smooth Divide the batter evenly among six greased muffin cups. Blueberries should be sprinkled on top. Bake for 10-12 minutes, or until the top is golden brown. Serve.

Nutrition: Cal 363; Net Carbs 4.5g; Fat 32g; Protein 22g

Cauliflower-Based Waffles

Servings: 2 and **Total Time:** approx. 25 minutes

Ingredients:

1 tbsp sesame seeds
2 tsp thyme, chopped
1 tbsp olive oil
2 eggs
½ head cauliflower
1 tsp garlic powder
1 cup zucchini, shredded and squeezed
1/3 cup Parmesan cheese
1 cup mozzarella, grated
2 green onions

Directions:

Chop the cauliflower into florets, toss in a food processor, and pulse until rice forms. Transfer to a clean kitchen towel and press to absorb excess moisture. Return to the food processor and pulse in the zucchini, green onions, and thyme until smooth.

Transfer to a mixing bowl. Stir in the remaining ingredients and mix well. Allow for a 10-minute rest. Warm the waffle iron and evenly spread the mixture on it. Cook for about 5 minutes, or until golden brown.

Nutrition: Cal 336; Net Carbs 7.2g; Fat 21g; Protein 32g

Vegan Recipes

Vegan Sandwich with Tofu

Servings: 2 and **Total Time:** approx. 20 min + chilling time

Ingredients:

¼ lb firm tofu, sliced	1 tbsp olive oil
Marinade	2 tbsp olive oil
Salt and black pepper to taste 1 tsp allspice	½ tbsp xylitol
	2 zero carb buns
1 tsp thyme, chopped	1 habanero pepper, seeded and minced
2 green onions, thinly sliced	½ tsp Dijon mustard
1 garlic clove	Lettuce slaw
½ small iceberg lettuce, shredded	½ carrot, grated
	Salt black pepper to taste
½ red onion, grated	1 tbsp lemon juice
2 tsp liquid stevia	2 tbsp olive oil

Directions:

Blend the marinade ingredients in a food processor for 1 minute. In a bowl, pour the mixture over the tofu slices.

Place in the fridge for 1 hour to marinate. Whisk together the lemon juice, stevia, olive oil, mustard, salt, and pepper in a large mixing bowl.

Set aside the lettuce, carrot, and onion. In a skillet over medium heat, heat 1 teaspoon of oil. Take the tofu out of the refrigerator and cook it for 6 minutes on all sides.

Transfer to a plate. Place the tofu on top of the buns, followed by the slaw. Serve.

Nutrition: Cal 487; Net Carbs 10.5g; Fat 38g; Protein 13g

Blackberries with Coconut Milk Shake

Servings: 2 and **Total Time:** approx. 5 minutes

Ingredients:

1 tbsp vegan protein powder	½ cup water
1 ½ cups coconut milk	1 cup fresh blackberries
	¼ tsp vanilla extract

Directions:

In a blender, combine all of the ingredients and blend until they are uniform and creamy. Pour into glasses and serve!

Nutrition: Cal 463; Net Carbs 9g; Fat 44g; Protein 7g

Grilled Cauliflower Steaks

Servings: 2 and **Total Time:** approx. 30 minutes

Ingredients:

1 head cauliflower, sliced lengthwise into 'steaks'	2 tbsp chili sauce
	1 tsp hot paprika
2 tbsp olive oil	1 tsp oregano
Salt and black pepper to taste 1 shallot, chopped	1 bunch haricots vert, trimmed
1 tbsp cilantro, chopped	1 tbsp fresh lemon juice

Directions:

Preheat the grill to medium. For 6 minutes, steam the haricots vert in salted water over medium heat. Drain, transfer to a mixing bowl, and toss with lemon juice.

Combine the olive oil, chilli sauce, hot paprika, and oregano in a mixing bowl. Brush the mixture over the cauliflower steaks. Place them on the grill, cover, and cook for 6 minutes. Cook for another 6 minutes after flipping the cauliflower. Place the grilled caulis on a plate and top with salt, black pepper, shallots, and cilantro. Serve with the haricots verts, which have been steamed.

Nutrition: Cal 184; Net Carbs 8.4g; Fat 16g; Protein 5g

Stir-Fry Tofu & Vegetable

Servings: 2 and **Total Time:** approx. 15 min + chilling time

Ingredients:

2 tbsp olive oil	1 ½ cups tofu, cubed
1 ½ tbsp flaxseed meal	Salt and black pepper to taste 1 garlic clove, minced
1 tbsp sesame seeds	
1 tbsp soy sauce, sugar-free	1 cup mushrooms, sliced
½ head broccoli, cut into florets	1 tsp onion powder

Directions:

Combine onion powder, tofu, salt, soy sauce, black pepper, flaxseed, and garlic in a mixing bowl. Allow the mixture to marinate in the fridge for 20-30 minutes, tossing it to coat.

Warm the olive oil in a pan over medium heat. Stir-fry the broccoli, mushrooms, and tofu mixture for 6 minutes.

It takes 8 minutes. Serve with sesame seeds on top.

Nutrition: Cal 423; Net Carbs 7.3g; Fat 31g; Protein 25g

Grilled Vegetables and Kebab

Servings: 4 and **Total Time:** approx. 30 min + chilling time

Ingredients:

- 1 yellow bell pepper, cut into chunks
- 1 cup zucchini, sliced
- 2 tbsp chives
- 1 red bell pepper, cut chunks
- 2 tbsp olive oil
- 1 cup barbecue sauce, sugar-free
- 10 oz tempeh, cut into chunks
- 1 red onion, cut into chunks

Directions:

Pour 2 cups of water into a pot set over medium heat. Bring to a boil, then remove from the heat and stir in the tempeh.

Cover the pot and steam the tempeh for 5 minutes to remove the bitterness. The tempeh should be drained. Pour the barbecue sauce into a bowl, then add the tempeh and coat with it.

Cover the bowl and place it in the refrigerator for 2 hours to marinate.

Preheat the grill to medium. Thread the tempeh, yellow bell pepper, and cilantro on a thread.

Zucchini, red bell pepper, and onion

Brush the grill grate with olive oil before placing the skewers on it and brushing with barbecue sauce.

Cook the skewers for 3 minutes on each side, rotating and brushing with additional barbecue sauce as needed. When the kabobs are ready, place them in a serving dish.

Nutrition: Cal 228; Net Carbs 3.6g; Fat 15g; Protein 13g

Vegan Smoothie

Servings: 4 and **Total Time:** approx. 10 minutes

Ingredients:

- 1 tbsp vegan protein powder, zero carbs
- 1 cup cantaloupe, chopped
- 1 cup fresh blueberries
- 2 cups coconut milk
- ½ cup coconut cream

Directions:

In a blender, combine all of the ingredients and blend until smooth. Serve.

Nutrition: Cal 341; Net Carbs 8g; Fat 28g; Protein 6g

Portobello Bun Mushroom Burgers

Servings: 4 and **Total Time:** approx. 30 minutes

Ingredients:

- ½ tsp dried oregano
- 2 tbsp olive oil
- 4 portobello mushroom caps 1 clove garlic
- 1 cup guacamole
- ¼ cup tofu, crumbled
- 2 tbsp Kalamata olives, chopped
- ½ cup roasted red peppers, sliced
- Salt and black pepper to taste 2 tomatoes, sliced
- 1 zucchini, sliced
- 1 tbsp red wine vinegar

Directions:

In a bowl, crush the garlic with the back of a spoon and season with salt. Brush the mushrooms and each inner side of the pan with 1 tablespoon of oil.

buns made from the mixture Place the mushrooms in a preheated grill pan and grill for 8 minutes on both sides, or until tender.

Drizzle the zucchini with olive oil, season with salt and pepper, and grill for 5-6 minutes on both sides.

Toss the red peppers, olives, tofu, vinegar, oregano, and remaining oil in a mixing bowl. Spread some guacamole on a mushroom bun slice, then add 1-2 zucchini slices, a scoop of the vegetable mixture, a slice of tomato, and another mushroom bun slice.

Serve and have fun!

Nutrition: Cal 221; Net Carbs 5.3g; Fat 20g; Protein 5g

Roasted Bake tomatoes

Servings: 4 and **Total Time:** approx. 20 minutes

Ingredients:

- 3 tomatoes, sliced
- 1 tsp garlic puree
- 1 tbsp nutritional yeast
- 2 tbsp parsley. chopped
- 2 tbsp olive oil
- ½ cup pepitas seeds
- Salt black pepper to taste

Directions:

Preheat the oven to 380 degrees Fahrenheit. Place the tomatoes in a baking dish and drizzle with the olive oil.

Add pepitas seeds, nutritional yeast, garlic puree, salt, and pepper to a food processor and pulse until the desired consistency is achieved. Firmly press the mixture onto each tomato slice.

Bake the tomato slices for 10 minutes on the prepared baking sheet. Garnish with parsley before serving.

Nutrition: Cal 165; Fat 15g; Net Carbs 3.2g; Protein

6.2g

Grilled Tofu Kabobs

Servings: 4 and **Total Time:** approx. 30 min + chilling time

Ingredients:

14 oz firm tofu, cut into strips 4 tsp sesame oil	1 lemon, juiced
½ cup sesame seeds	3 tsp garlic powder
	5 tbsp soy sauce, sugar-free
4 tbsp coconut flour	1 tbsp balsamic vinegar
Arugula salad	4 cups arugula, chopped
2 tsp extra virgin olive oil	2 tbsp pine nuts
Salt and black pepper to taste	

Directions:

Stick the tofu strips on the skewers and place them on the plate.

on a plate Combine sesame oil, lemon juice, soy sauce, garlic powder, and coconut flour in a mixing bowl. Pour the soy sauce mixture over the tofu and toss to coat. Refrigerate the dish for 2 hours, covered.

Heat the griddle pan on high. Toss the tofu in the sesame seeds and grill for 12 minutes, or until golden brown on both sides. Arrange the arugula on a plate to serve. Season with salt and black pepper and drizzle with olive oil and balsamic vinegar. To serve, sprinkle with pine nuts and top with tofu kabobs.

Nutrition: Cal 411; Net Carbs 7g; Fat 33g; Protein 22g

Thyme & Garlic Steamed Bok Choy

Servings: 4 and **Total Time:** approx. 15 minutes

Ingredients:

2 lb Bok choy, sliced	2 tbsp coconut oil
½ tsp red pepper flakes	2 tbsp soy sauce, sugar-free
1 tsp garlic, minced	
½ tsp thyme, chopped	Salt and black pepper to taste

Directions:

Warm the coconut oil in a pan over medium heat. Cook until the garlic is soft, about 1 minute.

Cook until the bok choy, red pepper, soy sauce, black pepper, salt, and thyme are heated through, about 5 minutes. Serve.

Nutrition: Cal 112; Net Carbs 4.5g; Fat 9g; Protein 5g

Cucumber & Tomato Salad Sticky with Tofu

Servings: 4 and **Total Time:** approx. 15 min + chilling time

Ingredients:

2 tbsp olive oil	12 oz tofu, sliced
1 tbsp sriracha sauce	1 cup green onions, chopped
2 tbsp vinegar	Salad
1 tbsp fresh lemon juice	2 tbsp extra virgin olive oil Salt and black pepper to taste
1 garlic clove, minced	
1 cucumber, sliced	2 tomatoes, sliced
1 tsp fresh dill weed	

Directions:

In a mixing bowl, combine the tofu slices, garlic, sriracha sauce, vinegar, and green onions.

Allow to settle for about 30 minutes in a bowl. In a skillet over medium heat, warm the olive oil. Tofu should be cooked for 5 minutes, or until golden brown.

Arrange tomatoes and cucumber slices on a salad plate, season with salt and pepper, drizzle with lemon juice and extra virgin olive oil, and scatter with dill.

Serve with the tofu on top.

Nutrition: Cal 371; Net Carbs 7.7g; Fat 31g; Protein 17g

Dip with Tofu and Swiss Chard

Servings: 4 and **Total Time:** approx. 20 minutes

Ingredients:

2 tbsp mayonnaise	1 cups Swiss chard
2 tbsp olive oil	½ cup tofu, crumbled
1 garlic clove, minced	¼ cup almond milk
½ tsp paprika	1 tsp nutritional yeast
Salt and pepper to taste	½ tsp mint leaves, chopped

Directions:

Bring a pot of salted water to a boil over medium heat. Cook for 5-6 minutes, or until the Swiss chard is wilted. In a food processor, puree all of the remaining

Ingredients except the mayonnaise. Season with salt and pepper to taste. To make a salad, combine the Swiss chard and mayonnaise in a mixing bowl.

mixture that is homogeneous Serve.

Nutrition: Cal 136; Net Carbs 7.3g; Fat 11g; Protein 3g

Ratatouille with Pecans

Servings: 4 and **Total Time:** approx. 50 minutes

Ingredients:

2 tbsp olive oil	1 eggplant, sliced
¼ cup pecans, chopped	1 zucchini, sliced
14 oz canned tomatoes	1 yellow bell pepper, sliced
1 red bell pepper, sliced	
¼ cup basil leaves, chop half	1 tbsp balsamic vinegar
2 sprigs thyme	1 red onion, sliced
½ lemon, zested	Salt and black pepper to taste
1 cloves garlic, sliced	

Directions:

Warm the olive oil in a casserole pot over medium heat. For 5 minutes, sauté the eggplants, zucchinis, and bell peppers. Place the vegetables in a large mixing bowl.

Sauté the garlic, onion, and thyme leaves for 5 minutes in the same pan before adding the cooked vegetables, canned tomatoes, balsamic vinegar, chopped basil, salt, and pepper to taste. Cover the pot and stir. Cook the

Ingredients for 30 minutes on low heat. Combine the remaining basil leaves and lemon zest in a mixing bowl. Seasoning should be adjusted. Serve and have fun!

Nutrition: Cal 188; Net Carbs 8.3g; Fat 13g; Protein 4.5g

Fennel & Celeriac with Chili Tomato Sauce

Servings: 4 and **Total Time:** approx. 35 minutes

Ingredients:

2 tbsp olive oil	1 garlic clove, crushed
½ celeriac, sliced	½ fennel bulb, sliced
¼ cup vegetable stock	Salt black pepper to taste
Sauce	2 tomatoes, halved
½ cup onions, chopped	1 bunch fresh basil, chopped
2 cloves garlic, minced	1 tbsp fresh cilantro, chopped
1 chili, minced	Salt and black pepper to taste
2 tbsp olive oil	

Directions:

Set a pan over medium-high heat and warm olive oil. Sauté the garlic for 1 minute. Stir in celeriac and fennel slices for 3-4 minutes, then pour in the stock; cook until softened, 5 minutes. Sprinkle with salt and pepper. Brush the tomato halves with olive oil. Microwave for 15 minutes; get rid of any excess liquid.

Remove the cooked tomatoes to a food processor; add the Ingredients for the sauce and puree to obtain the desired consistency. Serve the celeriac and fennel topped with tomato sauce.

Nutrition: Cal 175; Net Carbs 5.3g; Fat 15g; Protein 2g

Coleslaw with Poppy Seeds

Servings: 4 and **Total Time:** approx. 15 minutes

Ingredients:

Dressing	2 tbsp olive oil
¼ tsp dill, minced	1 cup poppy seeds
1 tbsp yellow mustard	2 tbsp green onions, chopped
1 lime, freshly squeezed	Salt and black pepper to taste
Salad	1 carrot, shredded
1 shallot, sliced	2 tbsp Kalamata olives, pitted
1 garlic clove, minced	
½ head white cabbage, shredded	

Directions:

In a mixing bowl, combine the green onions, olive oil, mustard, lime juice, garlic, salt, and black pepper. Mix in the poppy seeds, dill, and green onions.

In a mixing bowl, combine the cabbage, carrot, and shallot.

To serve, transfer to a salad plate, drizzle with dressing, and top with Kalamata olives.

Nutrition: Cal 285; Net Carbs 6.4g; Fat 22g; Protein 8g

Roasted Asparagus and Romesco sauce

Servings: 4 and **Total Time:** approx. 20 minutes

Ingredients:

1 lb asparagus spears, trimmed	Salt and black pepper to taste
½ tsp paprika	Romesco sauce
2 red bell peppers, roasted	2 tbsp almond flour
2 tsp olive oil	1 garlic clove, minced
½ cup scallions, chopped	1 tbsp lemon juice
½ tsp chili pepper	2 tbsp rosemary, chopped
Salt and black pepper to taste	2 tbsp olive oil

Directions:

In a food processor, combine the Ingredients: for the romesco sauce. Pulse until the

Ingredients are thoroughly combined. Place aside.

Preheat the oven to 390 degrees Fahrenheit. Preheat the oven to 350°F.

Line a baking sheet with parchment paper. Arrange asparagus spears on a baking sheet. Toss with 2 tablespoons olive oil, paprika, black pepper, salt, and pepper.

Bake for 9 minutes, or until thoroughly cooked. Transfer to a serving plate, drizzle with the sauce, and serve.

Nutrition: Cal 145; Net Carbs 5.9g; Fat 11g; Protein 4g

Vegetable Stew

Servings: 4 and **Total Time:** approx. 35 minutes

Ingredients:
- 2 tbsp olive oil
- 1 tbsp flaxseed meal
- 2 tomatoes, chopped
- 1 thyme sprig, chopped
- 1 cup wild mushrooms, sliced
- 4 cups vegetable stock
- ½ tsp chili pepper
- 1 tsp smoked paprika
- 1 turnip, chopped
- 1 onion, chopped
- 2 garlic cloves, pressed
- ½ cup celery, chopped
- 2 tbsp rosemary, chopped
- 1 carrot, chopped
- 2 tbsp dry white wine

Directions:

In a medium-sized pot, heat the olive oil and cook the onion, carrot, celery, mushrooms, paprika, chilli pepper, and garlic for 5-6 minutes, or until tender; set aside.

Pour in the wine and stir to deglaze the pan's bottom. Put in the thyme and rosemary. Bring the tomatoes, stock, reserved vegetables, and turnip to a boil.

Reduce the heat to low and cover the pan to allow the mixture to simmer for 15 minutes. 3 minutes later, add the flaxseed meal to thicken the stew.

Divide the dish into individual bowls and serve.

Nutrition: Cal 164; Net Carbs 8.2g; Fat 11g; Protein 3

Zucchini Loaded with Tofu & Hazelnut

Servings: 4 and **Total Time:** approx. 55 minutes

Ingredients:
- 2 tbsp olive oil
- 2 garlic cloves, pressed
- 2 cups crushed tomatoes
- ¼ tsp chili pepper
- Salt and black pepper to taste
- 2 tbsp cilantro, chopped
- 12 oz firm tofu, crumbled
- ½ cup onions, chopped
- ¼ tsp dried oregano
- 2 zucchinis, cut into halves, scoop out the insides
- ¼ cup hazelnuts, chopped

Directions:

Preheat the oven to 390 degrees Fahrenheit. In a skillet over medium heat, warm the olive oil and sauté the onion, garlic, and tofu for 5 minutes, or until softened. Place the scooped zucchini flesh, 1 cup of tomatoes, oregano, and chilli in a mixing bowl. Cook for 6 minutes, seasoning with salt and pepper. Fill a baking dish halfway with the remaining tomatoes.

Fill the zucchini shells with the tofu mixture. In the baking dish, arrange the zucchini boats. 30 minutes in the oven Continue baking for 5 to 6 minutes after adding the hazelnuts. To serve, sprinkle with cilantro.

Nutrition: Cal 234; Net Carbs 9g; Fat 18g; Protein 17g

Pumpkin & Bell Pepper Noodles

Servings: 4 and **Total Time:** approx. 20 minutes

Ingredients:
- 2 tbsp olive oil
- 2 tbsp sesame oil
- 2 avocados, chopped
- 1 lemon, juiced and zested
- 1 onion, chopped
- Salt and black pepper to taste
- ½ lb pumpkin, spiralized
- ½ lb bell peppers, spiralized
- 2 tbsp pumpkin seeds
- 2 tbsp cilantro, chopped
- 1 jalapeño pepper, minced

Directions:

Toast the pumpkin seeds in a dry nonstick skillet for a minute, stirring frequently, until golden; set aside. Sauté bell peppers and onions in oil.

8 minutes with the pumpkin Place on a serving platter. In a food processor, combine avocados, sesame oil, onion, jalapeo pepper, lemon juice, and lemon zest to make a creamy mixture.

Season to taste and pour over the vegetable noodles. Garnish with the pumpkin seeds and serve.

Nutrition: Cal 673; Net Carbs 9.8g; Fat 59g; Protein 23g

Mushrooms Bake & Curried Cauliflower

Servings: 4 and **Total Time:** approx. 35 minutes

Ingredients:
- 1 tsp chili paprika paste
- 1 cup mushrooms, halved
- 4 garlic cloves, minced
- ¼ cup coconut oil, melted
- Salt and black pepper to taste
- 1 head cauliflower, cut into florets
- 2 tomatoes, chopped
- ½ tsp curry powder
- 1 red onion, sliced

Directions:

Preheat the oven to 380°F. Toss the cauliflower, mushrooms, garlic, red onion, tomatoes, chilli paprika paste, curry powder, coconut oil, black pepper, and salt in a large mixing bowl to coat well.

Spread out on a baking dish and roast for 20-25 minutes, shaking once. Serve warm.

Nutrition: Cal 171; Net Carbs 5.9g; Fat 16g; Protein 3.5g

Roasted Cauliflower with Bell Peppers

Servings: 4 and **Total Time:** approx. 45 minutes

Ingredients:

1 lb cauliflower florets	2 bell peppers, halved
2 onions, quartered	¼ cup olive oil
½ tsp cayenne pepper	Salt and black pepper to taste

Directions:

Preheat the oven to 425 degrees Fahrenheit. Preheat the oven to 350°F. Line a large baking sheet with parchment paper.

Arrange the cauliflower, onion, and bell peppers on the baking sheet.

Toss with olive oil, black pepper, salt, and cayenne pepper until well combined. Roast for 35 minutes, tossing in between, until they begin to brown.

Nutrition: Cal 186; Fat 15g; Net Carbs 8.2g; Protein 4g

Tofu Vegetable Casserole

Servings: 4 and **Total Time:** approx. 55 minutes

Ingredients:

½ cup carrot, chopped	1 ½ lb Brussels sprouts, shredded
2 bay leaves	
2 tsp olive oil	10 oz tofu, pressed and cubed
1 cup leeks, chopped	½ cup celery, chopped
1 garlic clove, minced	2 ½ cups mushrooms, sliced
1 ½ cups vegetable stock	1 habanero pepper, chopped
2 tomatoes, chopped	2 thyme sprigs, chopped
1 rosemary sprig, chopped	Salt and black pepper to taste

Directions:

Warm the oil in a pot over medium heat. Sauté the garlic and leeks for 3 minutes, or until soft and translucent. Cook for another 4 minutes after adding the tofu. Combine the habanero pepper, celery, mushrooms, and carrots in a mixing bowl.

Cook for 5 minutes while stirring. Stir in the remaining ingredients Simmer for 25-35 minutes, or until the chicken is cooked through.

Take out the bay leaves and set them aside. Serve.

Nutrition: Cal 328; Net Carbs 9.7g; Fat 18g; Protein 21g

Coconut Green Soup

Servings: 4 and **Total Time:** approx. 30 minutes

Ingredients:

1 broccoli head, chopped	1 cup spinach
1 onion, chopped	1 garlic clove, minced
½ cup leeks	3 cups vegetable stock
1 bay leaf	½ cup coconut milk
2 tbsp coconut oil	Salt black pepper to taste
2 tbsp coconut yogurt	

Directions:

In a large pot over medium heat, warm the coconut oil. Cook for 5 minutes after adding the onion, leeks, and garlic.

Cook for 5 minutes more after adding the broccoli. Pour in the stock and garnish with the bay leaf.

Bring to a boil, then turn down to a low heat. Cook for about 10 minutes.

Cook for 3 minutes more after adding the spinach. Remove the bay leaf from the soup and puree it with a hand blender.

Adjust the seasoning with the coconut milk. Arrange in serving bowls and top with a swirl of coconut yoghurt. Serve and have fun!

Nutrition: Cal 232; Net Carbs 4.3g; Fat 25g; Protein 5g

Snacks Recipes & Appetizers Recipes

Walnuts & Cheese Mushrooms

Servings: 4 and **Total Time:** approx. 35 minute

Ingredients:

- ½ cup grated Pecorino Romano cheese
- ¼ cup olive oil
- 1 garlic cloves, minced
- Salt black pepper to taste
- ¼ cup ground walnuts
- 12 button mushrooms, stemmed
- ¼ cup pork rinds
- 2 tbsp chopped fresh parsley

Directions:

Preheat oven to 400 F. In a bowl, mix pork rinds, Pecorino Romano cheese, garlic, parsley, salt, and pepper.

Brush a baking sheet with some oil. Spoon the cheese mixture into the mushrooms and arrange them on the baking sheet.

Top with the ground walnuts and drizzle the remaining olive oil on the top. Bake for 20 minutes or until golden. Transfer to a platter and serve.

Nutrition: Cal 289; Net Carbs 4.9g; Fat 25g; Protein 8g

Meatball Shakshuka

Servings: 4 and **Total Time:** approx. 50 minutes

Ingredients:

- ¾ cup pork rinds
- ½ lb ground Italian sausage
- 1 tsp shallot powder
- 1 tbsp chopped parsley
- 3 tbsp olive oil
- Salt and black pepper to taste
- ½ lb ground beef
- ½ cup grated Pecorino cheese
- 1 tsp garlic powder
- 1 tsp ground cumin
- 2 ½ cups marinara sauce
- 5 eggs

Directions:

Combine ground beef, Italian sausage, pork rinds, Parmesan cheese, 1 egg, shallot powder, garlic powder, parsley, salt, pepper, and garlic powder in a mixing bowl.

cumin powder Form the mixture into meatballs. In a skillet, heat the olive oil and brown the meatballs for 10 minutes.

Cook for 20 minutes after adding the marinara sauce and submerging the meatballs in it. Cook for another 10 minutes after cracking the remaining eggs into the sauce. Serve.

Nutrition: Cal 652; Net Carbs 7.9; Fat 42g; Protein 43g

Avocado & Cauliflower Burritos

Servings: 2 and **Total Time:** approx. 15 minutes

Ingredients:

- 1 tbsp butter
- 2 pieces of zero carb flatbread
- 1 cup tomato salsa
- 1 tbsp cilantro, chopped
- 5 oz cauliflower florets
- 1 cup yogurt
- 1 avocado, sliced
- Salt and black pepper to taste

Directions:

Put the cauliflower in a food processor and pulse until it resembles rice. In a skillet, melt the butter and add the cauli rice. Sauté for 4-5 minutes until cooked through. Season with salt and black pepper.

On flatbread, spread the yogurt all over and distribute the salsa on top. Top with cauli rice and scatter the avocado slices and cilantro on top. Fold and tuck the burritos and cut them into two. Serve and enjoy!

Nutrition: Cal 457; Net Carbs 9.5g; Fat 31g; Protein 16g

Breakfast Bread "Naan"

Servings: 6 and **Total Time:** approx. 25 minutes

Ingredients:

- ¼ cup olive oil
- ¾ cup almond flour
- ½ tsp baking powder
- 2 cups boiling water
- 8 oz butter
- 2 tbsp psyllium husk powder
- 2 garlic cloves, minced
- 1 tsp salt

Directions:

Mix the almond flour, psyllium husk powder, ½ teaspoon of salt, and baking powder in a bowl. Pour in olive oil and boiling water to combine the ingredients like a thick porridge. Stir and allow the dough for 5 minutes. Divide the dough into 6 pieces and mold into balls.

Place the balls on wax paper and flatten. Melt half of the butter in a frying pan over medium heat and fry the naan on both sides to have a golden color. Transfer to a plate and keep warm. Add the remaining butter to

the pan and sauté garlic until fragrant, about 1 minute. Pour the garlic butter into a bowl and serve as a dip along with the naan.

Nutrition: Cal 329; Net Carbs 1.3g; Fat 21g; Protein 4g

Rosemary Feta Cheese Bombs

Servings: 4 and **Total Time:** approx. 50 minutes

Ingredients:

- 6 tbsp butter
- 1 cup crumbled feta cheese
- 1 tbsp olive oil
- 2 white onions, thinly sliced
- 1 tsp Swerve brown sugar
- 2/3 cup almond flour
- ½ cup heavy whip cream
- 2 sprigs rosemary
- 2 tbsp red wine vinegar
- 3 eggs

Directions:

Preheat oven to 350 F. Line a baking tray with parchment paper. In a saucepan, warm 1 cup of water and butter. Bring to a boil and add in almond flour, beating vigorously until ball forms. Turn the heat off; keep beating while adding the eggs, one at a time, until the dough is

smooth and slightly thickened. Scoop mounds of the dough onto the baking dish. Press a hole in the center of each mound. Bake for 20 minutes until risen and golden. Remove from the oven and pierce the sides of the buns with a toothpick. Return to the oven and bake for 2 minutes until crispy. Set aside to cool.

Tear out the middle part of the bun (keep the turnout part) to create a hole in the bun for the cream filling. Set aside. Heat olive oil in a saucepan and sauté onions and rosemary for 2 minutes. Stir in Swerve sugar and vinegar and cook to bubble for 3 minutes or until caramelized.

In a bowl, beat whipping cream and feta together. Spoon the mixture into a piping bag and press a spoonful of the mixture into the buns. Cover with the turnout portion of pastry and top with onion relish to serve.

Nutrition: Cal 379; Net Carbs 3.5g, Fat 37g, Protein 10g

Mushroom Feta Skewers

Servings: 2 and **Total Time:** approx. 20 minutes

Ingredients:

- ½ lb white button mushrooms, quartered
- 14 oz block feta cheese, cubed
- 1 lemon, juiced
- 2 tbsp olive oil
- 2 tbsp chopped parsley
- 2 red onions, cut into wedges
- 1 tsp Chinese five-spice

Directions:

Thread feta, mushrooms, and onions alternately on the skewers. In a bowl, mix olive oil, Chinese five-spice, and lemon juice. Brush the skewers with the mixture.

Cook in a grill pan over high heat until the vegetables lightly char, about 10 minutes. Garnish with parsley and serve.

Nutrition: Cal 368; Net Carbs 6.9g; Fat 27g; Protein 17g

Mushroom & Kale Pierogis

Servings: 4 and **Total Time:** approx. 45 minutes

Ingredients:

- 2 oz fresh kale
- ½ cup cream cheese
- 2 garlic cloves, minced
- 7 tbsp butter
- ½ cup almond flour
- 1 tsp baking powder
- 3 oz Bella mushrooms, sliced
- 2 cups Parmesan, grated
- 1 small red onion, chopped
- 3 eggs
- Salt and black pepper to taste
- 4 tbsp coconut flour

Directions:

Melt 2 tbsp of butter in a skillet and sauté garlic, red onion, mushrooms, and kale for 5 minutes. Season with salt and pepper and reduce the heat to low. Stir in cream cheese and ½ cup of Parmesan cheese; simmer for 1 minute. Set aside to cool.

In a bowl, combine almond and coconut flours, salt, and baking powder. Put a pan over low heat and melt the remaining Parmesan cheese and butter.

Turn the heat off. Pour the eggs into the cream mixture, continue stirring while adding the flour mixture until a firm dough forms. Mold the dough into balls, place on a chopping board, and use a rolling pin to flatten each into ½ inch thin round piece.

Spread a generous amount of stuffing on one-half of each dough, fold over the filling, and seal the dough with fingers. Brush with oil and bake for 20 minutes at 380 F.

Nutrition: Cal 538; Net Carbs 6g; Fat 51g; Protein 18g

Parmigiano Cauliflower Cakes

Servings: 4 and **Total Time:** approx. 25 minutes

Ingredients:

- 2 cups cauliflower florets
- 1 cup olive oil
- 1 large egg, beaten
- 2 tbsp chopped almonds
- Salt and black pepper to taste
- ½ cup grated Parmigiano cheese
- 2 green onions, chopped
- 1 cup golden flaxseed meal
- 1 tbsp chopped parsley

Directions:

Place cauliflower and 1 cup of water into a pot and bring to a boil until soft; drain. Transfer to a food processor.

Puree until smooth. Pour into a bowl and mix in salt, pepper, egg, green onions, parsley, cheese, and almonds. Make 12 small cakes from the mixture and coat with the flaxseed meal. Heat olive oil in a

deep pan and cook patties on both sides until golden,

6-8 minutes. Serve.

Nutrition: Cal 419; Net Carbs 5.5g; Fat 24g; Protein 14g

Triple Cheese Chips

SERVINGS 4 | **PREP TIME** 10 minutes | **COOK TIME** 7 minutes

Ingredients:

Olive oil spray
Pinch cayenne pepper
½ cup finely shredded Cheddar cheese
½ cup finely shredded Parmesan cheese
¼ cup finely shredded jalapeño Cheddar cheese

Directions:

Preheat the oven to 425°F. Lightly spray a baking sheet with oil and line with parchment paper. In a medium bowl, toss the Parmesan, Cheddars, and cayenne pepper until well mixed. Drop the cheese mixture onto the baking sheet, about 1½ tablespoons per chip.

Spread out the cheese with the back of a spoon, leaving a minimum of 1 inch between the edges. Bake until melted and bubbly, but do not brown, 5 to 7 minutes. Remove the chips from the baking sheet and cool on a baking rack.

Nutrition: Calories: 138; Fat: 11g; Protein: 10g; Total Carbs: 1g

Parmesan Zucchini Chips

SERVINGS 2 | **PREP TIME** 20 minutes | **COOK TIME** 20 minutes

Ingredients:

Nonstick cooking spray
1 teaspoon garlic powder
½ teaspoon salt
½ cup low-sugar marinara sauce
2 medium zucchini, cut into ¼-inch coins
1 cup grated Parmesan cheese

Directions:

Preheat the oven to 425°F. Spray a baking sheet with cooking spray. Put the zucchini slices in a medium bowl and sprinkle with the salt. Set aside for 15 minutes.

In a separate bowl, combine the Parmesan cheese and garlic powder. Blot the zucchini with a paper towel and place on the prepared baking sheet. Sprinkle each zucchini coin with a generous amount of the cheese mixture.

Bake for 15 to 20 minutes, or until the cheese topping is bubbling. Serve with the marinara sauce for dipping.

Nutrition: Calories: 249; Fat: 13g; Protein: 21g; Total Carbs: 12g

Crispy Kale Chips

SERVINGS 2 | **PREP TIME** 5 minutes | **COOK TIME** 25 minutes

Ingredients:

2 cups kale, cleaned, leaves trimmed from stalk
½ teaspoon freshly ground black pepper
½ teaspoon garlic powder
½ teaspoon salt
1 tablespoon olive oil
½ teaspoon onion powder

Directions:

Preheat the oven to 300°F. In a large bowl, add kale leaves and the olive oil. Toss to coat the leaves evenly with the oil. Add the salt, pepper, onion powder, and garlic powder to the bowl.

Toss again to coat the leaves evenly. On a parchment-lined baking sheet, spread the kale into an even layer. Place the sheet in the preheated oven. Bake for 10 minutes, rotate the baking sheet, then bake for an additional 15 minutes. Remove the baking sheet from the oven. Cool the kale on the tray for 3 minutes before serving.

Nutrition: Calories: 99; Fat: 7g; Total Carbs: 8.3g; Net Carbs: 7.2g

Margarita Pizza Chips

SERVINGS 8 | **PREP TIME** 10 minutes | **COOK TIME** 10 minutes

Ingredients:

16 slices deli salami
16 fresh basil leaves
Pinch pepper
2 medium tomatoes, cut into ¼-inch-thick slices
Pinch salt
8 ounces fresh mozzarella, cut into 16 pieces

Directions:

Preheat the oven to 375°F. Line a rimmed baking sheet with parchment paper. Line a plate with paper towels. Lay the salami on the parchment paper and bake for 9 minutes, until the salami browns on the edges and begins to shrink. While the salami bakes, season the tomatoes with salt and pepper and set aside.

Transfer the salami it to the prepared plate to drain excess oil for a couple of minutes. Turn the oven to broil. Place the crisp salami on the prepared baking sheet. Top each slice with a slice of tomato, a basil leaf, and a mozzarella slice. Return the baking sheet to the oven and broil for 60 to 90 seconds, until the cheese begins to bubble.

Allow the bites to cool for 2 to 3 minutes, then transfer to a dish and serve.

Nutrition: Calories: 155; Fat: 12g; Protein: 9g; Total Carbs: 1g;

Southern Fried Deviled Eggs

MAKES 16 | **PREP TIME** 15 minutes | **COOK TIME** 20 minutes

Ingredients:

- 4 to 5 cups avocado oil for frying (or enough to fill your pan about 2 inches deep)
- ¼ cup mayonnaise
- 2 teaspoons Dijon mustard
- 1 teaspoon salt
- 2 large eggs
- 1 cup finely crushed pork skins
- 8 hard-boiled eggs
- ¼ cup sour cream
- ½ teaspoon freshly ground black pepper
- Paprika, for garnish

Directions:

Pour the oil into a deep, medium heavy-bottomed pan, and place on the stove over medium heat. Cut the boiled eggs in half lengthwise. Scoop out the yolks, place the yolks in a small bowl, and set the yolks and egg white boats aside. Pour the crushed pork skins into a shallow bowl.

In another shallow bowl, whisk the two uncooked eggs. Take an egg white boat, dip both sides in the pork skins, then submerge it in the whisked eggs and then back in the pork skins. Place on a plate, and repeat with the remaining egg white boats. Using a slotted spoon, gently lower 2 or 3 of the boats into the oil. Cook for about 3 minutes, flipping halfway through, until golden brown.

Transfer onto another plate lined with paper towels. Working in batches, repeat with the remaining boats. With a fork, mash the egg yolks. Add the mayonnaise, sour cream, Dijon mustard, salt, and pepper, and mix well. Using a piping bag, resealable bag with the corner cut off, or spoon, fill each boat with yolk mixture, and garnish with paprika.

Nutrition: (2 deviled eggs): Calories: 257; Fat: 22g; Protein: 12g; Total Carbs: 1g

Antipasto Skewers

SERVINGS 12 | **PREP TIME** 10 minutes

Ingredients:

- 12 Kalamata olives
- 12 pimento-stuffed green olives
- 12 slices thick-cut summer sausage
- 12 slices thick-cut salami
- 12 marinated baby mozzarella balls
- 12 grape tomatoes

Directions:

On a 7-inch wooden or bamboo knotted skewer, thread the ingredients in this order: Kalamata olive, salami (end to end), green olive, mozzarella ball, summer sausage (end to end), grape tomato. Repeat with the remaining skewers. Plate and serve.

Nutrition: (1 skewer): Calories: 255; Fat: 22g; Protein: 11g; Total Carbs: 2.5g

Rosemary Roasted Almonds

SERVINGS 4 | **PREP TIME** 5 minutes | **COOK TIME** 15 minutes

Ingredients:

- 1½ cups almonds
- 1 tsp chopped fresh rosemary
- ½ teaspoon freshly ground black pepper
- 1 tablespoon olive oil
- ½ teaspoon salt
- ¼ teaspoon ground ginger

Directions:

Preheat the oven to 325°F. In a medium bowl, combine the almonds and olive oil. Mix until the almonds are evenly coated. Add the rosemary, salt, pepper, and ginger to the almonds. Stir to combine.

On a baking sheet covered with aluminum foil, spread the almonds into an even layer. Place the sheet in the preheated oven. Bake for 15 minutes, or until toasted.

Nutrition: (½ cup): Calories: 240; Fat: 21.5g; Protein: 7.6g; Total Carbs: 8.4g

Spicy Barbecue Pecans

SERVINGS 8 | **PREP TIME** 15 minutes | **COOK TIME** 20 minutes

Ingredients:

- 2½ tablespoons butter, melted
- 1 teaspoon kosher salt
- ½ teaspoon garlic powder
- ¼ teaspoon dry mustard
- 2 cups pecan halves
- 1 tablespoon gluten-free Worcestershire sauce
- ½ teaspoon chili powder
- ¼ teaspoon cayenne pepper
- 1 tablespoon tamari, or gluten-free soy sauce

Directions:

Preheat the oven to 325°F. Line a baking sheet with parchment paper. Set aside. In a medium bowl, stir the melted butter, Worcestershire sauce, tamari, salt, chili powder, garlic powder, cayenne, and mustard. Add the pecans and toss to coat well.

Pour the coated pecans on the baking sheet and spread into a single layer. Bake for 18 to 20 minutes, stirring once halfway through the cooking time. Keep a close eye on them to ensure they don't burn. Spread the pecan halves on paper towels to cool completely before packing in an airtight container for storage.

Nutrition: (¼ cup): Calories: 270; Fat: 26g; Protein: 4g; Total Carbs: 5g

Texas Trash

SERVINGS 10 TO 12 | **PREP TIME** 15 minutes | **COOK TIME** 1 hour, 15 minutes

Ingredients:

- 1½ (5-ounce) bags pork rinds, broken into bite-size pieces
- ½ cup raw pecans
- 6 tablespoons melted butter
- ½ teaspoon onion powder
- ½ teaspoon paprika
- ¼ teaspoon celery salt
- ½ cup raw almonds
- 2 tsp hot sauce or sriracha
- ½ cup raw Brazil nuts
- 2 tsp Worcestershire sauce
- ½ teaspoon garlic powder
- ½ teaspoon kosher salt
- 1½ cups Cheddar cheese crisps, purchased or homemade

Directions:

Preheat the oven to 250°F. Line a baking sheet with parchment paper. In a large bowl, mix the pork rinds, almonds, pecans, and Brazil nuts. In a small bowl, whisk the melted butter, Worcestershire sauce, hot sauce, onion powder, garlic powder, paprika, salt, and celery salt.

Pour the butter mixture over the pork rinds and nuts, and toss to coat. Pour everything onto the baking sheet and spread it evenly. Bake for 1 hour to 1 hour and 15 minutes, stirring every 15 minutes.

The pork rinds should be crispy, not soggy. Remove from the oven, add the cheese crisps, and gently toss to incorporate them into the warm mixture. Transfer the Texas trash onto paper towels to cool.

Nutrition: (⅓ cup): Calories: 388; Fat: 32g; Protein: 21g; Total Carbs: 4g

Marinated Artichokes

MAKES 2 CUPS | **PREP TIME** 10 minutes, plus 24 hours to marinate

Ingredients:

- 2 (13¾-ounce) cans artichoke hearts, drained and quartered
- 4 small garlic cloves, crushed with the back of a knife
- 1 tsp fresh rosemary leaves
- 1 teaspoon salt
- ¾ cup extra-virgin olive oil
- 1 teaspoon red pepper flakes
- 2 teaspoons chopped fresh oregano
- 1 teaspoon dried oregano

Directions:

In a medium bowl, combine the artichoke hearts, olive oil, garlic, rosemary, oregano, red pepper flakes (if using), and salt. Refrigerate in an airtight container and marinate for at least 24 hours before using. Refrigerate for up to 2 weeks.

Nutrition (¼ cup): Calories: 275; Fat: 27g; Protein: 4g; Total Carbs: 11g

Fennel and Orange Marinated Olives

SERVINGS 12 | **PREP TIME** 10 minutes | **COOK TIME** 2 hours

Ingredients:

- 1 cup almonds, preferably Marcona
- 1 orange, peeled and very thinly sliced
- 1 small red onion, thinly sliced
- 1 sprig fresh rosemary
- ¾ cup extra-virgin olive oil
- 2 tsp red wine vinegar
- ½ fennel bulb, thinly sliced
- Pinch red pepper flakes

Directions:

Preheat the oven to 300°F. In a shallow baking dish, toss all of the ingredients. Cover with foil and bake for 1½ hours.

Remove the foil and continue baking for another 20 to 30 minutes. Allow the mixture to cool to room temperature before serving.

Nutrition: (about ⅓ cup): Calories: 243; Fat: 24g; Protein: 3g; Total Carbs: 7g

Baked Olives and Feta

SERVINGS 6 | **PREP TIME** 5 minutes | **COOK TIME** 30 minutes

Ingredients:

- Nonstick cooking spray
- 1 (6-ounce) jar green olives, drained
- 2 tsp minced fresh thyme
- 1 (6-ounce) can black olives, drained
- 14 ounces feta cheese, crumbled

2 tablespoons minced fresh rosemary
2 tablespoons olive oil

Directions:

Preheat the oven to 350°F. Spray an 8-inch-square baking dish with cooking spray. Pour the olives into the prepared dish. Stir in the feta cheese, rosemary, and thyme.

Drizzle the olive oil on top and mix well until the olives and cheese are well coated. Bake for 22 to 25 minutes. Turn the oven to low broil and broil for an additional 2 to 4 minutes, or until the olives are browned.

Remove from the oven and serve warm.

Nutrition: Calories: 284; Fat: 24g; Protein: 10g; Total Carbs: 7g

Loaded Feta

MAKES 1½ CUPS | **PREP TIME** 5 minutes

Ingredients:

- ⅓ cup extra-virgin olive oil
- 1 teaspoon dried oregano
- 1 to 2 teaspoons red pepper flakes, to taste
- 1 teaspoon dried thyme
- 2 teaspoons dried rosemary
- ½ teaspoon salt
- 8 ounces feta cheese, cut into ½-inch cubes

Directions:

In a medium bowl or large glass jar, whisk the olive oil, rosemary, oregano, thyme, red pepper flakes, and salt.

Add the feta and toss to coat, being sure not to crumble the feta. Store, covered, in the refrigerator for up to 4 days. Let sit at room temperature for at least 30 minutes before serving to allow the oil to return to liquid.

Nutrition: (⅓ cup): Calories: 311; Fat: 30g; Protein: 8g; Total Carbs: 3g

Buffalo Roasted Cauliflower

SERVINGS 3 | **PREP TIME** 5 minutes | **COOK TIME** 20 minutes

Ingredients:

- 2 cups cauliflower florets
- 1 teaspoon onion powder
- 1 teaspoon garlic powder
- ¼ teaspoon salt
- ⅛ teaspoon freshly ground black pepper
- ⅓ cup hot sauce
- ¼ tsp Worcestershire sauce
- 2 tablespoons bleu cheese dressing
- ¼ cup butter
- 1 tablespoon olive oil
- 1 tablespoon white vinegar

For the bleu cheese sauce

- ⅛ cup crumbled bleu cheese
- 2 tablespoons sour cream

Directions:

Preheat the oven to 425°F. In a large bowl, combine the cauliflower florets, olive oil, garlic powder, onion powder, salt, and pepper. Mix well to season evenly.

On a parchment-lined baking sheet, spread the cauliflower into an even layer. Bake for 20 minutes, or until the edges of the cauliflower pieces begin to brown. In a large skillet over medium-high heat, add the butter and melt. Add the hot sauce, vinegar, and Worcestershire sauce.

Whisk over medium-high heat until the mixture is bubbling. Remove the skillet from the heat. In a small bowl, whisk the bleu cheese dressing and sour cream.

Fold in the crumbled bleu cheese. Cover and refrigerate until ready to serve. In a large bowl, toss the cooked cauliflower with the buffalo sauce to coat. Allow the cauliflower to cool for 1 to 2 minutes before serving with the bleu cheese sauce.

Nutrition: Calories: 340; Fat: 33g; Protein: 7g; Total Carbs: 7g;

Prosciutto and Cream Cheese Stuffed Mushrooms

SERVINGS 4 | **PREP TIME** 5 minutes | **COOK TIME** 20 minutes | TOTAL TIME: 27 minutes

Ingredients:

- ¾ cup cream cheese, at room temperature
- 4 slices prosciutto, chopped
- ¼ teaspoon salt
- 16 small button mushrooms, stemmed, gills removed
- ¼ cup sour cream
- 1 tablespoon olive oil
- 1 tsp chopped fresh parsley
- ⅛ teaspoon freshly ground black pepper

Directions:

Preheat the oven to 400°F. In a large bowl, mix the cream cheese and sour cream. Add the prosciutto, parsley, salt, and pepper. Stir to combine. Spoon equal amounts of the cream cheese and prosciutto mixture into the mushrooms. On a parchment-lined baking sheet, arrange the mushrooms, cream cheese-side up. Drizzle with the olive oil. Bake for 20 minutes, or until slightly browned. Remove the baking sheet from the oven. Cool for 1 to 2 minutes before serving.

Nutrition: (4 stuffed mushrooms): Calories: 279; Fat: 25g; Protein: 12g; Total Carbs: 3g

Jalapeño Poppers

SERVINGS 1 | **PREP TIME** 10 minutes | **COOK TIME** 15 minutes | TOTAL TIME: 25 minutes

Ingredients:

6 jalapeño peppers
2 tsp cream cheese
⅛ teaspoon freshly ground black pepper
½ teaspoon minced garlic
¼ teaspoon salt
1 teaspoon olive oil
4 ounces Monterey Jack cheese, cubed

Directions:

Preheat the oven to 450°F. Wash the jalapeños and cut off the tops. Using a small knife, cut the jalapeños top to bottom without cutting through to the other side. Gently open the peppers and remove the seeds and veins. Set the peppers aside.

To a small bowl, add the minced garlic, cream cheese, salt, and pepper. Mix well to combine. Stuff the jalapeños with the Monterey Jack cheese so they are full but will still close.

With a small spoon or knife, spread an equal amount of cream cheese inside each jalapeño, over the Monterey Jack, to help bind the pepper together. Close the peppers and place them on a baking sheet.

Drizzle the jalapeños with olive oil and place the baking sheet in the preheated oven. Bake for 15 minutes, or until browned.

Nutrition: (6 cheese-stuffed jalapeños): Calories: 254; Fat: 21.5g; Protein: 9.8g; Total Carbs: 7.8g

Garlic Breadsticks

MAKES 8 | **PREP TIME** 15 minutes, plus 30 minutes to rest | **COOK TIME** 15 minutes

Ingredients:

1 cup almond flour
2 teaspoons baking powder
¼ teaspoon salt
2 large eggs
½ cup grated Cheddar cheese 2 ounces (¼ cup) cream cheese
2 tablespoons coconut flour
1 teaspoon garlic powder
2½ cups grated mozzarella cheese
2 tablespoons garlic salt

Directions:

Preheat the oven to 400°F, and line a baking sheet with parchment paper. In a small bowl, stir the almond flour, coconut flour, baking powder, garlic powder, and salt. Set aside. In a medium microwave-safe bowl, combine the mozzarella, Cheddar, and cream cheese. Heat in 30-second increments until the mixture is melted and smooth.

Remove the cheese from the microwave, and stir to blend. Add half the flour mixture, and mix. Add the eggs and remaining flour mixture, and mix until incorporated. Let the dough rest for 30 minutes to make it easier to work with. Spread a piece of parchment paper on the counter. With damp hands, make a ball out of the dough, and split it in half.

Place half the ball on the parchment paper on the counter, and split it into 4 equal parts. Using your palms, roll each part into a 6- to 8-inch breadstick. Place the 4 breadsticks on the baking sheet. Repeat with the remaining dough to make 8 breadsticks total. Sprinkle the garlic salt over the breadsticks. Bake for 13 to 15 minutes, or until golden brown, turning halfway through. Remove from the oven, and serve.

Nutrition: (1 breadstick): Calories: 254; Fat: 20g; Protein: 14g; Total Carbs: 4g

Cheesy Baked Meatballs

SERVINGS 12 | **PREP TIME** 20 minutes | **COOK TIME** 40 minutes

Ingredients:

¼ cup olive oil, plus more for greasing
2 garlic cloves, minced
1 (8-ounce) can tomato sauce 1 teaspoon salt, divided
½ cup crushed pork skins
1½ pounds ground beef
½ teaspoon garlic powder
1 large egg
½ cup grated Parmesan cheese
1 (10-ounce) can diced tomatoes with green chiles, like Ro-tel
¼ teaspoon freshly ground black pepper, divided
¼ cup grated Parmesan cheese
½ cup grated mozzarella cheese

Directions:

Preheat the oven to 375°F, and lightly grease a 9-by-13-inch baking dish. In a medium pot over medium-low heat, heat the olive oil. Add the garlic, and sauté for 1 or 2 minutes.

Reduce heat to low, and add the diced tomatoes, tomato sauce, ½ teaspoon salt, and ⅛ teaspoon pepper. Cook, stirring occasionally, while you make the meatballs. In a large bowl, combine the ground beef, pork skins, Parmesan, egg, garlic powder, and remaining ½ teaspoon salt and ⅛ teaspoon pepper. Mix well, scoop, and roll into 24 balls about 1½ inches in diameter, and place side by side in the prepared baking dish.

Bake for 20 minutes, remove from the oven, cover with the sauce, and top with the grated mozzarella. Bake for another 20 minutes, covering lightly with aluminum foil if the cheese begins to get too brown. Garnish with the Parmesan, and serve.

Nutrition: (2 meatballs): Calories: 220; Fat: 15g; Protein: 16g; Total Carbs: 3.5g

Smoothies & Beverages Recipes

Almond Smoothie

Servings: 2 and **Total Time:** approx. 4 minutes

Ingredients:

- 2 cups almond milk
- 1 tsp cinnamon
- 4 tbsp flax meal
- Drops of stevia to taste
- 1 tbsp almond butter
- ½ cup Greek yogurt
- A handful of ice cubes
- 1 tsp almond extract

Directions:

In a blender, combine the yoghurt, almond milk, almond butter, flax meal, almond extract, and stevia. Blend for 30 seconds, or until uniform and smooth.

Pour into smoothie glasses, add ice cubes, and top with cinnamon. Serve and have fun!

Nutrition: Cal 412; Net Carbs 5.6g; Fat 31g; Protein 21g

Chocolate Protein Cocktail

Servings: 4 and **Total Time:** approx. 10 minutes

Ingredients:

- 4 mint leaves
- 1 tbsp vanilla protein powder
- 3 cups almond milk, chilled
- Whipping cream for topping
- 3 tbsp xylitol
- 1 avocado, pitted, peeled, sliced
- 3 tsp cocoa powder
- 1 cup coconut milk, chilled

Directions:

Blend the almond milk, cocoa powder, avocado, coconut milk, xylitol, and protein powder until smooth in a blender.

Place in serving glasses, top with whipping cream, and garnish with mint leaves.

Nutrition: Cal 287; Net Carbs 5.2g; Fat 15g; Protein 12g

Hot Chocolate

Servings: 2 and **Total Time:** approx. 10 minutes

Ingredients:

- 2 cups unsweetened almond milk
- 1 tbsp unsweetened cocoa powder
- ¼ cup heavy cream
- 2 tbsp stevia extract powder

Directions:

Place a saucepan over medium heat and add the almond milk and heavy cream. While stirring constantly, add the cocoa powder and cook for 2-3 minutes until slightly thickened. Whisk in stevia extract powder and serve hot.

Nutrition: Cal 98; Net Carbs 3g; Fat 10g; Protein 2g

Cold Matcha Latte

Servings: 4 and **Total Time:** approx. 10 minutes

Ingredients:

- 1 cup almond milk, cold
- 1 cup water
- 2 tsp sugar-free coconut syrup
- 2 tsp matcha green tea powder

Directions:

2 cups of water, warmed in the microwave Divide the matcha green tea powder between them and whisk until smooth. For an iced latte, add cold almond milk. Serve and have fun!

Warm the milk in a small saucepan, then pour it into the mug until it's nearly full. For an iced latte, use cold milk.

Nutrition: Cal 65; Net Carbs 4.3g; Fat 3g; Protein 2g

Double Chocolate Shake

SERVINGS 2 | TOTAL TIME: 10 minutes

Ingredients:

1 cup crushed ice, divided	¾ cup unsweetened almond milk
1 tsp unsweetened cocoa powder	1 tablespoon coconut oil
¼ cup heavy (whipping) cream	3 tablespoons unsweetened chocolate protein powder
1 tablespoon chopped 90 percent dark chocolate	1 tablespoon sugar-free chocolate syrup

Directions:

In a blender, blend ½ cup of ice, almond milk, heavy cream, and coconut oil. Add the protein powder, cocoa powder, dark chocolate, chocolate syrup, and remaining ½ cup of ice. Blend for 1 minute, or until smooth, and serve.

Nutrition: Calories: 451; Fat: 41g; Protein: 10g; Total Carbs: 19g

Chocolate Protein Shake

SERVING 1 | PREP TIME 5 minutes

Ingredients:

1 cup unsweetened full-fat coconut milk	1 teaspoon cacao powder
	1 scoop collagen powder
1 tablespoon MCT oil 1 cup fresh spinach	½ teaspoon stevia or 4 drops liquid stevia extract A few ice cubes (optional)

Directions:

Place the coconut milk, collagen, cacao powder, MCT oil, spinach, stevia, ice (if using), and blend until smooth.

Nutrition: Calories: 631; Fat: 55g; Protein: 19g; Total Carbs: 15g

Vanilla Bean Smoothie

SERVINGS 2 | PREP TIME 10 minutes

Ingredients:

1 cup almond milk	½ avocado
2 tablespoons egg white protein powder	Seeds of 1 vanilla bean
¼ teaspoon ground cinnamon 2 cups ice cubes	1 teaspoon coconut oil

Directions:

In a blender, blend the almond milk, avocado, egg white powder, coconut oil, vanilla bean seeds, and cinnamon until combined. Add the ice, and blend until smooth and thick.

Nutrition: Calories: 158; Fat: 13g; Protein: 6g; Total Carbs: 5g;

Vanilla Shake

SERVINGS 2 | TOTAL TIME: 10 minutes

Ingredients:

1 cup crushed ice, divided	1 cup unsweetened almond milk
1 tsp pure vanilla extract	
¼ cup heavy (whipping) cream	3 tablespoons unsweetened vanilla whey protein powder
1 tablespoon coconut oil	

Directions:

In a blender, blend ½ cup of ice, almond milk, heavy cream, and coconut oil. Add the protein powder, vanilla, and remaining ½ cup of ice. Blend for 1 minute, or until smooth, and serve.

Nutrition: Calories: 448; Fat: 41g; Protein: 17g; Total Carbs: 8g

Strawberries and Cream Shake

SERVINGS 2 | PREP TIME 10 minutes

Ingredients:

1 cup crushed ice, divided	¼ cup unsweetened almond milk
1 tablespoon coconut oil	
½ cup heavy (whipping) cream	½ cup strawberries
1 teaspoon pure vanilla extract	

Directions:

In a blender, blend ½ cup of ice, almond milk, heavy cream, and coconut oil. Add the strawberries, vanilla, and remaining ½ cup of ice. Blend for 1 minute, or until smooth, and serve.

Nutrition: Calories: 249; Fat: 25g; Protein: 2g; Total Carbs: 6g;

Cheesecake Smoothie

SERVINGS 2 | PREP TIME 10 minutes

Ingredients:

¾ cup unsweetened almond milk	¼ cup Greek yogurt
2 tablespoons cream cheese	2 (7g) stevia packets
2 cups ice cubes	1 tablespoon heavy (whipping) cream

Directions:

In a blender, blend the almond milk, yogurt, cream cheese, cream, and stevia until combined. Add the ice, and blend until smooth and blend until smooth, and serve.

Nutrition: Calories: 113; Fat: 9g; Protein: 5g; Total Carbs: 2g;

Peanut Butter Shake

SERVINGS 2 | **PREP TIME** 10 minutes

Ingredients:

1 cup crushed ice, divided
2 tablespoons coconut oil
¼ cup heavy (whipping) cream
¼ cup powdered peanut butter (such as PB2)
1 cup unsweetened almond milk

Directions:

In a blender, blend ½ cup of ice, powdered peanut butter and heavy cream. Add the coconut oil, almond milk, and remaining ½ cup of ice. Blend for 1 minute, or until smooth, and serve.

Nutrition: (½ of finished smoothie recipe): Calories: 535; Fat: 51g; Protein: 13g; Total Carbs: 17g

Peanut Butter Cup Protein Smoothie

SERVINGS 2 | **PREP TIME** 5 minutes

Ingredients:

1 cup water
1 scoop chocolate protein powder
¾ cup coconut cream
2 tablespoons natural peanut butter
3 ice cubes

Directions:

Put the water, coconut cream, protein powder, peanut butter, and ice in a blender and blend until smooth.

Nutrition: Calories: 486; Fat: 40g; Protein: 30g; Total Carbs: 11g

Chocolate, Peanut Butter, and Banana Shake

SERVINGS 2 | TOTAL TIME: 10 minutes

Ingredients:

1 cup crushed ice, divided
1 tsp unsweetened peanut butter
1 tablespoon coconut oil
½ tsp pure vanilla extract
1 cup unsweetened almond milk
3 tablespoons unsweetened chocolate protein powder
1½ teaspoons cocoa powder
¼ cup heavy (whipping) cream
1 teaspoon banana extract

Directions:

In a blender, blend ½ cup of ice, protein powder, peanut butter, and coconut oil. Add the cocoa powder, almond milk, heavy cream, banana extract, vanilla, and remaining ½ cup of ice. Blend for 1 minute, or until smooth, and serve.

Nutrition: Calories: 473; Fat: 46g; Protein: 10g; Total Carbs: 11g

Chocolate-Mint Smoothie

SERVINGS 2 | **PREP TIME** 10 minutes

Ingredients:

1 cup unsweetened almond milk
1 teaspoon chopped fresh mint
2 (7g) stevia packets
2 tablespoons cocoa powder
2 tablespoons almond butter
1 cup ice cubes

Directions:

In a blender, blend the almond milk, almond butter, cocoa powder, mint, and stevia until combined. Add the ice, and blend until smooth.

Nutrition: Calories: 129; Fat: 11g; Protein: 5g; Total Carbs: 6g; Fiber: 3g; Net Carbs: 3g

Almond Butter and Cacao Nib Smoothie

SERVINGS 1 | **PREP TIME** 5 minutes

Ingredients:

1 cup unsweetened almond milk
2 tablespoons unsweetened almond butter
1 tablespoon unsweetened cocoa powder
½ teaspoon almond extract (optional)
¼ cup heavy (whipping) cream
1 to 2 teaspoons monk fruit extract or sugar-free sweetener (optional)
1 tablespoon cacao nibs
½ teaspoon ground cinnamon

Directions:

In a blender combine the almond milk, cream, almond butter, cocoa powder, cacao nibs, sweetener (if using), almond extract (if using), and cinnamon. Blend until smooth and creamy, adding more almond milk if needed. Serve garnished with additional cacao nibs if desired.

Nutrition: Calories: 506; Fat: 47g; Protein: 11g; Total Carbs: 16g

In a blender, combine the avocado slices, blueberries, coconut milk, coconut cream, and erythritol and blend until smooth. Pour the smoothie into serving glasses and top with coconut flakes.

Nutrition: Cal 392; Net Carbs 8.6g; Fat 32g; Protein 10g

Vegan Chocolate Smoothie

Servings: 2 and **Total Time:** approx. 10 minutes

Ingredients:

- 1 tbsp unsweetened cocoa powder
- ¾ cup coconut milk
- 1 ½ cups watercress
- ¼ cup pumpkin seeds
- 2 tsp vegan protein powder
- ¼ cup water
- 1 tbsp chia seeds

Directions:

Blend all Ingredients except the chia seeds in a blender until creamy and uniform. Chill before serving in two glasses, dusted with chia seeds.

Nutrition: Cal 335; Net Carbs 5.7g; Fat 29g; Protein 7g

Quick Raspberry Vanilla Shake

Servings: 2 and **Total Time:** approx. 5 minutes

Ingredients:

- 1 cup raspberries
- 6 raspberries to garnish
- 2/3 tsp vanilla extract
- 2 tbsp erythritol
- ½ cup cold almond milk
- ½ cup heavy whipping cream

Directions:

In a large blender, process the raspberries, milk, vanilla extract, whipping cream, and erythritol for 2 minutes; work in two batches if needed. The shake should be frosty. Pour into glasses, stick in straws, garnish with raspberries and serve.

Nutrition: Cal 213; Net Carbs 8.7g; Fat 13g; Protein 4g

Blueberry Coconut Smoothie

Servings: 2 and **Total Time:** approx. 5 minutes

Ingredients:

- 1 avocado, pitted and sliced
- 1 cup coconut milk
- 6 tbsp coconut cream
- 1 cup blueberries
- 2 tbsp erythritol
- 2 tbsp coconut flakes

Directions:

Creamy Vanilla Cappuccino

Servings: 2 and **Total Time:** approx. 6 minutes

Ingredients:

- 2 cups unsweetened vanilla almond milk, chilled
- 1 tsp swerve sugar
- 1 cup cottage cheese, cold
- ¼ tsp xanthan gum
- Unsweetened chocolate shavings to garnish
- ½ tbsp powdered coffee
- ½ tsp vanilla bean paste

Directions:

Blend the almond milk, swerve sugar, cottage cheese, coffee, vanilla bean paste, and xanthan gum for 1 minute on high speed until smooth. Serve immediately in tall shake glasses topped with chocolate shavings.

Nutrition: Cal 253; Net Carbs 6.2g; Fat 18g; Protein 5g

Turmeric Latte

Servings: 2 and **Total Time:** approx. 10 minutes

Ingredients:

- 2 cups almond milk
- ½ cup brewed coffee
- ¼ tsp turmeric powder
- 1/3 tsp cinnamon powder
- 1 tsp xylitol
- Nutmeg powder to garnish

Directions:

Add the almond milk, cinnamon powder, coffee, turmeric, and xylitol to the blender. Blend the Ingredients: at medium speed for 50 seconds and pour the mixture into a saucepan. Over low heat, set the pan and heat through for 6 minutes, without boiling. Keep swirling the pan to prevent it from boiling. Turn the heat off, and serve in latte cups topped with nutmeg powder.

Nutrition: Cal 73; Net Carbs 3.9g; Fat 4.5g; Protein 3g

Detox Drink

Servings: 2 and **Total Time:** approx. 5 minutes

Ingredients:

1 small cucumber, peeled and chopped	2 large ripe avocados, halved and pitted
2 tbsp Swerve sugar	¼ cup cold almond milk
½ tsp vanilla extract	1 tbsp cold heavy cream

Directions:

In a blender, add the avocado pulp, cucumber, Swerve sugar, almond milk, vanilla extract, and heavy cream. Process until smooth. Pour the mixture into 2 tall serving glasses, garnish with strawberries, and serve immediately.

Nutrition: Cal 423; Net Carbs 8.5g; Fat 34g; Protein 7g

Loaded Denver Omelet

SERVINGS 1 | **PREP TIME** 5 minutes | **COOK TIME** 5 minutes

Ingredients:

1 tablespoon butter Freshly ground black pepper 2 tablespoons diced ham	3 large eggs Sea salt 1 scallion, white and green parts thinly sliced
¼ bell pepper, seeds and ribs removed, thinly sliced	2 tablespoons shredded Cheddar cheese

Directions:

Melt the butter in a small nonstick skillet over medium heat. Whisk the eggs in a small bowl and season with salt and pepper. Pour the eggs into the skillet and cook for 1 to 2 minutes, or until barely set around the edges. Lift up the edges with a spatula and tilt the pan so the liquid eggs slide underneath. Sprinkle the ham, scallion, bell pepper, and shredded cheese over the eggs and continue cooking for another minute. Fold the omelet in half and cook for 1 minute. Flip carefully and cook for 1 more minute or until the center of the omelet is no longer watery.

Nutrition: Calories: 415; Fat: 33g; Protein: 26g; Total Carbs: 4g

Baked Omelet with Pancetta and Swiss Cheese

SERVINGS 4 | **PREP TIME** 10 minutes | **COOK TIME** 40 minutes

Ingredients:

1 tablespoon butter, plus more for greasing	10 large eggs
1 cup canned coconut milk	1 cup diced pancetta
2 teaspoons chopped chives	1 cup shredded Swiss cheese
Freshly ground black pepper	Pinch sea salt

Directions:

Preheat the oven to 350°F. Lightly grease a 9-inch-square baking dish with butter, and set aside. In a large skillet over medium-high heat, melt the butter. Cook the pancetta, stirring, until it is crispy, about 4 minutes. Remove the skillet from the heat, and transfer the pancetta to a medium bowl.

Add the eggs, coconut milk, cheese, and chives to the bowl, and whisk to blend. Season the egg mixture with salt and pepper. Pour the egg mixture into the baking dish, and bake the omelet until it is set, puffy, and golden, about 30 minutes, and serve.

Nutrition: Calories: 496; Fat: 41g; Protein: 27g; Total Carbs: 6g

Skillet-Baked Eggs with Yogurt and Spinach

SERVINGS 4 | **PREP TIME** 10 minutes | **COOK TIME** 25 minutes

Ingredients:

½ cup plain Greek-style yogurt	1 teaspoon freshly squeezed lemon juice
¼ teaspoon chili powder	2 tablespoons extra-virgin olive oil
2 tablespoons butter	4 large eggs
½ white onion, diced	
8 cups spinach	1 tsp chopped cilantro

Directions:

In a small bowl, stir the yogurt, lemon juice, and chili powder, and set aside. Preheat the oven to 350°F. In a large, ovenproof skillet over medium heat, heat the butter and olive oil.

Add the onion, and sauté until soft, about 5 minutes. Stir in the spinach, and sauté, tossing frequently, until wilted, about 5 minutes. Push the spinach to the side of the skillet, and spoon out any extra liquid. Arrange the spinach so it covers the entire bottom of the skillet, and use a spoon to make 4 wells in the greens.

Break the eggs into the wells, and place the skillet in the oven. Bake until the whites are set, about 10 minutes. Spoon the yogurt mixture over the eggs, top with the cilantro, and serve.

Nutrition: Calories: 241; Fat: 23g; Protein: 9g; Total Carbs: 5g;

Mediterranean Frittata

SERVINGS 2 | **PREP TIME** 10 minutes | **COOK TIME** 15 minutes

Ingredients:

- 4 large eggs
- 1 teaspoon dried herbs
- 8 cherry tomatoes, halved
- ¼ teaspoon salt
- ¼ cup extra-virgin olive oil, divided
- 4 ounces quartered artichoke hearts, rinsed, drained, and thoroughly dried
- 2 tablespoons fresh chopped herbs, such as rosemary, thyme, oregano, basil
- Freshly ground black pepper
- 1 cup fresh spinach, arugula, kale, or other leafy greens
- ½ cup crumbled soft goat cheese

Directions:

Preheat the oven to broil on low. In a small bowl, whisk the eggs, herbs, salt, and pepper. Set aside. In a 4- to 5-inch oven-safe skillet heat 2 tablespoons of olive oil over medium heat.

Add the spinach, artichoke hearts, and cherry tomatoes and sauté until just wilted, 1 to 2 minutes. Pour in the egg mixture and let it cook undisturbed over medium heat for 3 to 4 minutes, until the eggs begin to set on the bottom. Sprinkle the goat cheese across the top of the egg mixture and transfer the skillet to the oven. Broil for 4 to 5 minutes, or until the frittata is firm in the center and golden brown on top.

Remove from the oven and run a rubber spatula around the edge. Invert onto a large plate or cutting board and slice in half. Serve warm and drizzled with the remaining 2 tablespoons olive oil.

Nutrition: Calories: 527; Fat: 47g; Protein: 21g; Total Carbs: 10g

Asparagus Frittata

SERVINGS 4 | **PREP TIME** 10 minutes | **COOK TIME** 20 minutes

Ingredients:

- ½ cup extra-virgin olive oil, divided
- 1 pound medium-thin asparagus, rough stalks trimmed, cut 1-inch pieces
- 2 tablespoons vegetable broth 1 teaspoon salt
- ¼ cup Zesty Orange for serving
- ¼ cup finely chopped white onion (about ½ small onion)
- 6 large eggs
- 2 medium garlic cloves, minced
- ½ teaspoon freshly ground black pepper
- ½ cup chopped herbs (basil, parsley, or mint), for garnish (optional)

Directions:

In a large skillet, heat ¼ cup of olive oil over medium heat. Add the onion and sauté for 3 to 4 minutes, until the onion begins to soften. Add the asparagus and garlic and cook until the asparagus is tender, 5 to 6 minutes.

Transfer the cooked vegetables to a bowl and let cool. In a medium bowl, whisk the eggs, vegetable broth, salt, and pepper. Add the cooled asparagus and mix until well combined. In the same skillet, heat 2 tablespoons of olive oil over medium-high heat.

Pour the egg mixture into the skillet and reduce the heat to medium-low. Let the eggs cook undisturbed for 2 to 3 minutes, or until the bottom begins to set. Cook, continuously moving the uncooked egg mixture until the top is a little wet but not liquid, 3 to 5 minutes.

Place a large flat plate or cutting board on top of the skillet and quickly invert the tortilla. Add the remaining 2 tablespoons of olive oil to the skillet and carefully slide the tortilla back into the pan, uncooked-side down.

Cook over low heat until cooked through, another 2 to 3 minutes. Transfer back to the plate or cutting board. Rest for 5 minutes before slicing. Serve warm.

Nutrition: Calories: 444; Fat: 40g; Protein: 12g; Total Carbs: 9g

Keto's Other Favorites

Tofu and Avocado Sandwiches

Servings: 2 and **Total Time:** approx. 10 minutes

Ingredients:

- 4 little gem lettuce leaves
- 1 tsp chopped parsley
- ½ oz butter, softened
- 4 tofu slices
- 1 avocado, sliced
- 1 large red tomato, sliced

Directions:

Place the lettuce on a flat serving plate. Smear each leaf with butter and arrange tofu slices on the leaves. Top with the avocado and tomato slices. Garnish the sandwiches with parsley and serve.

Nutrition: Cal 390; Net Carbs 4g; Fat 29g; Protein 12g

Broccoli Mushroom Risotto

Servings: 4 and **Total Time:** approx. 30 minutes

Ingredients:

- 1 cup cremini mushrooms, chopped
- 2 garlic cloves, minced
- ¾ cup white wine
- ¾ cup grated Parmesan
- Salt and black pepper to taste
- 4 oz butter
- 1 head broccoli, grated
- 1 red onion, finely chopped
- 1 cup coconut cream
- 1 teaspoon chopped thyme

Directions:

Melt the butter in a saucepan over medium heat. Sauté mushrooms until golden, 5 minutes. Add in garlic and onion and cook for 3 minutes until fragrant and soft.

Mix in broccoli, 1 cup of water, and white wine. Season with salt and pepper and simmer for 10 minutes. Mix in coconut cream and simmer until most of the cream evaporates. Turn heat off and stir in Parmesan and thyme. Serve warm.

Nutrition: Cal 519; Net Carbs 12g; Fat 39g; Protein 15g

Quick Strawberry Mousse

Servings: 4 and **Total Time:** approx. 10 min + chilling time

Ingredients:

- 1 large egg white
- 2 cups frozen strawberries
- 2 cups whipped cream
- 2 tbsp Swerve sugar

Directions:

Pour 1 ½ cups strawberries and swerve sugar in a blender; process until smooth. Pour in the egg white and transfer the mixture to a bowl. Use an electric hand mixer to whisk until fluffy. Spoon the mixture into dessert glasses and top with whipped cream and strawberries. Serve chilled.

Nutrition: Cal 150; Net Carbs 4.8g; Fats 7g; Protein 2g

Beef Ceeseburgers

Servings: 2 and **Total Time:** approx. 20 minutes

Ingredients:

- 1 tbsp olive oil
- 2 sprigs parsley, chopped
- 1 tsp yellow mustard
- 1 spring onion, chopped
- Salt, black pepper, and cayenne pepper to taste
- ½ lb ground beef
- 1 oz cheddar cheese, grated

Directions:

To a mixing bowl, add ground beef, cayenne pepper, black pepper, spring onion, parsley, and salt. Shape into 2 balls, then flatten to make burgers.

In a separate bowl, mix mustard and cheddar cheese. Split the cheese mixture between the prepared patties.

Wrap the meat mixture around the cheese to ensure that the filling is sealed inside.

Warm oil in a skillet over medium heat. Cook the burgers for 5 minutes on each side.

Nutrition: Cal 386; Net Carbs 3.3g; Fat 25g; Protein 32g

Baked Sausage & Peppers

Servings: 2 and **Total Time:** approx. 35 minutes

Ingredients:

1 cucumber, sliced	1 large tomato, chopped
2 teaspoon dried parsley	2 red bell peppers
Salt black pepper to taste	1 teaspoon dried basil
1 teaspoon butter, melted	1 lb sausages, sliced
1 teaspoon mayonnaise	2 teaspoon Greek yogurt

Directions:

Preheat the oven's broiler to 420 F and line a baking sheet with parchment paper.

Arrange the bell peppers and sausages on the baking sheet, drizzle with the melted butter, and season with basil, salt, and black pepper.

Bake in the oven for 20 minutes.

Meanwhile, in a salad bowl, combine the Greek yogurt, mayonnaise, cucumber, tomato, salt, black pepper, and parsley; set aside. When the bake is ready, remove it from the oven and serve with the salad.

Nutrition: Cal 463; Net Carbs 5.3g; Fat 40g; Protein 20g

Beef Bolognese Squashed

Servings: 4 and **Total Time:** approx. 65 minutes

Ingredients:

Bolognese	2 teaspoon olive oil
1 onion, chopped	1 garlic clove, minced
1 small carrot, chopped	½ lb ground beef
2 teaspoon tomato paste	1 ½ cups tomatoes, crushed
12 oz butternut squash	Salt and black pepper to taste
2 tbsp butter	1 tbsp dried basil

Directions:

Pour the olive oil into a saucepan and heat over medium heat. Add in the onion, garlic, and carrot. Sauté for 3 minutes or until the onion is soft and the carrot caramelized.

Pour in the ground beef, tomato paste, tomatoes, salt, black pepper, and basil. Stir and cook for 15 minutes, or simmer for 30 minutes. Mix in some water if the mixture is too thick and simmer for 20 minutes.

Melt the butter in a skillet over medium heat and toss the butternut squash quickly in the butter, for about 1 minute only. Season with salt and black pepper. Divide the butternut squash into serving plates and spoon the sauce on top. Serve the dish immediately.

Nutrition: Cal 295; Net Carbs 12.5g; Fat 21g; Protein 13g

Ricotta Balls

Servings: 2 and **Total Time:** approx. 20 minutes

Ingredients:

Cheese balls	1/3 cup ricotta cheese, crumbled
1 tsp lemon juice	2 tbsp Grana Padano cheese, shredded
1 egg	
Salt to taste	
1/3 cup almond flour	1/3 tsp flax meal
Salt and black pepper to taste	Salad
2 cups arugula leaves	½ tsp mustard
1 small cucumber, thinly sliced	1 tomato, sliced
	2 tbsp mayonnaise
1 green onion, sliced	4 radishes, sliced

Directions:

In a mixing dish, combine ricotta cheese, Grana Padano cheese, flax meal, and almond flour.

Add in the egg, salt, and black pepper and stir well. Form balls out of the mixture. Set the balls on a parchment-lined baking sheet and bake for 10 minutes at 380 F. Lay arugula leaves on a large salad platter; add in radishes, tomato, cucumber, and green onion.

In a small bowl, mix the mayonnaise, salt, lemon juice, and mustard. Sprinkle this mixture over the vegetables. Add cheese balls on top and serve.

Nutrition: Cal 255; Net Carbs 3.9g; Fat 19g; Protein 13g

Broccoli Creamy Cheese Soup

Servings: 2 and **Total Time:** approx. 25 minutes

Ingredients:

2 tbsp peanut butter	1 tbsp olive oil
¾ cup heavy cream	1 garlic, minced
4 cups veggie broth	4 cups chopped broccoli
2 ¾ cups cheddar, grated	Salt black pepper to taste
¼ cup cheddar, to garnish	½ bunch fresh mint, chopped
1 onion, diced	

Directions:

Warm the olive oil and peanut butter in a pot over medium heat. Sauté onion and garlic for 3 minutes, stirring occasionally.

Season with salt and pepper. Add the broth and broccoli and bring to a boil.

Reduce the heat and simmer for 10 minutes. Puree the soup with a hand blender until smooth. Add in the cheese and cook for about 1 minute.

Stir in the heavy cream. Serve in bowls with the reserved grated cheddar cheese and sprinkled with fresh mint.

Nutrition: Cal 552; Net Carbs 6.9g; Fat 49g; Protein 25g

Crunchy Cauliflower with Mash

Servings: 6 and **Total Time:** approx. 55 minutes

Ingredients:

- 2 tbsp sesame oil
- 1 lb parsnips, quartered
- 1 tsp cumin powder
- ¼ tsp cayenne pepper
- 1 cup coconut cream
- ½ cup grated cheddar cheese
- 20 oz cauliflower florets
- ½ cup almond milk
- ¼ cup coconut flour
- ½ cup almond breadcrumbs
- 3 tbsp melted butter
- A pinch of nutmeg

Directions:

Preheat oven to 425 F. Line a baking sheet with parchment paper. In a bowl, combine almond milk, coconut flour, and cayenne. In another

bowl, mix breadcrumbs and cheddar cheese. Dip each cauliflower floret into the milk mixture, and then into the cheese mixture.

Place breaded cauliflower on the baking sheet and bake for 30 minutes, turning once. Pour 4 cups of slightly salted water into a pot and add in parsnips. Bring to boil and cook for 15 minutes. Drain and transfer to a bowl.

Add in melted butter, cumin, nutmeg, and coconut cream. Mash the ingredients using a potato mash. Spoon the mash into plates and drizzle with sesame oil. Serve with baked cauliflower.

Nutrition: Cal 390; Net Carbs 8g; Fat 30g; Protein 10g

Mixed Mushroom Pizza with Pepperoni

Servings: 2 and **Total Time:** approx. 25 minutes

Ingredients:

- ¾ cup mozzarella, shredded
- 2 oz mixed mushrooms, sliced
- 2 tbsp olive oil
- 2 (1 pack) cauliflower pizza crusts
- 1 tbsp basil pesto
- Salt black pepper to taste
- 4 oz pepperoni, sliced

Directions:

Preheat the oven to 350 F. Grease two baking dishes with cooking spray. Add in the two cauliflower crusts.

In a bowl, mix the mushrooms with pesto, olive oil, salt, and black pepper. Divide the mozzarella cheese on top of the pizza crusts.

Spread the mushroom mixture and cover with the pepperoni slices.

Bake the pizzas in batches until the cheese has melted, about 8 minutes. Remove when ready, cut, and serve with a spinach salad.

Nutrition: Cal 512; Net Carbs 4.6g; Fat 41g; Protein 28g

Cauliflower & Mushroom Arancini

Servings: 4 and **Total Time:** approx. 25 minutes

Ingredients:

- 1 cup cauliflower rice
- 1 garlic clove, minced
- 4 tbsp ground flax seeds
- 4 tbsp sunflower seeds
- 1 tsp mustard
- ½ cup Pecorino cheese, grated
- 2 tbsp butter, softened
- 1 cup mushrooms, chopped
- 4 tbsp hemp seeds
- 1 tbsp dried basil
- 1 egg

Directions:

Set a pan over medium heat and warm 1 tablespoon of butter. Add in mushrooms and garlic and sauté until there is no more water in the mushrooms. Remove to a bowl and let cool for a few minutes. Place in

Pecorino cheese, cauliflower rice, hemp seeds, mustard, egg, sunflower seeds, flax seeds, and basil. Create balls from the mixture.

In a pan, warm the remaining butter; fry the balls for 7 minutes. Flip them over with a wide spatula and cook for 6 more minutes. Serve and enjoy!

Nutrition: Cal 283; Net Carbs 7.2g; Fat 29g; Protein 15g

Brussels Sprouts with Spiced Halloumi

Servings: 2 and **Total Time:** approx. 35 minutes

Ingredients:

- 1 tbsp coconut oil
- 4 oz butter
- 10 oz halloumi cheese, sliced
- 1 tsp chili powder
- ½ tsp onion powder
- ½ cup unsweetened coconut, shredded
- ½ lb Brussels sprouts, halved
- Lemon wedges for serving
- Salt and black pepper to taste

Directions:

In a bowl, mix the shredded coconut, chili powder, salt, coconut oil, and onion powder. Then, toss the halloumi slices in the spice mixture.

Heat a grill pan over medium heat and cook the coated halloumi cheese for 2-3 minutes. Transfer to a plate to keep warm. In a skillet, melt half of the butter, add, and sauté the Brussels sprouts until slightly caramelized. Season with salt and pepper.

Dish the Brussels sprouts into serving plates with the halloumi cheese and lemon wedges. Melt the remaining butter in the skillet and drizzle over the Brussels sprouts and halloumi cheese. Serve.

Nutrition: Cal 574; Net Carbs 6.2g; Fat 47g; Protein 21g

Pecan Arugula Pizza

Servings: 4 and **Total Time:** approx. 35 minutes

Ingredients:

1 tbsp olive oil	1 cup grated mozzarella
1 tomato, thinly sliced	½ cup almond flour
2 tbsp ground psyllium husk	1 cup basil pesto
1 zucchini, cut into half-moons	1 cup baby arugula
	¼ tsp red chili flakes
2 tbsp chopped pecans	

Directions:

Preheat oven to 390 F. Line a baking sheet with parchment paper. In a bowl, mix almond flour, psyllium powder, olive oil, and 1 cup of lukewarm water until dough forms.

Spread the mixture on the sheet and bake for 10 minutes. Spread pesto on the crust and top with mozzarella cheese, tomato slices, and zucchini. Bake until the cheese melts, 15 minutes. Top with arugula, pecans, and red chili flakes.

Nutrition: Cal 191; Net Carbs 3g; Fat 14g; Protein 9g

Spinach Pesto

Servings: 2 and **Total Time:** approx. 10 minutes

Ingredients:

2 cups baby spinach	3 garlic cloves, minced
¼ cup pine nuts	¼ cup grated Parmesan cheese
Salt and black pepper to taste	
½ cup extra-virgin olive oil	

Directions:

In a food processor, place all the Ingredients except for the olive oil; pulse until the mixture is finely chopped. While the food processor is running, pour in the olive oil in a thin stream and blend until the pesto is smooth.

Nutrition: Cal 655; Net Carbs 3.5g; Fat 65g; Protein 8g

Pepperoni Fat Head Pizza

Servings: 4 and **Total Time:** approx. 30 minutes

Ingredients:

1 egg, beaten	1 ½ cups grated mozzarella
4 tbsp tomato sauce	2 tbsp cream cheese, softened
1 tsp dried oregano	¾ cup almond flour
½ cup sliced pepperoni	

Directions:

Preheat oven to 420 F. Line a round pizza pan with parchment paper. Microwave the mozzarella cheese and cream cheese for 1 minute.

Stir in egg and add in the almond flour; mix well. Transfer the pizza "dough" onto a flat surface and knead until smooth. Spread it on the pizza pan. Bake for 6 minutes. Top with tomato sauce, remaining mozzarella, oregano, and pepperoni. Bake for 15 minutes. Serve sliced.

Nutrition: Cal 230; Net Carbs 3.4g; Fat 17g; Protein 16g

Berry Pancakes

Servings: 4 and **Total Time:** approx. 25 minutes

Ingredients:

1 cup of strawberries and raspberries, mashed	1 handful fresh strawberries and raspberries for topping
1 egg	½ cup almond flour
1 tbsp Swerve sugar	1 tsp baking soda
A pinch of cinnamon powder	½ cup almond milk
1 cup Greek yogurt	A pinch of salt
2 tsp butter	

Directions:

In a mixing bowl, combine almond flour, baking soda, salt, Swerve sugar, and cinnamon. Whisk in mashed berries, egg, and milk until smooth. Melt ½ tsp of butter

in a skillet and pour 1 tbsp of the mixture into the pan. Cook until small bubbles appear, flip, and cook until golden. Transfer to a plate and proceed using up the remaining batter for pancakes. Top pancakes with yogurt and whole berries.

Nutrition: Cal 229; Net Carbs 8.6g; Fat 15g; Protein 10g

Sweets Recipes And Desserts Recipes

Creamy Avocado Custard

Servings: 4 and **Total Time:** approx. 10 min + chilling time

Ingredients:
- 3 soft avocados
- ½ cup heavy cream
- ½ cup water
- 1 tsp agar agar powder
- ½ lime, juiced
- Salt and black pepper to taste

Directions:

Place ¼ cup of the water in a bowl and sprinkle agar agar powder on top; set aside to dissolve. Core, peel avocados, and add the flesh to a food processor. Add in heavy cream, lime juice, salt, and pepper.

Process until smooth and pour in agar agar liquid. Blend further until smooth. Divide the mixture between 4 ramekins and chill overnight. Serve and enjoy!

Nutrition: Cal 302; Net Carbs 4.9g; Fat 27g; Protein 2.9g

Blackberry Scones

Servings: 4 and **Total Time:** approx. 30 min + cooling time

Ingredients:
- 2 eggs, beaten
- 2 tsp erythritol
- 1 ½ tsp baking powder
- ½ cup blackberries, halves
- 1 ½ tsp pure vanilla extract
- 1 cup almond flour

Directions:

Preheat oven to 350 F. Line a baking sheet with parchment paper. In a food processor, mix almond flour, eggs, erythritol, vanilla, and baking powder until smooth. Fold in blackberries.

Pour and spread the mixture on the sheet. Cut into 8 wedges like a pizza; bake for 20 minutes or until set and golden brown. Let cool and serve.

Nutrition: Cal 164; Net Carbs 4.3g; Fat 11g; Protein 9g

Strawberries Ricotta Parfait

Servings: 4 and **Total Time:** approx. 10 minutes

Ingredients:
- 1 cup ricotta cheese
- 2 tbsp sugar-free maple syrup
- 2 cups strawberries, chopped
- 2 tbsp balsamic vinegar

Directions:

Place half of the strawberries in each of four small glasses and top with ricotta cheese. Finish with the remaining strawberries and drizzle with maple syrup and balsamic vinegar. Serve.

Nutrition: Cal 159; Net Carbs 7g; Fats 8g; Protein 7g

Coconut Panna Cotta Caramel

Servings: 4 and **Total Time:** approx. 65 min + chilling time

Ingredients:
- 4 eggs
- 2 cups coconut milk
- 1 tbsp lemon zest
- 2 cups heavy whipping cream Mint leaves, to serve
- 1/3 cup erythritol
- 1 tbsp vanilla extract
- ½ cup erythritol, for custard

Directions:

In a deep pan, heat the erythritol for the caramel. Add two tablespoons of water and bring to a boil. Lower the heat and cook until the caramel turns to a golden brown color. Divide between 4 metal tins, set aside and let cool. In a bowl, mix the eggs, remaining erythritol, lemon zest, and vanilla. Beat in the coconut milk until well combined.

Preheat your oven to 350 F. Pour the custard into each caramel-lined ramekin and place them into a deep baking tin. Fill over the way with the remaining hot water. Bake in the oven for around 45 minutes.

Carefully take out the ramekins with tongs and refrigerate for at least 3 hours. Run a knife slowly around the edges to invert onto a dish. Serve with dollops of whipped cream and scattered with mint leaves.

Nutrition: Cal 558; Net Carbs 6.5g; Fat 55g; Protein 9g

Almond Cookies

Servings: 4 and **Total Time:** approx. 40 minutes

Ingredients:

1 large egg	1 cup butter, softened
1 tsp baking powder	2 ¼ cups almond flour
1 cup Swerve sugar	¾ tsp almond extract
½ tsp salt	

Directions:

Preheat oven to 380 F. Line a baking sheet with parchment paper. In a bowl, mix almond flour, baking powder, and salt.

In another bowl, mix butter, Swerve sugar, egg, and almond extract until well smooth. Combine both mixtures until soft dough forms.

Lay a parchment paper on a flat surface, place the dough, and cover with another parchment paper. Using a rolling pin, flatten it into the ½- inch thickness and cut it into squares.

Arrange on the baking sheet with 1-inch intervals and bake in the oven until the edges are set and golden brown, about 25 minutes. Serve cooled.

Nutrition: Cal 430; Net Carbs 0.4g; Fat 46g; Protein 1.4g

Chocolate Vanilla Cake

Servings: 4 and **Total Time:** approx. 55 min + cooling time

Ingredients:

½ cup dark chocolate, melted	3 large eggs
½ cup olive oil	1 cup almond flour
1 cup Swerve sugar	2 tsp vanilla bean paste
½ tsp salt	2 tsp cinnamon powder
½ cup boiling water	2 tbsp erythritol powder

Directions:

Preheat oven to 370 F. Grease a springform pan and line with parchment paper. In a bowl, combine olive oil, almond flour, dark chocolate, Swerve, vanilla bean paste, salt, cinnamon, and boiling water.

Beat in the eggs one after the other until smooth.

Pour batter into the springform pan and bake for 25-35 minutes or until an inserted toothpick comes out clean.

Remove from oven and allow cooling in the pan completely. Run a wooden spatula along the sides and turn over onto a plate. Dust with erythritol powder; serve.

Nutrition: Cal 361; Net Carbs 3g, Fat 35g, Protein 15g

Cowboy Cookies

Servings: 8 and **Total Time:** approx. 30 minutes

Ingredients:

2 large eggs	2 cups almond flour
2 tsp baking powder	1 tsp baking soda
1 cup butter, softened	1 cup Swerve white sugar
1 cup Swerve brown sugar	1 tbsp vanilla extract
1 tbsp cinnamon powder	1 cup sugar-free chocolate chips
1 tsp salt	2 cups golden flaxseed meal
1 cup peanut butter chips	
1 ½ cups coconut flakes	2 cups chopped walnuts

Directions:

Preheat the oven to 380 degrees Fahrenheit. Preheat the oven to 350°F. Line a baking sheet with parchment paper. In a large mixing bowl, cream the butter, Swerve white and brown sugar, and vanilla extract with a hand mixer until light and fluffy.

Slowly incorporate the vanilla and eggs until smooth. Mix almond flour, baking powder, baking soda, cinnamon, and salt in a separate bowl.

Fold in the chocolate chips, peanut butter chips, flaxseed meal, coconut flaxseeds, and walnuts. Roll the dough into 12-inch balls and place at 2-inch intervals on a baking sheet. Bake for 10-12 minutes, or until the top is lightly golden. Cool before serving.

Nutrition: Cal 440; Net Carbs 4.6g; Fat 40g; Protein 16g

Buttery Dark Chocolate Cookies

Servings: 4 and **Total Time:** approx. 35 minutes

Ingredients:

2 eggs	1 cup dark chocolate chips
1 ½ cups almond flour	½ cup cocoa powder
1 tsp baking soda	12 tbsp butter, softened
¾ cup Swerve sugar	1 tsp vanilla extract

Directions:

Preheat oven to 360 F. Line a baking sheet with parchment paper. In a bowl, mix almond flour, cocoa powder, and baking soda. In a separate bowl, cream the butter and Swerve sugar until light and fluffy. Mix in the eggs, vanilla extract and then combine both mixtures. Fold in the chocolate chips until well distributed. Roll the dough into 1 ½-inch balls and arrange on the sheet at 2-inch intervals. Bake for 22 minutes until lightly golden.

Nutrition: Cal 269; Net Carbs 3.7g; Fat 29g; Protein 7g

Cranberries Cheesecake Bars

Servings: 4 and **Total Time:** approx. 35 min + chilling time

Ingredients:
- For the crust
- 2 tbsp Swerve confectioner's
- For the cheesecake layer
- 8 oz cream cheese
- 1 egg yolk
- 2 tsp pure vanilla extract
- 8 tbsp melted butter
- 1 ¼ cups almond flour
- For the cranberry layer
- 1 cup unsweetened cranberry sauce
- 1/3 cup Swerve confectioner's

Directions:

For the crust, preheat oven to 360 F. Line a baking sheet with parchment paper. In a bowl, mix butter, almond flour, and Swerve sugar. Spread and press the mixture onto the baking sheet and bake for 13 minutes or until golden brown.

For the cheesecake layer, whisk cream cheese, egg yolk, Swerve sugar, and vanilla in a bowl using an electric hand mixer until smooth. Spread the mixture on the crust when ready. Bake further for 15 minutes or until the filling sets. Remove from the oven, spread cranberry sauce on top, and refrigerate for 1 hour. Cut into bars and serve.

Nutrition: Cal 431; Net Carbs 4.5g; Fat 35g; Protein 20g

Blueberry Soufflé

Servings: 4 and **Total Time:** approx. 35 minutes

Ingredients:
- 4 egg yolks
- 1 cup frozen blueberries
- 5 tbsp erythritol
- ½ lemon, zested
- 3 egg whites
- 1 tsp olive oil

Directions:

Place a saucepan over medium heat and pour in the blueberries, 2 tbsp erythritol, and 1 tbsp water. Cook until the berries soften and become syrupy, 8-10 minutes. Set aside. Preheat oven to 350 F. In a bowl, beat egg yolks and 1 tbsp of erythritol until thick and pale. In another bowl, whisk egg whites until foamy.

Add in remaining erythritol and whisk until soft peak forms, 3-4 minutes. Fold egg white mixture into egg yolk mixture. Heat olive oil in a pan over low heat. Add in olive oil and pour in the egg mixture; swirl to spread. Cook for 3 minutes and transfer to the oven; bake for 2-3 minutes or until puffed and set. Plate soufflé and spoon blueberry sauce all over. Garnish with lemon zest.

Nutrition: Cal 102; Net Carbs 4.8g; Fat 6g; Protein 5.5g

Ginger Fudge with Chocolate

Servings: 4 and **Total Time:** approx. 30 minutes

Ingredients:
- 1 cup unsweetened dark chocolate, melted
- 1 cup Swerve sugar
- 1/3 cup coconut flour
- ¼ tsp ginger extract
- 4 large eggs
- ½ cup butter, melted

Directions:

Preheat the oven to 350 degrees Fahrenheit and line a rectangular baking sheet with parchment paper. Cream the eggs with the Swerve sugar in a mixing bowl until smooth. Whisk in the melted chocolate, butter, and ginger extract until well combined.

Fold in the coconut flour carefully, then pour the mixture into the baking tray. Bake for 20 minutes, or until a toothpick inserted into the centre comes out clean. Allow to cool in the tray after removing from the oven. Following that, cut into squares and serve.

Nutrition: Cal 427; Net Carbs 8.8g; Fat 42g; Protein 7g

Chocolate Energy Balls with Lime

Servings: 4 and **Total Time:** approx. 15 min + chilling time

Ingredients:
- 1/3 cup dark chocolate, chopped
- 1 lime, zested
- 1/4 tsp salt
- 1/3 cup heavy cream
- 1 tsp lime extract
- 2 tbsp cocoa powder
- 1 tbsp Swerve sugar

Directions:

Mix the cocoa powder with Swerve sugar in a small bowl and set aside. Heat the heavy cream in a small pan over low heat until tiny bubbles form around the edges of the pan. Turn the heat off.

Pour the dark chocolate and salt into the pan, swirl the pan to allow the hot cream over the chocolate, and then stir the mixture until smooth. Mix in the lime extract and transfer the mixture to a bowl.

Refrigerate for 4 hours and more. Line a baking tray with parchment paper. Pour the cocoa powder mixture into a shallow dish and the lime zest in a separate one.

Take out the chocolate mixture; form bite-size balls out of the mix and roll all around in the lime zest, and then completely coat in the cocoa powder. Place the truffles on the baking tray and chill in the fridge for 30 minutes before serving.

Nutrition: Cal 134; Net Carbs 7.6g; Fat 11g; Protein 2g

American Cheesecake

Servings: 4 and **Total Time:** approx. 25 min + chilling time

Ingredients:

For the crust	2 cups almond flour
6 tbsp butter, melted	1/3 cup xylitol
1 tsp cinnamon powder	For the filling
¼ cup Swerve confectioner's sugar	1 cup softened cream cheese
	1 cup halved strawberries
½ cup heavy cream	1 tsp vanilla extract

Directions:

Preheat oven to 360 F. In a food processor, blend butter, almond flour, xylitol, and cinnamon until the dough mixture resembles a ball-like shape. Stretch out the dough in a greased round pan covering the sides. With a fork, stab the bottom of the crust. Bake for 15 minutes.

Remove the crust after cooking and let cool.

For the filling, in a bowl, whisk cream cheese, heavy cream, Swerve sugar, and vanilla. Pour the filling into the crust, gently tap on a flat surface to release air bubbles, and refrigerate for 1 hour. Remove tart from the fridge and top with strawberries.

Nutrition: Cal 398; Net Carbs 6g; Fat 33g; Protein 5g

Chocolate Chips Walnut Biscuits

Servings: 4 and **Total Time:** approx. 30 minutes

Ingredients:

4 oz butter, softened	1 egg
2/3 cup dark chocolate chips	2 tbsp Swerve sugar
	½ cup chopped walnuts
2 tbsp Swerve brown sugar	1 tsp vanilla extract
½ cup almond flour	½ tsp baking soda

Directions:

Preheat oven to 360 F. In a bowl, whisk butter, serve sugar, and serve brown sugar until smooth. Beat in the egg and mix in the vanilla extract. In another bowl, combine almond flour with baking soda and mix into the wet Ingredients.

Fold in chocolate chips and walnuts. Spoon tablespoons full of the batter onto a greased baking sheet, leaving 2-inch spaces between each spoon. Press down each dough to flatten slightly. Bake for 15 minutes.

Transfer to a wire rack to cool completely.

Nutrition: Cal 429; Net Carbs 3.5g; Fat 39g; Protein 6g

Almond Cheesecake with Chocolate

Servings: 4 and **Total Time:** approx. 25 min + chilling time

Ingredients:

½ cup butter, melted	1 cup dark chocolate, chopped
1 cup raw almonds	
2 tbsp + ½ cup Swerve sugar 2 gelatin sheets	2 tbsp lime juice
	1 cup Greek yogurt
1 ½ cups cream cheese	1 tbsp mint extract

Directions:

Preheat oven to 360 F. In a blender, process the almonds until finely ground. Mix with butter and 2 tbsp of Swerve. Press the crust mixture on the bottom of a cake pan until firm. Bake for 5 minutes.

Place in the fridge to chill. In a pot, combine gelatin with lime juice and 1 tbsp of water. Let sit for 5 minutes and place the pot over medium heat to dissolve the gelatin. Microwave the dark chocolate for 1 minute; set aside. In another bowl, beat cream cheese and remaining Swerve sugar using an electric mixer until smooth. Stir in yogurt and gelatin until combined. Fold in melted chocolate and then the mint extract.

Remove the pan from the fridge and pour the cream mixture on top. Tap the side gently to release any trapped air bubbles and transfer to the fridge to chip for 3 hours or more. Remove and release the pan's locker, top with more dark chocolate. Serve chilled.

Nutrition: Cal 241g, Net Carbs 3.8g, Fat 14g, Protein 7g

Chocolate Fat Bombs

Servings: 6 and **Total Time:** approx. 10 min + chilling time

Ingredients:

2 tbsp coconut butter	2 tbsp coconut oil
1 tbsp cacao powder	¼ tsp vanilla extract
2 tbsp ghee	1/8 tsp nutmeg
¼ tsp red chili flakes	¼ tsp ground cinnamon
1 tbsp stevia	¼ tsp salt

Directions:

Melt the coconut butter, coconut oil, and ghee in a small pan over low heat. Stir in cacao powder, vanilla, nutmeg, cinnamon, stevia, and salt.

Divide the mixture between muffin cups. Top with red chili flakes and place in the freezer for 1 hour or until firm. Unmold before serving.

Nutrition: Cal 147; Net Carbs 0.6g, Fat 15g, Protein 2g

Dark Chocolate Cheesecake Bites

Servings: 6 and **Total Time:** approx. 10 min + cooling time

Ingredients:

½ cup half and half
1 tsp vanilla extract
½ cup Swerve sugar
20 oz cream cheese, softened
10 oz dark chocolate chips

Directions:

In a saucepan, melt the chocolate with half and a half over low heat for 1 minute. Turn the heat off. In a bowl, whisk the cream cheese, Swerve sugar, and vanilla with a hand mixer until smooth.

Stir into the chocolate mixture. Spoon into silicone muffin tins and freeze for 4 hours until firm.

Nutrition: Cal 239; Net Carbs 3.1g; Fat 22g; Protein 5g

Viennese Coffee Bites

Servings: 6 and **Total Time:** approx. 5 min + cooling time

Ingredients:

½ cup melted ghee
3 tbsp cocoa powder
6 tbsp brewed coffee
1 ½ cups mascarpone cheese
¼ cup erythritol

Directions:

Beat the ghee, mascarpone, cocoa powder, erythritol, and coffee with a hand mixer until creamy and fluffy, about 1 minute. Fill in muffin tins and freeze for 3 hours until firm.

Nutrition: Cal 250; Net Carbs 2g; Fat 24g; Protein 6g

Blueberry Sorbet

Servings: 8 and **Total Time:** approx. 15 min + chilling time

Ingredients:

½ lemon, juiced
1 cup Swerve sugar
4 cups frozen blueberries
½ tsp salt

Directions:

Blend the blueberries, Swerve, lemon juice, and salt in a food processor until smooth. Pour into a bowl after straining through a colander. Allow for a three-hour chilling period.

Fill an ice cream maker halfway with chilled juice and churn until the mixture resembles ice cream.

Pour into a bowl and chill for another 3 hours.

Nutrition: Cal 40; Net Carbs 6.3g; Fat 1g; Protein 1g

Coconut Waffles with Cranberry

Servings: 4 and **Total Time:** approx. 16 minutes

Ingredients:

2/3 cup coconut flour
2 eggs
½ tsp vanilla extract
1 ½ cups almond milk
A pinch of salt
1 tsp lemon zest
2 tsp baking powder
6 tbsp unsalted butter, melted and cooled slightly
¼ cup fresh cranberries
2/3 cup erythritol
Greek yogurt for topping

Directions:

Put cranberries, erythritol, 3/4 cup water, vanilla, and lemon zest in a saucepan. Bring to a boil and reduce the temperature; simmer for 15 minutes or until the cranberries break and a sauce forms set aside.

In a bowl, mix coconut flour, baking powder, and salt. In another bowl, whisk eggs, almond milk, and butter and pour the mixture into the flour mixture.

Combine until a smooth batter forms. Preheat a waffle iron and brush with butter. Pour some of the batter and cook until golden and crisp, 4 minutes. Repeat with the remaining batte. Plate the waffles, spoon a dollop of yogurt on top, followed by the cranberry sauce.

Nutrition: Cal 280; Net Carbs 8.9g; Fat 19g; Protein 6g

Peanut Butter Ice Cream

Servings: 6 and **Total Time:** approx. 10 min + cooling time

Ingredients:

½ cup smooth peanut butter
3 cups half and half
1 pinch of salt
½ cup erythritol
½ cups raspberries
1 tsp vanilla extract

Directions:

In a bowl, beat peanut butter and erythritol with a hand mixer until smooth. Gradually whisk in half and half until thoroughly combined. Add in vanilla and salt and mix. Transfer the mixture to a loaf pan and freeze for 50 minutes until firmed up. Scoop into glasses when ready and serve topped with raspberries.

Nutrition: Cal 296; Net Carbs 9g; Fat 25g; Protein 9g

Chocolate Cupcakes

Servings: 4 and **Total Time:** approx. 45 minutes

Ingredients:

2 tbsp unsweetened cocoa powder
1 cup almond flour
1 tsp baking powder
½ cup plain yogurt
3 oz unsweetened dark chocolate chips
2 tbsp stevia
1 egg
2 tbsp butter, melted

Directions:

Preheat the oven to 350 F.

Line muffin cups with parchment paper and set aside.

In a medium bowl, whisk the almond flour, stevia, cocoa powder, and baking powder together.

In a separate bowl, whisk the egg, yogurt, and butter, and pour the mixture gradually into the flour mixture while mixing with a spatula just until well incorporated. Try not to over-mix. Fold in some chocolate chips and fill the muffin cups with the batter - ¾ way up.

Top with the remaining chocolate chips, place on a baking tray, and bake for 20 minutes. Let the muffins cool for 15 minutes before serving.

Nutrition: Cal 210; ; Net Carbs 9.2g; Fat 13g Protein 4g

Strawberry Mini Cakes

Servings: 4 and **Total Time:** approx. 50 minutes

Ingredients:

4 eggs
2 cups strawberries
1 cup almond flour
½ tsp vanilla powder
2 tsp coconut oil
¼ cup xylitol
1 cup coconut milk
¼ tsp powdered sugar
A pinch of salt

Directions:

Place all ingredients except coconut oil, berries, and powdered sugar, in a blender; pulse until smooth. Fold in strawberries. Preheat oven to 330 F. Grease a baking dish with oil. Pour the mixture into the pan and bake for 40 minutes. Sprinkle with powdered sugar and cut into mini cakes.

Nutrition: Cal 211; Net Carbs 7.4g; Fat 18g; Protein 14g

Mascarpone Red Velvet Cakes

Servings: 6 and **Total Time:** approx. 35 minutes

Ingredients:

6 eggs
½ cup butter
1 cup Swerve sugar
½ cup coconut flour
2 tbsp baking powder
1 tbsp red food coloring
2 tbsp heavy cream
½ cup erythritol
1 cup Greek yogurt
1 tsp vanilla extract
1 cup almond flour
2 tbsp cocoa powder
¼ tsp salt
For the frosting
1 cup mascarpone cheese
1 tsp vanilla extract

Directions:

Preheat oven to 380 F. Grease 2 heart-shaped cake pans with butter. In a bowl, beat butter, eggs, vanilla, Greek yogurt, and Swerve sugar until smooth.

In another bowl, mix the almond and coconut flours, cocoa, salt, baking powder, and red food coloring. Combine both mixtures until smooth and divide the batter between the two cake pans.

Bake in the oven for 25 minutes or until a toothpick inserted comes out clean. In a bowl, using an electric mixer, whisk the mascarpone cheese and erythritol until smooth. Mix in vanilla and heavy cream. Transfer to a wire rack, let cool, and spread the frosting on top. Serve.

Nutrition: Cal 449; Net Carbs 5.2g; Fat 40g; Protein 17g

Chocolate Frosting Cakes

Servings: 4 and **Total Time:** approx. 30 minutes

Ingredients:

½ cup almond flour
1 tsp baking powder
1 tsp cinnamon, ground
A pinch of salt

½ cup butter, melted
1 tsp pure almond extract
1 cup heavy cream
¼ cup erythritol
½ tsp baking soda
A pinch of ground cloves
1 egg
½ cup buttermilk
Frosting

1 cup dark chocolate, flaked

Directions:

Grease a donut pan with cooking spray and preheat the oven to 360 F. Mix the cloves, almond flour, baking powder, salt, baking soda, erythritol, and cinnamon in a bowl. In a separate bowl, combine the almond extract, butter, egg, and buttermilk. Mix the wet mixture into the dry mix. Evenly spoon the batter into the donut pan. Bake for 17 minutes. Set a pan over medium heat and warm heavy cream; simmer for 2 minutes. Fold in the chocolate flakes; combine until all the chocolate melts; and let cool. Spread the frosting on top of the cakes.

Nutrition: Cal 341; Net Carbs 3.2g; Fat 36g; Protein 3g

Coconut Macadamia Bars

Servings: 12 and **Total Time:** approx. 10 min + chilling time

Ingredients:
- ½ cup smooth peanut butter
- 1 cup macadamia, chopped
- 1 cup coconut flakes
- 2 tsp vanilla bean paste
- ½ cup pepitas
- ¼ cup coconut oil, solidified
- 1 tsp cinnamon powder

Directions:

Combine macadamia nuts, pepitas, coconut flakes, cinnamon powder, peanut butter, coconut oil, and vanilla bean paste in a mixing bowl.

Preheat the oven to 350°F. Line a baking sheet with parchment paper. Spread the mixture onto the baking sheet and place in the refrigerator for at least 1 hour to firm up. Cut the bars into bars and serve.

Nutrition: Cal 241; Net Carbs 7.5g; Fat 22g; Protein 6g

Almond Butter & Chocolate Bars

Servings: 12 and **Total Time:** approx. 5 min + chilling time

Ingredients:
- ¼ cup melted butter
- 1 ½ cups chocolate chips
- 1 cup chopped walnuts
- ¼ cup almond butter
- ½ cup sugar-free maple syrup
- 1 tbsp sesame seeds

Directions:

Combine chocolate chips, almond butter, maple syrup, butter, seeds, and walnuts in a mixing bowl. Preheat the oven to 350°F. Line a baking sheet with parchment paper. Spread the mixture onto the baking sheet and place in the refrigerator for 1 hour, or until firm. Cut the dough into bars.

Nutrition: Cal 189; Net Carbs 6g; Fat 20g; Protein 4g

Blueberry Ice Balls

Servings: 2 and **Total Time:** approx. 15 min + cooling time

Ingredients:
- ½ tsp vanilla extract
- 1 cup cold water
- 2 tbsp heavy whipping cream
- 3 tbsp mashed blueberries
- 2 packets gelatine, sugar-free
- 1 cup water
- 2 cups crushed Ice

Directions:

Boil the water over medium heat and dissolve the gelatine inside. Transfer to a blender and add the remaining ingredients. Pulse until smooth and make balls. Freeze them for 3 hours.

Nutrition: Cal 82; Net Carbs 5.8g; Fat 9g; Protein 3g

Buckeye Fat Bomb Bars

Servings: 12 and **Total Time:** approx. 15 min + chilling time

Ingredients:
- 6 oz heavy cream
- 1 ¼ cups peanut butter
- 1 tsp vanilla extract
- 1/8 tsp salt
- ½ cup butter, melted
- ½ cup almond flour
- 1 tsp Swerve sugar
- 6 oz dark chocolate chips

Directions:

In a food processor, mix peanut butter, butter, almond flour, vanilla, and Swerve sugar. Line a baking sheet with parchment paper. Spread the vanilla mixture onto the sheet and refrigerate to firm, 30 minutes.

Add the chocolate chips, heavy cream, and salt to a pot and melt over low heat until bubbles form around the edges. Let cool for 5 minutes and whisk until smooth. Pour over the butter mixture and refrigerate for 1 hour. Cut into bars and serve.

Nutrition: Cal 379; Net Carbs 8.5g; Fat 34g; Protein 9g

Small Keto Appliance Recipes

Beef Meatballs

Servings: 6 and **Total Time:** approx. 8 hours 25 minutes

Ingredients:

2 lb ground beef
4 cloves garlic, minced
1 onion, finely chopped
4 tbsp chopped parsley
Salt and pepper to taste
2 (6 oz) tomato paste
1 tsp red pepper flakes
3 bay leaves
4 (24 oz) crushed tomatoes
1 lb ground pork
1 cup zero carb breadcrumbs
1 cup grated Parmesan cheese
1 tsp Italian seasoning
2 tbsp chopped basil
2 tbsp grated Parmesan cheese
4 eggs, cracked into a bowl

Directions:

In a bowl, add the beef, pork, onions, garlic, breadcrumbs, parsley, eggs, cheese, salt, and pepper. Use your hands to mix the ingredients and form 2-inch meatballs out of the mixture. Lightly grease the baking tray with cooking spray and put the meatballs on it. Tuck the baking tray into the oven and broil the meatballs on high heat for about 5 minutes on each side.

After, remove the meatballs from the oven and put them in your slow cooker. Top it with crushed tomatoes, red pepper flakes, tomato paste, bay leaves, and Italian seasoning. Close the lid and cook the meatballs and other ingredients on Low for 8 hours.

When ready, open the lid and adjust the taste with salt and pepper. Stir the mixture gently with a spoon. Then, dish the meatballs with tomato sauce into a serving bowl and garnish it with the chopped basil and parmesan cheese. Serve it on a good lump of steamed squash spaghetti.

Nutrition: Cal 635; Net Carbs 7.6g; Fat 44g; Protein 54g

Chicken Stew with Sorrel

Servings: 6 and **Total Time:** approx. 4 hours 20 minutes

Ingredients:

4 chicken breasts, cut into thin strips 2 tbsp olive oil
4 cups chicken broth
Salt and pepper to taste
1 large leek, chopped 1 lb sorrel
2 cups chopped daikon radish

Directions:

First, season the chicken with salt and pepper. Warm the olive oil in a skillet over medium heat and add the chicken strips. Brown the chicken strips for about 6 minutes; transfer to your slow cooker. Top it with the leek, sorrel, daikon radish, and chicken broth. Close the lid and cook the ingredients on High for 4 hours. Once ready, open the pot and adjust the taste with salt and pepper. Spoon the stew into serving bowls and serve it with some cauliflower rice.

Nutrition: Cal 410; Net Carbs 4.3g; Fat 22g; Protein 42g

Chipotle Chicken

Servings: 4 and **Total Time:** approx. 4 hours 10 minutes

Ingredients:

1 lb chicken breasts, cubed
1 tsp chipotle chili powder
½ cup chicken broth
¼ tsp garlic powder
5 tbsp tomato paste
1/3 tsp liquid
Salt to taste
¼ tsp onion powder
¼ tsp cumin stevia

Directions:

Pour the chipotle powder, onion powder, cumin powder, garlic powder, salt, stevia, and tomato paste into your slow cooker. Gradually add the chicken broth while continually mixing the ingredients with a spoon until smooth paste forms. Then, add the remaining chicken broth and stir it again. Put the chicken breasts in the sauce mixture, making sure to coat it with the sauce using a spoon. Close the lid and cook the chicken on High for 4 hours.

When the chicken is ready, open the lid, and use two forks to shred the chicken. You can do this in the cooker. Adjust the seasoning and stir. Spoon the chipotle chicken onto serving plates and serve with a side of steamed cauli rice if desired.

Nutrition: Cal 240; Net Carbs 3g; Fat 11g; Protein 25g

Green Bean Beef Soup

Servings: 6 and **Total Time:** approx. 30 minutes

Ingredients:

- 2 tbsp olive oil
- 2 garlic cloves, minced
- 1 tsp thyme
- 2 cups green beans, chopped
- Salt and black pepper to taste
- 2 cups diced tomatoes
- 1lb ground beef
- 1 tsp oregano
- 1 onion, chopped
- 6 cups beef broth
- 3 tbsp Parmesan cheese, grated

Directions:

Warm the olive oil in your Instant Pot on Sauté. Add the beef and brown it for 5-6 minutes. Stir in onion and garlic for 2 minutes. Pour in the tomatoes, broth, green beans, thyme, and oregano.

Close the lid, secure the pressure valve, and select Manual on High for 15 minutes. Once done, quickly release pressure, and open the lid. Adjust taste with pepper and salt. Sprinkle with Parmesan cheese and serve.

Nutrition: Cal 170; Net Carbs 3.7g; Fat 9g; Protein 16g

Pork Ragout

Servings: 4 and **Total Time:** approx. 8 hours 20 minutes

Ingredients:

- 1 lb pork tenderloin
- 5 cloves garlic, smashed
- 1 onion, chopped
- 2 bay leaves
- 1 tbsp chopped parsley
- Salt and pepper to taste
- ½ cup roasted red Peppers
- 1 cup crushed tomatoes
- 2 sprigs fresh thyme
- 1 tsp olive oil

Directions:

Season the tenderloin with salt and pepper. Put a skillet over medium heat and add the olive oil and garlic to it.

Sauté the garlic and onion until fragrant, about 3 minutes, and transfer them to your slow cooker.

Put the tenderloin in the skillet and brown it on both sides for 4 minutes. Place it into the slow cooker. Top with roasted red peppers, tomatoes, bay leaves, fresh thyme, and half of the parsley.

Close the lid and cook the Ingredients on Low for 8 hours. Open the lid after it is done and use a spoon to remove the bay leaves and thyme sprigs. Shred the pork with 2 forks and stir in the remaining parsley.

Dish the pork ragout over a bed of zucchini noodles and serve.

Nutrition: Cal 197; Net Carbs 5.2g; Fat 5g; Protein 31g

Worcestershire Pork Loin

Servings: 4 and **Total Time:** approx. 8 hours 15 minutes

Ingredients:

- 1 lb pork loin
- 1/3 cup Worcestershire sauce
- Salt and pepper to taste
- 1 tsp garlic powder
- 3 slices smoked bacon, diced
- 2 cups mushroom cream soup
- ½ tbsp olive oil

Directions:

Warm the oil in a skillet over medium heat. Season the pork loin with salt, garlic powder, and pepper. Place it in the heated oil and sear it on both sides to be slightly brown for 5 minutes. While the pork loin sears, pour the mushroom soup cream and Worcestershire sauce in your slow cooker and use a spoon to mix them evenly.

When the pork is ready, put it in the mixed sauces. Cover the lid and cook them on Low for 8 hours.

After 6 hours, open the cover and add in the smoked bacon. Continue cooking for 2 hours on Low. Remove the pork afterward onto a plate, let it sit for 3 minutes and then slice it with a knife.

Plate the pork slices, spoon the sauce with the bacon over them and serve it with a creamy parsnip mash and roasted green beans.

Nutrition: Cal 427; Net Carbs 9g; Fat 26g; Protein 35g

Pork Neck Casserole

Servings: 4 and **Total Time:** approx. 8 hours 10 minutes

Ingredients:

- 1 lb pork neck
- 2 cups sliced mushrooms
- 4 carrots, diced
- 8 Baby turnips, peeled
- 1 red onion, diced
- 1 greed bell pepper, diced
- 1 cup chicken stock
- 1 small bouquet garni blend Salt and pepper to taste

Directions:

Season the pork neck with salt and pepper and put it in your slow cooker. Top it with the bouquet garni, onion, mushrooms, carrots, bell pepper, and turnips. Pour the chicken broth over everything. Close the lid and cook on Low mode for 8 hours.

When ready, remove the pork, let it sit for 2 minutes before slicing.

Plate with the vegetables and spoon some amount of sauce over and serve.

Nutrition: Cal 463; Net Carbs 10g; Fat 23g; Protein 35g

Beef & Broccoli Stew

Servings: 4 and **Total Time:** approx. 4 hours 20 minutes

Ingredients:

tbsp olive oil	1 lb ground beef
½ cup leeks, chopped	1 head broccoli, cut into florets Salt and black pepper to taste
1 tsp yellow mustard	
2 tomatoes, chopped	
1 tsp Worcestershire sauce	8 oz tomato sauce
1 tbsp rosemary, chopped	½ tsp dried oregano

Directions:

Coat the broccoli with black pepper and salt. Set them into a bowl, drizzle over the olive oil, and toss to combine. In a separate bowl, combine the beef with Worcestershire sauce, leeks, salt, mustard, and

black pepper, and stir well. Press on your slow cooker's bottom. Scatter in the broccoli, add the tomatoes, oregano, and tomato sauce. Cook for 4 hours on High; covered. Serve the casserole with scattered rosemary.

Nutrition: Cal 326; Net Carbs 7g; Fat 22g; Protein 25g

Chicken Stew with Veggies

Servings: 4 and **Total Time:** approx. 4 hours 15 minutes

Ingredients:

2 garlic cloves, minced	1 cup mushrooms, chopped
¼ tsp celery seeds, ground	1 cup chicken stock
1 carrot, chopped	1 cup sour cream
1 cup leeks, chopped	1 pound chicken breasts
2 tbsp fresh parsley, chopped Salt and black pepper to taste	1 tsp dried thyme
4 zucchinis, spiralized	

Directions:

Season the chicken with salt, black pepper, and thyme and place it into your slow cooker. Stir in leeks, sour cream, celery seeds, garlic, carrot, mushrooms, and stock. Cook on High for 4 hours.

Heat a pot with salted water over medium heat and bring to a boil. Stir in the zucchini pasta, cook for 1 minute, and drain. Transfer to a plate, top with chicken mixture, and sprinkle with parsley to serve.

Nutrition: Cal 312; Net Carbs 8.4g; Fat 17g; Protein 26g

Chicken Jardiniere

Servings: 4 and **Total Time:** approx. 8 hours 40 minutes

Ingredients:

4 chicken thighs	3 bacon slices, chopped
Salt and pepper to taste	¼ tsp dried thyme
3 cloves garlic, minced	1 cup chicken broth
½ cup dry white wine	3 Button mushrooms, sliced
2 tsp butter	
20 small pearl onions, peeled	¾ cup chopped green beans
¼ cup sliced asparagus	8 small turnips, peeled

Directions:

Put a skillet over medium heat and add the bacon. Fry the bacon until it is crispy and browned for about 4 minutes. Remove with a slotted spoon to your slow cooker while maintaining the grease derived from it. Add the butter to the skillet and fry the chicken until golden brown on both sides, about 8-10 minutes.

Turn off the heat and put the chicken in your slow cooker too. Top the bacon and chicken with garlic, thyme, chicken broth, white wine, mushrooms, turnips, pearl onions, green beans, and asparagus. Close the lid and cook on Low for 8 hours. Once ready, stir the ingredients: with a spoon and adjust the taste with salt and pepper.

Dish the chicken and vegetables into a serving platter. Serve the chicken with a celeriac mash if desired.

Nutrition: Cal 460; Net Carbs 14g; Fat 21g; Protein 47g

Chicken with Garlic Sauce

Servings: 6 and **Total Time:** approx. 8 hours 10 minutes

Ingredients:

2 lb chicken breasts, halved	1 cup roasted red bell pepper
2 tbsp olive oil	1 cup chicken broth
1 tsp Swerve sweetener	½ tsp dried oregano
4 cloves garlic, minced	Salt to taste

Directions:

Pour the chicken broth, roasted bell pepper, Swerve sweetener, oregano, and garlic in your blender and process until a smooth liquid is achieved, about 2 minutes. Lightly season the chicken with salt and put it in your slow cooker. Pour the blended mixture over it along with the olive oil and cook covered on Low for 8 hours.

After, dish the chicken with sauce into a serving bowl and serve it with a mix of sautéed broccoli florets, asparagus, and green beans if desired.

Nutrition: Cal 326; Net Carbs 2g; Fat 20g; Protein 32g

Lamb Shoulder

Servings: 4 and **Total Time:** approx. 4 hours 20 minutes

Ingredients:
- 1 lb lamb shoulder, deboned Salt and black pepper to taste 2 tbsp olive oil
- 1 sprig rosemary
- 1 garlic clove, crushed
- 1 sprig thyme

Directions:

Prepare a water bath and place the Sous Vide Cooker in it. Set the Sous Vide Cooker to 145 F. Rub the lamb with pepper and salt.

Place the lamb and the remaining listed ingredients in a vacuum-sealable bag. Release air by the water displacement method, seal, and submerge the bag in the water bath. Set the timer for 4 hours. Once the timer has stopped, remove the bag and transfer the lamb to a baking dish; slice-it. Strain the juices into a saucepan and cook over medium heat for 2 minutes. Preheat a grill to high. Grill the shoulder until golden. Serve with sauce.

Nutrition: Cal 245; Net Carbs 0g; Fat 16g; Protein 23g

Pork & Kraut

Servings: 4 and **Total Time:** approx. 8 hours 5 minutes

Ingredients:
- 1 lb pork tenderloin
- ¼ cup butter
- 1 (20 oz) sauerkraut, undrained
- Salt and pepper to taste

Directions:

Put the pork in your slow cooker, pour the sauerkraut with its juice butter, 1 cup of water, salt, and pepper. Cover the lid and cook the ingredients on Low for 8 hours.

Open the lid and use two forks to shred the tenderloin. Also, add some water if the mixture is dry, and stir it with a spoon. Serve the pork with mashed turnips and some steamed rapini if desired.

Nutrition: Cal 285; Net Carbs 2.5g; Fat 15g; Protein 32g

Goat Cheese Lamb Ribs

Servings: 4 and **Total Time:** approx. 4 hours 10 minutes

Ingredients:
- 2 lb lamb ribs
- 1 clove garlic, minced
- ½ tsp cayenne pepper
- 1 tbsp ground fennel seeds
- 3 tbsp parsley, chopped
- 2 tbsp vegetable oil
- 2 tbsp rosemary, chopped
- Salt and black pepper to taste 8 oz Goat cheese, crumbled
- 2 oz roasted walnuts, chopped

Directions:

Make a water bath, place the Sous Vide Cooker in it, and set to 134 F. Mix the listed lamb ingredients except for the lamb. Pat dry the lamb using a napkin and rub the meat with the spice mixture.

Place the meat in a vacuum-sealable bag, release air by the water displacement method, seal, and submerge the bag in the water bath. Set the timer for 4 hours.

Once the timer has stopped, remove the bag and remove the lamb. Oil and preheat a grill on high heat. Place the lamb on it and sear to become golden brown. Cut the ribs between the bones.

Garnish with goat cheese, walnuts, and parsley. Serve with a hot sauce dip, if desired.

Nutrition: Cal 796; Net Carbs 3.4g; Fat 58g; Protein 64g

Shredded BBQ Roast

Servings: 4 and **Total Time:** approx. 30 hrs 16 minutes

Ingredients:
- 1 medium chuck roast
- 1 tbsp blackened rub
- 3 tbsp butter

Directions:

Make a water bath, place the Sous Vide Cooker in it, and set to 135 F. Pat dry the meat using a napkin and season with blackened rub.

Place the meat in a vacuum-sealable bag, release air by the water displacement method and seal the bag. Submerge bag in the water bath. Set the timer for 30 hours.

Once the timer has stopped, remove the bag and unseal it. Remove the meat and pat it dry. Warm the butter in a skillet over medium heat. Sear the beef for 2-3 minutes on all sides. remove and let it sit for 5 minutes before slicing. Serve.

Nutrition: Cal 318; Net Carbs 0g; Fat 20g; Protein 36g

Pork with Mushroom Sauce

Servings: 4 and **Total Time:** approx. 80 minutes

Ingredients:

- 4 pork chops
- 6 oz mushrooms, sliced
- 2 tbsp Worcestershire sauce
- 3 tbsp chives, chopped
- Black pepper to taste
- ½ cup beef stock
- 3 tbsp butter, unsalted

Directions:

Make a water bath, place a Sous Vide cooker in it, and set it at 140 F.

Rub pork chops with salt and pepper and place them in a vacuum- sealable bag. Release air by the water displacement method, seal, and submerge the bag in the water bath. Set the timer for 55 minutes.

Once the timer has stopped, remove and unseal the bag.

Remove the pork and pat it dry using a napkin. Discard the juices. Place a skillet over medium heat and add 1 tablespoon butter. Once the butter has melted, add pork and sear for 2 minutes on both sides. Place aside.

Add the mushrooms to the skillet and cook for 5 minutes. Turn heat off, add the remaining butter and swirl until butter melts. Season with pepper and salt. Serve pork chops with mushroom sauce.

Nutrition: Cal 427; Net Carbs 3g; Fat 27g; Protein 43g

Touch of Spice Pulled Pork

Servings: 6 and **Total Time:** approx. 8 hours 20 minutes

Ingredients:

- 3 lb pork butt, extra fat removed
- ¼ tbsp xylitol
- 4 cloves garlic, crushed
- Salt and pepper to taste
- Green salad to serve
- 1 tbsp hot sauce
- 1 onion, cut into wedges

Directions:

Rub the pork butt with salt, pepper, and xylitol. Let it sit for 10 minutes and then put it in your slow cooker.

Pour in ¼ cup of water and add onion, garlic, and hot sauce. Cover and cook them on Low for 8 hours.

When ready, remove the pork and use two forks to shred it. Serve the pulled pork on a bed of green salad.

Nutrition: Cal 581; Net Carbs 4.2g; Fat 40g; Protein 55g

Buffalo Chicken Wings

Servings: 6 and **Total Time:** approx. 1 hour 20 minutes

Ingredients:

- 3 lb chicken wings
- 2 tsp garlic powder
- ½ cup hot sauce
- ½ cup olive oil for frying
- Salt to taste
- 2 tbsp smoked paprika
- 2 ½ cups almond flour
- 5 tbsp butter

Directions:

Make a water bath, place a Sous Vide cooker in it, and set it at 144 F. Combine the wings, garlic, salt, sugar, and smoked paprika. Coat the chicken evenly. Place the chicken in a sizable vacuum-sealable bag, release air by the water displacement method and seal the bag.

Submerge the bag in the water. Set the timer to cook for 1 hour. Once the timer has stopped, remove and unseal the bag. Pour about the flour into a large bowl, add the chicken and toss to coat the chicken evenly.

Heat oil in a pan over medium heat, fry the chicken in the oil until golden brown. Remove and place aside. In another pan, melt the butter and add the hot sauce. Coat the wings with butter and hot sauce. Serve.

Nutrition: Cal 772; Net Carbs 5g; Fat 55g; Protein 59g

Whole Chicken

Servings: 6 and **Total Time:** approx. 6 hours 20 minutes

Ingredients:

- 3 mixed bell peppers, diced
- 3 cups celery, diced
- 3 cups leeks, diced
- Salt to taste
- 1 (4 lb) whole chicken, trussed
- 1 ¼ tsp black peppercorns
- 2 bay leaves
- 5 cups chicken stock

Directions:

Make a water bath, place a Sous Vide machine in it, and set it at 150 F. Season the chicken with salt. Place all the listed ingredients and chicken in a sizable vacuum-sealable bag. Release air by the water displacement method and seal the vacuum bag.

Drop the bag in the water bath and set the timer for 6 hours. Cover the water with a plastic bag to reduce evaporation and water every 2 hours to the bath. Once the timer has stopped, remove and unseal the bag. Preheat a broiler. Broil the chicken until the skin is golden brown, about 8 minutes. Carve and serve.

Nutrition: Cal 390; Net Carbs 10g; Fat 24g; Protein 31g

Chicken Provencal

Servings: 4 and **Total Time:** approx. 8 hours 25 minutes

Ingredients:

- 1 eggplant, cut into 1-inch chunks
- 4 chicken thighs
- 4 bacon slices, chopped
- 1 red chili, minced
- 3 cloves garlic, minced
- ½ cube chicken stock, crushed
- ¼ cup chopped parsley
- 1 tbsp olive oil
- 1 zucchini, cut in chunks
- 2 cups passata
- 1 red onion, cut in wedges
- 2 tsp mixed herb seasoning

Directions:

Warm the olive oil in a skillet over medium heat and fry the bacon until it is browned and crispy, about 4 minutes. Add the chicken, red chili, red onion, eggplant, zucchini, and garlic and sauté for 5-6 minutes.

Remove to your slow cooker. Pour in the passata, 1 cup of water, chicken stock cube, and mixed herbs seasoning.

Stir the Ingredients lightly with a spoon, close the lid, and cook them for 8 hours on Low. Once ready, open the lid and stir in the parsley.

Dish the chicken with sauce and veggies into a serving bowl and serve it with some creamy broccoli mash if desired.

Nutrition: Cal 330; Net Carbs 9g; Fat 20g; Protein 22

Chicken in Wine Sauce

Servings: 6 and **Total Time:** approx. 6 hours 10 minutes

Ingredients:

- 1 (14.5 oz) can cream of mushroom soup
- 2 tbsp milk
- 2 tsp dried parsley
- 2 tsp onion powder
- Salt and pepper to taste
- 4 chicken breasts, boneless
- 1/3 cup white wine
- 2 (4 oz) cans mushrooms, drained
- ½ tsp garlic powder

Directions:

In your slow cooker, pour the mushroom soup, mushrooms, white wine, milk, onion powder, garlic powder, and dried parsley. Season with salt and pepper and stir it with a spoon.

Put the chicken in the sauce and use the spoon to cover the chicken with some of the sauce. Close the lid and cook it on High for 4 hours.

Open the lid after and dish the chicken with the sauce into serving bowls. Serve on a bed of zoodles or squash spaghetti if desired.

Nutrition: Cal 226; Net Carbs 5g; Fat 21g; Protein 42g

Chicken Cacciatore

Servings: 4 and **Total Time:** approx. 4 hours 50 minutes

Ingredients:

- 1 cup sliced Cremini mushrooms
- 1½ lb chicken thighs, boneless
- 1 yellow onion, chopped
- 3/4 cup chicken broth
- 1 green bell pepper, chopped
- 2 tbsp chopped parsley
- Salt and pepper to taste
- 3 cloves garlic, minced
- 1 tsp rosemary
- 1 ½ tsp balsamic vinegar
- 1 ½ cup crushed tomatoes
- 3/4 dry red wine
- 2 ½ tbsp olive oil
- 2 tbsp grated Parmesan cheese

Directions:

Put a skillet over medium heat and add two tablespoons of olive oil to warm. As it heats, season the chicken with salt and pepper and brown it on both sides for 6 minutes in total. Transfer the chicken to your slow cooker.

Then take the skillet over the heat and use a paper towel to wipe it, return the skillet to heat, and heat the remaining olive oil. Pour in the onion and garlic and cook until softened for 2 minutes, then add 1 tablespoon of balsamic vinegar. Cook until the vinegar reduces, 1-2 minutes. Pour the mixture into the cooker.

Add in the tomatoes, mushrooms, bell pepper, rosemary, chicken broth, and wine and stir. Close the lid and cook them on High mode for 4 hours. Serve the chicken garnished with chopped parsley and Parmesan cheese.

Nutrition: Cal 518; Net Carbs 5g; Fat 40g; Protein 31g

Turnip Soup with Sour Cream

Servings: 4 and **Total Time:** approx. 8 hours 30 minutes

Ingredients:

2 tbsp olive oil	1 cup onion, chopped
2 garlic cloves, minced	2 turnips, peeled and chopped
1 celery, chopped	
4 tsp sour cream	3 cups vegetable broth
¼ cup ground almonds	1 tbsp fresh cilantro, chopped
1 cup almond milk	

Directions:

Warm the olive oil in a skillet over medium heat and sauté celery, garlic, and onion for 6 minutes. Transfer to your slow cooker.

Pour in the broth and turnips. Close the cover and cook on Low for 8 hours. When ready, puree the soup with an immersion blender. Stir in the ground almonds and almond milk. Serve garnished with sour cream and cilantro.

Nutrition: Cal 165; Net Carbs 7.7g; Fat 11g; Protein 8g

Smoky Zucchini Chips

SERVINGS 6 | **PREP TIME** 15 minutes | **COOK TIME** 8 to 10 minutes | **TEMPERATURE:** 400°F

Ingredients:

2 large eggs	1 cup almond flour
½ cup Parmesan cheese	1 teaspoon garlic powder
½ teaspoon smoked paprika	¼ teaspoon freshly ground black pepper
1½ teaspoons sea salt	2 zucchini, cut into ¼-inch-thick slices
Avocado oil spray	

Directions:

Beat the eggs in a shallow bowl. In another bowl, stir the almond flour, Parmesan cheese, salt, garlic powder, smoked paprika, and black pepper.

Dip the zucchini slices in the egg mixture, then coat them with the almond flour mixture. Set the air fryer to 400°F. Place the zucchini chips in a single layer in the air fryer basket, working in batches if necessary.

Spray the chips with oil and cook for 4 minutes. Flip the chips and spray them with more oil. Cook for 4 to 6 minutes more.

Nutrition: Calories: 181; Fat: 14g; Protein: 11g; Total Carbs:

Lemon-Garlic Mushrooms

SERVINGS 6 | **PREP TIME** 10 minutes | **COOK TIME** 10 to 15 minutes | **TEMPERATURE:** 375°F

Ingredients:

12 ounces sliced mushrooms	Freshly ground black pepper
1 tablespoon avocado oil	3 tablespoons unsalted butter
Sea salt	1 teaspoon minced garlic
1 tsp freshly squeezed lemon juice	½ teaspoon red pepper flakes
2 tablespoons chopped fresh parsley	

Directions:

Place the mushrooms in a medium bowl and toss with the oil. Season to taste with salt and pepper. Place the mushrooms in a single layer in the air fryer basket.

Set your air fryer to 375°F and cook for 10 to 15 minutes, until the mushrooms are tender. While the mushrooms cook, melt the butter in a small pot or skillet over medium-low heat. Stir in the garlic and cook for 30 seconds. Remove the pot from the heat and stir in the lemon juice and red pepper flakes. Toss the mushrooms with the lemon-garlic butter and garnish with the parsley before serving.

Nutrition: Calories: 80; Fat: 8g; Protein: 1g; Total Carbs: 1g;

Buttery Green Beans

SERVINGS 6 | **PREP TIME** 5 minutes | **COOK TIME** 8 to 10 minutes | **TEMPERATURE:** 400°F

Ingredients:

1 pound green beans, trimmed	1 teaspoon garlic powder
Sea salt	1 tablespoon avocado oil
	Freshly ground black pepper
¼ cup unsalted butter, melted	¼ cup freshly grated Parmesan cheese

Directions:

In a large bowl, toss the green beans, avocado oil, and garlic powder and season with salt and pepper. Set the air fryer to 400°F. Arrange the green beans in a single layer in the air fryer basket.

Cook for 8 to 10 minutes, tossing halfway through. Transfer the beans to a large bowl and toss with the melted butter. Top with the Parmesan cheese and serve warm.

Nutrition: Calories: 134; Fat: 11g; Protein: 3g; Total Carbs: 6g;

Sweet and Spicy Pecans

SERVINGS 8 | **PREP TIME** 7 minutes | **COOK TIME** 15 minutes | **TEMPERATURE:** 275°F

Ingredients:

3 tablespoons unsalted butter, melted	¼ cup brown sugar substitute, such as Swerve or Sukrin Gold
2 cups pecan halves	
¼ teaspoon cayenne	1½ teaspoons Maldon

pepper, more or less to taste

sea salt (or regular sea salt if you like)

Directions:

Line your air fryer basket with parchment paper or an air fryer liner. Place the melted butter in a small pot and whisk in the brown sugar substitute, sea salt, and cayenne pepper. Stir until well combined. Place the pecans in a medium bowl and pour the butter mixture over them. Toss to coat. Set the air fryer to 275°F.

Place the pecans in the air fryer basket in a single layer, working in batches if necessary, and cook for 10 minutes. Stir, then cook for 5 minutes more. Transfer the pecans to a parchment paper–lined baking sheet and allow them to cool completely before serving.

Nutrition: Calories: 225; Fat: 24g; Protein: 3g; Total Carbs: 16g

Spiced-Pumpkin Chicken Soup

SERVINGS 6 | **PREP TIME** 15 minutes | **COOK TIME** 6 hours on low

Ingredients:

- 1 tablespoon extra-virgin olive oil
- 1 pound pumpkin, diced
- 1 tablespoon grated fresh ginger
- ¼ teaspoon ground nutmeg
- ¼ teaspoon salt Pinch ground allspice
- 2 cups chopped cooked chicken
- 2 cups coconut milk
- 4 cups chicken broth
- ½ sweet onion, chopped
- ½ teaspoon ground cinnamon
- 2 teaspoons minced garlic
- ¼ tsp ground black pepper
- 1 cup heavy (whipping) cream

Directions:

Lightly grease the insert of the slow cooker with the olive oil. Place the broth, coconut milk, pumpkin, onion, ginger, garlic, cinnamon, nutmeg, pepper, salt, and allspice in the insert. Cover and cook on low for 6 hours.

Using an immersion blender or a regular blender, purée the soup.

If you removed the soup from the insert to purée, add it back to the pot, and stir in the cream and chicken. Keep heating the soup on low for 15 minutes to heat the chicken through.

Nutrition: Calories: 389; Fat: 32g; Protein: 16g; Total Carbs: 10g

Cheesy Bacon-Cauliflower Soup

SERVINGS 6 | **PREP TIME** 15 minutes | **COOK TIME** 6 hours on low

Ingredients:

- 1 tablespoon extra-virgin olive oil
- 2 cups chopped cooked chicken
- 3 teaspoons minced garlic
- 2 cups shredded Cheddar cheese
- 2 cups coconut milk
- 4 cups chicken broth
- 2 cups chopped cauliflower
- 1 sweet onion, chopped
- ½ cup cream cheese, cubed
- 1 cup chopped cooked bacon

Directions:

Lightly grease the insert of the slow cooker with the olive oil. Place the broth, coconut milk, chicken, bacon, cauliflower, onion, and garlic in the insert.

Cover and cook on low for 6 hours. Stir in the cream cheese and Cheddar and serve.

Nutrition: Calories: 540; Fat: 44g; Protein: 35g; Total Carbs: 7g

Turkey-Potpie Soup

SERVINGS 8 | **PREP TIME** 20 minutes | **COOK TIME** 7 to 8 hours on low

Ingredients:

- 1 tablespoon extra-virgin olive oil
- 4 cups chicken broth
- 2 celery stalks, chopped
- 2 teaspoons minced garlic
- 1 carrot, diced
- 2 cups heavy (whipping) cream
- Freshly ground black pepper, for seasoning
- ½ pound skinless turkey breast, cut into ½-inch chunks
- 1 sweet onion, chopped
- 2 teaspoons chopped fresh thyme
- 1 cup green beans, cut into 1-inch pieces Salt, for seasoning
- 1 cup cream cheese, diced

Directions:

Lightly grease the insert of the slow cooker with the olive oil. Place the broth, turkey, celery, carrot, onion, garlic, and thyme in the insert.
Cover and cook on low for 7 to 8 hours. Stir in the cream cheese, heavy cream, and green beans. Season with salt and pepper and serve.
Nutrition: Calories: 415; Fat: 35g; Protein: 20g; Total Carbs: 7g

Faux Lasagna Soup

SERVINGS 6 | **PREP TIME** 20 minutes | **COOK TIME** 6 hours on low

Ingredients:

3 tablespoons extra-virgin olive oil, divided
2 teaspoons minced garlic
4 cups beef broth
1½ tablespoons dried basil
2 teaspoons dried oregano
4 ounces cream cheese
½ sweet onion, chopped
1 pound ground beef
1 (28-ounce) can diced tomatoes, undrained
1 cup shredded mozzarella
1 zucchini, diced

Directions:

Lightly grease the insert of the slow cooker with 1 tablespoon of the olive oil. In a large skillet over medium-high heat, heat the remaining 2 tablespoons of the olive oil.

Add the ground beef and sauté until it is cooked through, about 6 minutes. Add the onion and garlic and sauté for an additional 3 minutes.

Transfer the meat mixture to the insert. Stir in the broth, tomatoes, zucchini, basil, and oregano. Cover and cook on low for 6 hours. Stir in the cream cheese and mozzarella and serve.

Nutrition: Calories: 472; Fat: 36g; Protein: 30g; Total Carbs: 9g

Pork Kebabs

SERVINGS 4 | **PREP TIME** 15 minutes, plus 2 hours to marinate | **COOK TIME** 6 to 8 minutes | **TEMPERATURE**: 375°F

Ingredients:

¼ cup coconut aminos
2 tablespoons freshly squeezed lime juice
1 teaspoon minced garlic
Sea salt
1 cup stevia-sweetened ginger ale, such as Zevia brand (optional) 1 pound pork tenderloin, cut into 1½-inch cubes
¼ cup sugar-free ketchup
2 tablespoons brown sugar substitute, such as Swerve or Sukrin Gold
ground black pepper
1 red bell pepper, cut into 1½-inch pieces 1 small red onion, cut into 1½-inch pieces

Directions:

In a small bowl, whisk the coconut aminos, ketchup, lime juice, brown sugar substitute, garlic, and salt and pepper to taste. Whisk in the ginger ale (if using).

Place the pork in a shallow dish and pour the marinade over top. Cover the dish with plastic wrap and let the pork marinate in the refrigerator for 2 to 4 hours. Thread the marinated pork cubes, red bell pepper, and onion on skewers, alternating as you go. Set the air fryer to 375°F. Place the kebabs in the air fryer basket in a single layer and cook for 6 to 8 minutes, until an instant-read thermometer reads 145°F.

Nutrition: Calories: 271; Fat: 9g; Protein: 34g; Total Carbs: 14g;

Pork-and-Sauerkraut Casserole

SERVINGS 6 | **PREP TIME** 15 minutes | **COOK TIME** 9 to 10 hours on low

Ingredients:

3 tablespoons extra-virgin olive oil, divided
1 (28-ounce) jar sauerkraut, drained
2 tablespoons butter
¼ cup granulated erythritol
2 pounds pork shoulder roast
½ sweet onion, thinly sliced
1 cup chicken broth

Directions:

Lightly grease the insert of the slow cooker with 1 tablespoon of the olive oil. In a large skillet over medium-high heat, heat the remaining 2 tablespoons of the olive oil and the butter. Add the pork to the skillet and brown on all sides for about 10 minutes.

Transfer to the insert and add the sauerkraut, broth, onion, and erythritol. Cover and cook on low for 9 to 10 hours. Serve warm.

Nutrition: Calories: 516; Fat: 42g; Protein: 28g; Total Carbs: 7g

Cream Cheese Sausage Balls

SERVINGS 12 | **PREP TIME** 10 minutes | **COOK TIME** 10 minutes | **TEMPERATURE**: 350°F

Ingredients:

1¾ cups almond flour
½ teaspoon sea salt
¼ teaspoon cayenne pepper
8 ounces Cheddar cheese, shredded
8 ounces cream cheese, at room temperature, cut into chunks
1 tablespoon baking powder
¼ tsp ground black pepper
1 pound fresh pork sausage, casings removed, crumbled

Directions:

In a large mixing bowl, combine the almond flour, baking powder, salt, black pepper, and cayenne pepper. Add the sausage, Cheddar cheese, and cream cheese. Stir to combine, and then, using clean hands, mix until all of the ingredients are well incorporated.

Form the mixture into 1½-inch balls. Set the air fryer to 350°F. Arrange the sausage balls in a single layer in the air fryer basket, working in batches if necessary. Cook for 5 minutes. Flip the sausage balls and cook for 5 minutes more.

Nutrition: Calories: 386; Fat: 27g; Protein: 16g; Total Carbs: 5g

Bacon-and-Eggs Breakfast Casserole

SERVINGS 8 | **PREP TIME** 15 minutes | **COOK TIME** 5 to 6 hours on low

Ingredients:

- 1 tablespoon bacon fat or extra-virgin olive oil
- 1 pound bacon, chopped and cooked crisp
- 2 teaspoons minced garlic
- ⅛ teaspoon salt
- 1 cup coconut milk
- 12 large eggs
- ½ sweet onion, chopped
- ¼ tsp black pepper
- Pinch red pepper flakes

Directions:

Lightly grease the insert of the slow cooker with the bacon fat or olive oil. In a medium bowl, whisk together the eggs, coconut milk, bacon, onion, garlic, pepper, salt, and red pepper flakes.

Pour the mixture into the slow cooker. Cover and cook on low for 5 to 6 hours. Serve warm.

Nutrition: Calories: 526; Fat: 43g; Protein: 32g; Total Carbs: 3g

Carnitas

SERVINGS 8 | **PREP TIME** 15 minutes | **COOK TIME** 9 to 10 hours on low

Ingredients:

- 3 tablespoons extra-virgin olive oil, divided
- 2 cups chicken broth
- 2 chipotle peppers, chopped Juice of 1 lime
- ½ teaspoon salt
- 2 cups diced tomatoes
- 2 tablespoons chopped cilantro, for garnish
- 1 teaspoon ground cumin
- 2 pounds pork shoulder, cut into 2-inch cubes
- ½ sweet onion, chopped
- 1 teaspoon ground coriander
- 1 avocado, peeled, pitted, and diced, for garnish
- 1 cup sour cream, for garnish

Directions:

Lightly grease the insert of the slow cooker with 1 tablespoon of the olive oil. In a large skillet over medium-high heat, heat the remaining 2 tablespoons of the olive oil. Add the pork and brown on all sides for about 10 minutes.

Transfer to the insert and add the tomatoes, broth, onion, peppers, lime juice, coriander, cumin, and salt. Cover and cook on low for 9 to 10 hours. Shred the cooked pork with a fork and stir the meat into the sauce. Serve topped with the avocado, sour cream, and cilantro.

Nutrition: Calories: 508; Fat: 41g; Protein: 29g; Total Carbs: 7g

Lemon Pork

SERVINGS 6 | **PREP TIME** 15 minutes | **COOK TIME** 7 to 8 hours on low

Ingredients:

- 3 tablespoons extra-virgin olive oil, divided
- ½ teaspoon salt
- ¼ cup chicken broth
- Juice and zest of 1 lemon
- ½ cup heavy (whipping) cream
- 2 pounds pork loin roast
- 1 tablespoon butter
- ¼ tsp black pepper
- 1 tablespoon minced garlic

Directions:

Lightly grease the insert of the slow cooker with 1 tablespoon of the olive oil. In a large skillet over medium-high heat, heat the remaining 2 tablespoons of the olive oil and the butter.

Lightly season the pork with salt and pepper. Add the pork to the skillet and brown the roast on all sides for about 10 minutes. Transfer it to the insert. In a small bowl, stir the broth, lemon juice and zest, and garlic. Add the broth mixture to the roast.

Cover, and cook on low for 7 to 8 hours. Stir in the heavy cream and serve.

Nutrition: Calories: 448; Fat: 31g; Protein: 39g; Total Carbs: 1g

Smoky Pork Tenderloin

SERVINGS 6 | **PREP TIME** 5 minutes | **COOK TIME** 19 to 22 minutes | **TEMPERATURE:** 400°F

Ingredients:

- 1½ pounds pork tenderloin
- 1 teaspoon smoked paprika
- 1 teaspoon garlic powder
- 1 tsp ground black
- 1 teaspoon chili powder
- 1 teaspoon sea salt
- 1 tablespoon avocado oil

pepper

Directions:

Pierce the tenderloin all over with a fork and rub the oil all over the meat. In a small dish, stir the chili powder, smoked paprika, garlic powder, salt, and pepper.

Rub the spice mixture all over the tenderloin. Set the air fryer to 400°F. Place the pork in the air fryer basket and cook for 10 minutes.

Flip the tenderloin and cook for 9 to 12 minutes more, until an instant-read thermometer reads at least 145°F. Allow the tenderloin to rest for 5 minutes, then slice and serve.

Nutrition: Calories: 255; Fat: 12g; Protein: 34g; Total Carbs: 1g

Slow Cooker Spanakopita Frittata

SERVINGS 8 | **PREP TIME** 10 minutes | 5 to 6 hours on low

Ingredients:

1 tablespoon extra-virgin olive oil

1 cup heavy (whipping) cream

2 teaspoons minced garlic

Cherry tomatoes, halved, for garnish (optional)

Yogurt, for garnish (optional)

12 large eggs

½ cup feta cheese

Parsley, for garnish (optional

2 cups chopped spinach)

Directions:

Lightly grease the insert of the slow cooker with the olive oil. In a medium bowl, whisk the eggs, heavy cream, garlic, spinach, and feta.

Pour the mixture into the slow cooker. Cover and cook on low 5 to 6 hours. Serve topped with the tomatoes, a dollop of yogurt, and parsley, if desired.

Nutrition: Calories: 247; Fat: 22g; Protein: 11g; Total Carbs: 2g

Appendix 1   Measurement Conversion Chart

VOLUME EQUIVALENTS (DRY)

US STANDARD	METRIC (APPROXIMATE)
1/8 teaspoon	0.5 mL
1/4 teaspoon	1 mL
1/2 teaspoon	2 mL
3/4 teaspoon	4 mL
1 teaspoon	5 mL
1 tablespoon	15 mL
1/4 cup	59 mL
1/2 cup	118 mL
3/4 cup	177 mL
1 cup	235 mL
2 cups	475 mL
3 cups	700 mL
4 cups	1 L

VOLUME EQUIVALENTS (LIQUID)

US STANDARD	US STANDARD (OUNCES)	METRIC (APPROXIMATE)
2 tablespoons	1 fl.oz.	30 mL
1/4 cup	2 fl.oz.	60 mL
1/2 cup	4 fl.oz.	120 mL
1 cup	8 fl.oz.	240 mL
1 1/2 cup	12 fl.oz.	355 mL
2 cups or 1 pint	16 fl.oz.	475 mL
4 cups or 1 quart	32 fl.oz.	1 L
1 gallon	128 fl.oz.	4 L

WEIGHT EQUIVALENTS

US STANDARD	METRIC (APPROXIMATE)
1 ounce	28 g
2 ounces	57 g
5 ounces	142 g
10 ounces	284 g
15 ounces	425 g
16 ounces (1 pound)	455 g
1.5 pounds	680 g
2 pounds	907 g

TEMPERATURES EQUIVALENTS

FAHRENHEIT (F)	CELSIUS (C) (APPROXIMATE)
225 °F	107 °C
250 °F	120 °C
275 °F	135 °C
300 °F	150 °C
325 °F	160 °C
350 °F	180 °C
375 °F	190 °C
400 °F	205 °C
425 °F	220 °C
450 °F	235 °C
475 °F	245 °C
500 °F	260 °C

Appendix 2   Dirty Dozen and Clean Fifteen

The Environmental Working Group (EWG) is a nonprofit, nonpartisan organization dedicated to protecting human health and the environment Its mission is to empower people to live healthier lives in a healthier environment. This organization publishes an annual list of the twelve kinds of produce, in sequence, that have the highest amount of pesticide residue-the Dirty Dozen-as well as a list of the fifteen kinds of produce that have the least amount of pesticide residue-the Clean Fifteen.

THE DIRTY DOZEN

- The 2016 Dirty Dozen includes the following produce. These are considered among the year's most important produce to buy organic:

Strawberries	Spinach
Apples	Tomatoes
Nectarines	Bell peppers
Peaches	Cherry tomatoes
Celery	Cucumbers
Grapes	Kale/collard greens
Cherries	Hot peppers

- The Dirty Dozen list contains two additional items kale/collard greens and hot peppers-because they tend to contain trace levels of highly hazardous pesticides.

THE CLEAN FIFTEEN

- The least critical to buy organically are the Clean Fifteen list. The following are on the 2016 list:

Avocados	Papayas
Corn	Kiw
Pineapples	Eggplant
Cabbage	Honeydew
Sweet peas	Grapefruit
Onions	Cantaloupe
Asparagus	Cauliflower
Mangos	

- Some of the sweet corn sold in the United States are made from genetically engineered (GE) seedstock. Buy organic varieties of these crops to avoid GE produce.

30-DAY MEAL PLAN

Please note: refer to the index to find the number of the page corresponding to the recipe. Repeat for another 30 days from the beginning.

We trust that this nutritional plan is to your liking!

	Breakfast	Lunch	Dinner	Total Calories
DAY 1	Coconut Crêpes with Vanilla Cream Calories: 326	Creamy Avocado "Pasta" Calories: 569	Lemon Pork Calories: 448	1343
DAY 2	Lemon Crepes Calories: 421	Spinach and Brussels Sprout Salad Calories: 511	Cream Cheese Sausage Balls Calories: 386	1318
DAY 3	Florentine Breakfast Sandwich Calories: 548	Chicken Salad with Parmesan Calories: 529	Spiced-Pumpkin Chicken Soup Calories: 389	1466
DAY 4	Pastrami Gofres and Peanut Butter Calories: 411	Spinach Salad with Goat Cheese and Nuts Calories: 540	Turkey-Potpie Soup Calories: 415	1366
DAY 5	Sausage Cakes with Poached Eggs Calories: 583	Cream of Cauliflower Gazpacho Calories: 505	Whole Chicken Calories: 390	1478
DAY 6	Chorizo Egg Cups Calories: 452	Chicken Breasts Calories: 571	Avocado Pesto Chargrilled Zucchini Calories: 394	1417

DAY 7	Bacon and Artichoke Omelet Calories: 447	Paprika Chicken and Pancetta in a Skillet Calories: 523	Buckeye Fat Bomb Bars Calories: 379	1349
DAY 8	Ham and Swiss Waffles Calories: 583	Sausage Verde Casserole Calories: 566	Chocolate Frosting Cakes Calories: 346	1495
DAY 9	Lemon Crepes Calories: 421	Sausage Verde Casserole Calories: 566	Avocado Pesto Chargrilled Zucchini Calories: 394	1381
DAY 10	Coconut Crêpes with Vanilla Cream Calories: 326	Chicken Breasts Calories: 571	Lemon Pork Calories: 448	1345
DAY 11	Florentine Breakfast Sandwich Calories: 548	Paprika Chicken and Pancetta in a Skillet Calories: 523	Whole Chicken Calories: 390	1461
DAY 12	Pastrami Gofres and Peanut Butter Calories: 411	Creamy Avocado "Pasta" Calories: 569	Turkey-Potpie Soup Calories: 415	1395
DAY 13	Sausage Cakes with Poached Eggs Calories: 583	Spinach and Brussels Sprout Salad Calories: 511	Chocolate Frosting Cakes Calories: 346	1440
DAY 14	Chorizo Egg Cups Calories: 452	Chicken Salad with Parmesan Calories: 529	Cream Cheese Sausage Balls Calories: 386	1367
DAY 15	Bacon and Artichoke Omelet Calories: 447	Spinach Salad with Goat Cheese and Nuts Calories: 540	Spiced-Pumpkin Chicken Soup Calories: 389	1376

DAY 16	Ham and Swiss Waffles Calories: 583	Cream of Cauliflower Gazpacho Calories: 505	Buckeye Fat Bomb Bars Calories: 379	1467
DAY 17	Coconut Crêpes with Vanilla Cream Calories: 326	Chicken Breasts Calories: 571	Lemon Pork Calories: 448	1345
DAY 18	Florentine Breakfast Sandwich Calories: 548	Paprika Chicken and Pancetta in a Skillet Calories: 523	Whole Chicken Calories: 390	1461
DAY 19	Lemon Crepes Calories: 421	Sausage Verde Casserole Calories: 566	Avocado Pesto Chargrilled Zucchini Calories: 394	1381
DAY 20	Pastrami Gofres and Peanut Butter Calories: 411	Creamy Avocado "Pasta" Calories: 569	Turkey-Potpie Soup Calories: 415	1395
DAY 21	Chorizo Egg Cups Calories: 452	Chicken Salad with Parmesan Calories: 529	Cream Cheese Sausage Balls Calories: 386	1367
DAY 22	Sausage Cakes with Poached Eggs Calories: 583	Spinach and Brussels Sprout Salad Calories: 511	Chocolate Frosting Cakes Calories: 346	1440
DAY 23	Bacon and Artichoke Omelet Calories: 447	Spinach Salad with Goat Cheese and Nuts Calories: 540	Spiced-Pumpkin Chicken Soup Calories: 389	1376
DAY 24	Ham and Swiss Waffles Calories: 583	Cream of Cauliflower Gazpacho Calories: 505	Buckeye Fat Bomb Bars Calories: 379	1467

DAY 25	Florentine Breakfast Sandwich Calories: 548	Paprika Chicken and Pancetta in a Skillet Calories: 523	Whole Chicken Calories: 390	**1461**
DAY 26	Lemon Crepes Calories: 421	Sausage Verde Casserole Calories: 566	Avocado Pesto Chargrilled Zucchini Calories: 394	**1381**
DAY 27	Coconut Crêpes with Vanilla Cream Calories:326	Chicken Breasts Calories: 571	Lemon Pork Calories: 448	**1345**
DAY 28	Pastrami Gofres and Peanut Butter Calories: 411	Creamy Avocado "Pasta" Calories: 569	Turkey-Potpie Soup Calories: 415	**1395**
DAY 29	Florentine Breakfast Sandwich Calories: 548	Paprika Chicken and Pancetta in a Skillet Calories: 523	Whole Chicken Calories: 390	**1461**
DAY 30	Sausage Cakes with Poached Eggs Calories:583	Spinach and Brussels Sprout Salad Calories: 511	Chocolate Frosting Cakes Calories: 346	**1440**

Appendix 3　Index

#

30-DAY MEAL PLAN 109

A

Almond Butter & Chocolate Bars 95
Almond Butter and Cacao Nib Smoothie 80
Almond Cheesecake with Chocolate 92
Almond Cookies 90
Almond Smoothie 78
American Cheesecake 92
Ancho T-Bone Steak 45
Antipasto Skewers 73

Appendix 1　Measurement Conversion Chart
.... 107

Appendix 2　Dirty Dozen and Clean Fifteen
.... 108

Appendix 3　Index 113

Artichoke Salad 18
Asian Broccoli Spiced Beef 41
Asparagus Frittata 83
Asparagus Gouda Frittata 10
Asparagus, Mushroom & Fennel Frittata 10
Avocado & Cauliflower Burritos 70
Avocado and Eggs with Shredded Chicken 6
Avocado Chili Omelet 5
Avocado Mousse "Croutons" 15
Avocado Pesto Chargrilled Zucchini 61

B

Baby Spinach Lasagna with Feta 57
Bacon & Mushrooms Beef Steaks 44
Bacon and Artichoke Omelet 5
Bacon Broccoli Crustless Quiche Cups 11
Bacon Cheddar Egg Muffins 16
Bacon Eggs Benedict Cups 12
Bacon Kale Pizza 35
Bacon-and-Eggs Breakfast Casserole 105
Bacon-Wrapped Egg Cups 8
Baked Chicken Tenders 29
Baked Eggs in Ham Cups 6
Baked Nutty Halibut 53
Baked Olives and Feta 74
Baked Omelet with Pancetta and Swiss Cheese 7
Baked Omelet with Pancetta and Swiss Cheese ... 82
Baked Pork Sausage 33
Baked Sausage & Peppers 85
Baked Trout and Asparagus Foil 48
Baked Zucchini, Chicken and Cheese 25
Barbecued Pork Chops 34

Basic Recipes & Simple Recipes 13

Basil Chicken Zucchini "Pasta" 31
BBQ Chicken Skewers 31
BBQ Rib Sweet Steak 45
Beef & Broccoli Stew 98
Beef Bolognese Squashed 85
Beef Ceeseburgers 84
Beef Cheese & Egg Casserole 43
Beef Cheeseburger 39
Beef Chili 40
Beef Meatballs 96
Beef Pepper & Green Beans Ragout 41
Beef Pho 22

Beef Recipes AND Lamb Recipes 39

Beef Sausage & Okra Casserole 42
Beef Stew 43
Beef, Bell Pepper & Mushroom Kebabs 43
Bell Peppers Stuffed with Enchilada Beef 40
Berry Pancakes 87
Blackberries with Coconut Milk Shake 63
Blackberry Scones 89
Blueberry Coconut Smoothie 81
Blueberry Ice Balls 95
Blueberry Sorbet 93
Blueberry Soufflé 91
Bread with Pumpkin and Zucchini 3
Breakfast Bread "Naan" 70
Broccoli & Bell Pepper Crispy Salmon 46
Broccoli & Mushroom Pizza 59
Broccoli & Peppers Balsamic Zoodles 56
Broccoli Asparagus Flan 61
Broccoli Beef 14
Broccoli Cheddar Soup 20
Broccoli Creamy Cheese Soup 85
Broccoli Mushroom Risotto 84
Broccoli Nachos Salsa 57
Brown Butter–Lime Tilapia 51
Brussels Sprouts & Ground Beef Scrambled Eggs 8
Brussels Sprouts with Spiced Halloumi 86
Buckeye Fat Bomb Bars 95
Buffalo Chicken Wings 30
Buffalo Chicken Wings 100
Buffalo Roasted Cauliflower 75
Butternut Squash Roast 60
Buttery Dark Chocolate Cookies 90
Buttery Green Beans 102

C

Cabbage and Broccoli Chicken Casserole 26
Carnitas 105
Cauliflower & Mushroom Arancini 86
Cauliflower-Based Waffles 62
Cauliflower-Cheddar Soup 19
Cheese Cauliflower Risotto with Mushroom ... 58
Cheese Cloud Eggs 5
Cheesecake Smoothie 79
Cheesy Bacon-Cauliflower Soup 103
Cheesy Baked Meatballs 76
Cheesy chicken Pinwheels 24
Cheesy Pork Quiche 36
Cheesy Sausage & Egg Muffins 9
Cheesy Zucchini Muffins 54
Chia Seeds Coconut-Lime Ice Cream 56
Chicken Bacon Burgers 28
Chicken Breasts 23
Chicken Cacciatore 101
Chicken Cordon Bleu Casserole 32
Chicken in Wine Sauce 101
Chicken Jardiniere 98
Chicken Nuggets 24
Chicken Nuggets 28
Chicken Provencal 101
Chicken Salad with Parmesan 16
Chicken Stew with Sorrel 96
Chicken Stew with Veggies 98
Chicken Thigh Chili with Avocado 28
Chicken with Garlic Sauce 98
Chicken with Mushrooms, Port, and Cream ... 29
Chili Pork Belly with sauce 36
Chilled Avocado-Cilantro Soup 22
Chilli Dressing Roasted Cauliflower 55
Chimichurri Tiger Shrimp 49

Chinese Style Pork with Noodles..35
Chipotle Chicken...96
Chocolate Chips Walnut Biscuits.....................................92
Chocolate Cupcakes..94
Chocolate Energy Balls with Lime..................................91
Chocolate Fat Bombs..92
Chocolate Frosting Cakes..94
Chocolate Protein Cocktail..78
Chocolate Protein Shake..79
Chocolate Vanilla Cake..90
Chocolate, Peanut Butter, and Banana Shake..............80
Chocolate-Mint Smoothie...80
Chorizo Egg Cups..5
Chorizo Egg Muffins...11
Cilantro Beef Balls...41
Cilantro Sauce Coconut Fried Shrimp...........................49
Citrus Pork with tomatoes Cabbage..............................34
Coconut Avocado Tart...58
Coconut Butter Coffee...15
Coconut Chicken...31
Coconut Flaxseed Waffles...6
Coconut Green Soup..68
Coconut Macadamia Bars...95
Coconut Panna Cotta Caramel......................................89
Coconut Saffron Mussels...53
Coconut Waffles with Cranberry...................................93
Coconut-Olive Beef with Mushrooms..........................44
Cod with Parsley Pistou..50
Cold Matcha Latte..78
Coleslaw with Poppy Seeds..66
Cowboy Cookies..90
Cranberries Cheesecake Bars...91
Cranberry Sauce and Herb Pork Chops.......................33
Cream Cheese Sausage Balls..104
Cream of Cauliflower Gazpacho....................................22
Creamed Turkey with Swiss Chard Soup....................27
Cream-Poached Trout..52
Creamy Asparagus Soup...19
Creamy Avocado "Pasta"...14
Creamy Avocado Custard..89
Creamy Broccoli, Bacon, and Cheese Soup.................20
Creamy Chicken and Spinach Bake..............................29
Creamy Tomato Soup..21
Creamy Vanilla Cappuccino...81
Crispy Avocado with Parmesan Sauce.........................59
Crispy Chicken Thighs with Radishes and Mushrooms.28
Crispy Fried Cod...50
Crispy Kale Chips..72
Crunchy Cauliflower with Mash....................................86
Cucumber & Tomato Salad Sticky with Tofu.............65
Curried Chicken Salad...30

D
Dark Chocolate Cheesecake Bites.................................93
Deli Ham Eggs...5
Detox Drink..81
Dijon Sauce Blackened Salmon......................................46
Dinner Vegetarian Pasta Mix...55
Dip with Tofu and Swiss Chard.....................................65
Double Chocolate Shake..79

E
Easy Herbed Tomato Bisque..21
Egg & Cheese Biscuit Casserole.......................................9
Egg and Pork Stuffed Zucchini......................................36
Eggplant Beef Lasagna...44
Eggs with Goat Cheese & Asparagus..............................7

F
Faux Lasagna Soup...103
Fennel & Celeriac with Chili Tomato Sauce................66
Fennel and Orange Marinated Olives..........................74
Fennel Chicken Wrapped in Bacon...............................26
Feta & Olive Pizza..61

Fish Recipes And Seafood Recipes...............46
Flank Steak Roll..43
Flavored Stuffed Mushrooms filled with Cajun.............62
Florentine Breakfast Sandwich..7
French Toast Egg Muffins...9

G
Garlic Breadsticks...76
Garlic Parmesan Crusted Salmon..................................52
Ginger Fudge with Chocolate..91
Gingery Pork Stir-Fry..37
Goat Cheese Lamb Ribs..99
Golden Saffron Cauli Rice...15
Grandma Bev's Ahi Poke...47
Grandma's Meatballs...44
Green Bean Beef Soup...97
Green Bean Broccoli Chicken Stir-Fry..........................24
Green Cheese Bowls..13
Green Pork Bake...38
Green Sauté...59
Green Smoothie..13
Green Tuna Traybake..48
Grilled Asparagus & Carrots..56
Grilled Beef on Skewers and salad................................41
Grilled Cauliflower Steaks..63
Grilled Salmon with salad..47
Grilled Steak and Green Beans......................................42
Grilled Tofu Kabobs...65
Grilled Vegetables and Kebab.......................................64
Guacamole...14

H
Halibut Curry..53
Ham and Cheese Poached Egg Cups............................11
Ham and Swiss Waffles...6
Herby Veggies Chicken Casserole.................................25
Hot Chocolate...78

I
Italian Meatballs...38

J
Jalapeño Poppers..76

K
Keto's Other Favorites.....................................84
King Burgers..39

L
Lamb Shoulder..99
Lemon Chicken and Asparagus Stir-Fry......................29
Lemon Crepes...3
Lemon Pork..105
Lemon Salmon and Asparagus......................................48
Lemon-Garlic Mushrooms..102
Lettuce Wraps with Pork & Dill Pickles.......................36
Loaded Chicken and Cauliflower Nachos...................30
Loaded Denver Omelet...7
Loaded Denver Omelet...82
Loaded Feta...75
Loaded Miso Soup with Tofu and Egg.........................21

M
Margarita Pizza Chips...72
Marinated Artichokes..74
Mascarpone Red Velvet Cakes......................................94
Meat Lover Sausage Pizza..37
Meatball Shakshuka..70
Mediterranean Eggplant Squash Pasta........................62
Mediterranean Frittata..83

Mediterranean Tilapia Bake 46
Mexican Egg Casserole 9
Miso Magic 20
Mixed Mushroom Pizza with Pepperoni 86
Morning Chia Pudding 3
Moroccan Salmon with Cauliflower Rice Pilaf 47
Mushroom & Herb Pizza 57
Mushroom & Kale Pierogis 71
Mushroom & Zucchini with Spinach Dip 60
Mushroom and Bacon Frittata 8
Mushroom Feta Skewers 71
Mushrooms Bake & Curried Cauliflower 67
Mushrooms Broccoli Noodles 59
Mustard-Crusted Cod with Roasted Broccoli 50
Mustardy Crab Cakes 49

O
Oven-Roast Veggie Chuck Beef 40

P
Paprika Chicken and Pancetta in a Skillet 25
Parmesan Zucchini Chips 72
Parmesan-Crusted Tilapia with Sautéed Spinach 51
Parmigiano Cauliflower Cakes 71
Pastrami Gofres and Peanut Butter 4
Peanut Butter Cup Protein Smoothie 80
Peanut Butter Ice Cream 93
Peanut Butter Shake 80
Pecan Arugula Pizza 87
Pepper-Crusted Salmon with Wilted Kale 47
Pepperoni Fat Head Pizza 87
Poached Cod over Brothy Veggie Noodles 51
Pork & Kraut 99
Pork Chops with Tomato Sauce 33
Pork Kebabs 104
Pork Kofta with Spiced Yogurt 34
Pork Neck Casserole 97
Pork Ragout 97

Pork Recipes 33
Pork Shoulder 37
Pork Steaks and Mushroom Sauce 37
Pork with Mozzarella 35
Pork with Mushroom Sauce 100
Pork-and-Sauerkraut Casserole 104
Portobello Bun Mushroom Burgers 64

Poultry Recipes 23
Prosciutto and Cream Cheese Stuffed Mushrooms 75
Prosciutto Pizza 38
Pumpkin & Bell Pepper Noodles 67

Q
Quick Raspberry Vanilla Shake 81
Quick Strawberry Mousse 84

R
Raspberry Yogurt Parfait 14
Ratatouille with Pecans 66
Red Wine Vegetables Beef Roast 45
Ricotta Balls 85
Roast Turkey 32
Roasted Asparagus and Romesco sauce 66
Roasted Bake tomatoes 64
Roasted Cauliflower Gratin 58
Roasted Cauliflower with Bell Peppers 68
Roasted Pork Stuffed with Ham & Cheese 34
Root Mash Veggie Beef Stew 39
Rosemary Feta Cheese Bombs 71
Rosemary Roasted Almonds 73
Rosemary Thyme Juicy Beef 45

S

Salads Recipes & Soups Recipes 18
Salmon and Egg Scramble 10
Sausage and Cheese Frittata 12
Sausage Cakes with Poached Eggs 4
Sausage Verde Casserole 12
Savory Sausage Balls 13
Scrambled Eggs Smoked Salmon 15
Scrambled Eggs with Mackerel 11
Sesame Pork Bites 35
Sesame-Crusted Tuna with Sweet Chili Vinaigrette 53
Shirataki Fettucine with Salmon 48
Shirataki Mussels Pasta 50
Shredded BBQ Roast 99
Shredded Chicken 30
Skillet-Baked Eggs with Yogurt and Spinach 82
Sliced Garlic & Cheezy Turkey Breast 27
Slow Cooker Spanakopita Frittata 106

Small Keto Appliance Recipes 96
Smoked Mackerel Lettuce Cups 16
Smoky Pork Tenderloin 105
Smoky Zucchini Chips 102

Smoothies & Beverages Recipes 78

Snacks Recipes & Appetizers Recipes 70
Southern Fried Deviled Eggs 73
Spiced Pumpkin Soup 19
Spiced-Pumpkin Chicken Soup 103
Spicy Barbecue Pecans 73
Spicy Beef Lettuce Cups 40
Spicy Crab Cakes 54
Spinach and Brussels Sprout Salad 16
Spinach Pesto 87
Spinach Salad with Goat Cheese and Nuts 18
Spinach, Mushroom, and Cheddar Frittata 8
Spiralized Zucchini in Bolognese Sauce 46
Stir-Fry Tofu & Vegetable 63
Strawberries and Cream Shake 79
Strawberries Ricotta Parfait 89
Strawberry Mini Cakes 94
Stuffed Chicken Breasts 23
Stuffed Zucchini with Cheddar 55
Sweet and Spicy Pecans 102

Sweets Recipes And Desserts Recipes 89
Swordfish in Tarragon-Citrus Butter 54

T
Texas Trash 74
Thai-Style Prawn Salad 18
Three Cheesy Pizza 60
Thyme & Garlic Steamed Bok Choy 65
Thyme Mushroom and turnip Chicken 25
Tilapia Tortillas with Cauliflower Rice 49
Tofu and Avocado Sandwiches 84
Tofu Parsnip Spaghetti a la "Bolognese" 57
Tofu Roasted Pepper 61
Tofu Stir-Fry 60
Tofu Vegetable Casserole 68
Tomato Basil Soup 20
Tomato Gratin with Eggplant 55
Touch of Spice Pulled Pork 100
Triple Cheese Chips 72
Tuna Pesto Caprese Salad 14
Tuna Slow-Cooked in Olive Oil 52
Turkey Egg Scramble 12
Turkey Meatloaf Muffins 32
Turkey Patties with Cucumber Salad 26
Turkey Salad 18
Turkey-Potpie Soup 103
Turmeric Latte 81

  Turnip and Thyme Soup..21
  Turnip Greens Artichoke Chicken 24
  Turnip Soup with Sour Cream 101

V
  Vanilla Bean Smoothie 79
  Vanilla Shake 79
  Vegan Chocolate Smoothie 81

Vegan Recipes 63
  Vegan Sandwich with Tofu 63
  Vegan Smoothie 64
  Vegetable Keto Pasta Gratin..................................56
  Vegetable Medley with Grilled Beef Steaks 42

Vegetable Sides & Dairy Recipes.................. 54
  Vegetable Stew...67
  Vegetarian French Onion Soup...........................19
  Veggie Bake with Sausage.....................................38
  Viennese Coffee Bites 93

W
  Walnuts & Cheese Mushrooms............................70
  Whole Chicken 100
  Winter Squash Pancakes 4
  Worcestershire Pork Loin......................................97
  wrap classic pigs..15

Z
  Zesty Zucchini Bread with Nuts............................4
  Zucchini Loaded with Tofu & Hazelnut............67
  Zucchini Pasta Puttanesca....................................13

Made in the USA
Monee, IL
13 December 2022

21240742R00070